PILGRIMAGE

PILGRIMAGE

PAST AND PRESENT

*Sacred travel and sacred space
in the world religions*

Simon Coleman and John Elsner

BRITISH MUSEUM PRESS

Acknowledgements

We would like to thank Glenn Bowman, Liz Edwards, Silvia Frenk, Rupert Gethin, Lindy Grant, John Guy, Shelley Hales, Anita Herle, Monica Jakowski, Ian Jenkins, Thupten Jinpa, Bob Knox, Kristin Norget, Filippo Osella, Caroline Osella, Amanda Sealy and Dr P. Starkey for their help and advice with matters textual or photographic. At an important stage we received excellent advice and encouragement from readers for both British Museum Press and Harvard University Press – their identities remain anonymous, but they nonetheless deserve our thanks. Throughout the process of writing this book, it has been a pleasure to work with the team at British Museum Press – with Celia Clear, who commissioned the book, Teresa Francis and Joanna Champness (respectively our editor and picture editor), Julie Young and Emma Way.

Finally, we would like to dedicate this book to our parents – Dante and Renée Elsner, John and Rochelle Coleman.

© 1995 Simon Coleman and John Elsner

Published by British Museum Press
A division of British Museum Publications Ltd
46 Bloomsbury Street
London WC1B 3QQ

British Library Cataloguing in Publication Data
A catalogue record for this book is available from the British Library

ISBN 0-7141-1738-2

Designed by Behram Kapadia

Phototypeset in Linotron Palatino by Rowland Phototypesetting Ltd
Bury St Edmunds, Suffolk
Printed in Italy by Imago Publishing Ltd

FRONTISPIECE *Sinhalese Buddhist monk before the colossal standing Buddha at Awkana, Sri Lanka. The statue, which according to local tradition was cut from the living rock in the 12th century AD, is 46 foot (14 metres) high, including the pedestal. It faces due east and the Buddha's right hand is raised in the abhaya mudra, the gesture of granting freedom from fear.*

Contents

Introduction:
Landscapes Surveyed

Imagine that reaching the goal of a pilgrimage is like attaining the summit of a mountain. The path of any one pilgrim treads only on a single slope and cannot but exclude the views from the other faces. Nor can the climber be fully aware of the other tracks mapped out in the same terrain by pilgrims of the past and future. Our aim in this book has been a little analogous to that of a cartographer tracing out the broad lines (and a few of the minute details) etched by pilgrims over the landscape and through the history of any given religion.

A pilgrimage is not just a journey; it also involves the confrontation of travellers with rituals, holy objects and sacred architecture. In approaching our theme, we shall examine how these elements interrelate and reinforce each other in the pilgrimage traditions of the world religions. Moreover, pilgrimage is as much about returning home with the souvenirs and narratives of the pilgrim's adventure, and we specifically focus on pilgrims' own recollections in this account. We therefore follow the pilgrims of the various faiths as they make their journeys, guided by existing 'sacred geographies' but also creating new ones.

The physical journey through time and space that is an essential part of pilgrimage can also have metaphorical resonances on many levels. A pilgrimage may be a rite of passage involving transformations of one's inner state and outer status; it may be a quest for a transcendent goal; it may entail the long-desired healing of a physical or spiritual ailment. On their return, pilgrims frequently bring back a token of the place, both as proof that the journey has been completed and as a physical manifestation of the charisma of a sacred centre. In this way, the sacred landscape becomes diffused, permeating even the everyday lives of those who have never been to, say, Mecca or Jerusalem.

One important aspect of the objects of pilgrimage – relics, talismans and amulets – is that they help to reconstruct the sacred journey in the imagination. For the actual pilgrim this is an act of memory; for the aspiring pilgrim such objects provide an imaginative link with a sacred goal which, it is hoped, will be encountered in the future. Equally powerful are texts – those accounts which pilgrims in all the major religions have left as testimony. These writings perhaps inspire future generations, but they can also serve as practical guides both to the physical journey and to its interpretation.

Our main theme focuses on the practices of established religious traditions with a scriptural basis. The opening chapter, on the classical

1 OPPOSITE Cracow, Poland, early May 1989. Worshippers carrying an icon in a procession between churches. This procession, which took place towards the end of the Communist period, was part of the local celebrations accompanying the legalisation of Solidarity.

world, treats what seems at first to be an incongruous case, since ancient Graeco-Roman religion did not make universalist claims or have written scriptures. However, we hope by this example not only to shed light on an ancestor of the Muslim and Christian religious practices of the eastern Mediterranean, but also to present an instance of pilgrimage in the context of a *culture* rather than a religion.

The structure of the book broadly reflects a movement from those religions – Christianity and Islam – which emphasise the paradigmatic quality of a single canonical text, to those with a multiplicity of sacred scriptures, like Hinduism and Buddhism. The chapters are intended to give an introductory guide to some of the major themes in each religion. However, we do not claim to give a comprehensive account in so brief a space, nor that it is possible to encapsulate the 'essence' of any religion. Not only do religions change through history, but their practices and scriptures are constantly subject to evolving, contested and even sometimes incompatible interpretations. Any overview, such as those presented in this book, is inevitably a generalisation.

Our aim, then, is initially to provide a text through which readers can construct their own paths of interpretation. Although occasional cross-references to other religions are provided, we have decided to make each chapter self-contained, and to avoid imposing an overarching theoretical framework on to the accounts themselves. In this way, we hope that readers will be able not only to focus on those religious systems which particularly interest them, but also decide for themselves whether common structures and meanings exist between the various traditions.

In order to allow the book to be read on a second, different level, there are six picture sections, placed in between the main chapters, which explicitly juxtapose and compare pilgrimage practices in the various religions. These explore three main areas. Firstly, how do pilgrimage sites embody 'the sacred', not only in permanently fixed locations like temples and shrines, but also in movable objects such as amulets, relics and even holy persons?[1] And how do such embodiments vary in different cultures? Secondly, can we see sacred centres as arenas not only for religious consensus but also for conflict, both within a single religion and between different faiths? And do such conflicts reflect important secular and political issues as well as strictly spiritual concerns? Finally, how does the physical practice of pilgrimage compare with its depiction and representation, both in narratives (textual or oral) and in art?

The Epilogue treats the subject of pilgrimage on yet another level. Here we discuss the broader theoretical and comparative literature on the subject in an attempt to show the strengths and weaknesses of various scholarly approaches, and also provide our own suggestions as to the viability of perceiving pilgrimage as a unitary phenomenon with features that exist across different cultures and religions.

The literature on pilgrimage is enormous and incorporates a wide range of approaches – academic, confessional, personal and canonical.[2] A danger of any one approach is that it provides a limited and therefore misleading view. In effect, it may cast light on only one part of the pilgrimage landscape. We have attempted, as part of our project of constructing an overview, to make space for the expression of different, even competing, views and discourses. For example, the *hajj* or pilgrimage to Mecca is prescribed in the Koran as one of the five pillars of Islam: the scripture enjoins not only the activity but also how it should be done, in righteousness, eagerness and praise of Allah, without loose talk, transgression or contention. However, not every pilgrim's experience need always match this ideal. Likewise, while an academic geographer may be more interested in how pilgrims travel and where they stay, the pilgrims themselves may frame their accounts purely in terms of their relationship to the *haram*, or sacred space, of Mecca.

A further problem in using such accounts, and in translating any pilgrim's experience into a text, is that one risks losing the spontaneity and multilayered richness of human religious activity. Any written account almost inevitably simplifies and overclarifies the ambiguities and evocative associations of symbols, rituals and experience. No book written in prose can be fully free of this difficulty in representing the dynamic character of human behaviour. Poetry might capture the feeling, but would blur the distinctive features of the landscape. However, in using the words and writings through which pilgrims over the centuries have themselves testified to their experience, and by extensive use of the visual images of pilgrimage, we hope to evoke as well as to describe and analyse the process of sacred travel.

1

Piety and Identity: Sacred Travel in the Classical World

'The hero of the tale which I beg the Muse to help me tell is that resourceful man who roamed the wide world after he had sacked the holy citadel of Troy. He saw the cities of many people and he learnt their ways. He suffered many hardships on the high seas in his struggles to preserve his life and bring his comrades home.'

ODYSSEY I, 1

Thus opens Homer's account of the wanderings of Odysseus: not a pilgrimage in any conventional sense, and yet perhaps an archetypal myth of journeying and return. Odysseus had spent ten years at the siege of Troy, away from his island home in Ithaca, and was then fated to spend ten further years in an arduous epic voyage home. Many of the themes of pilgrimage – the sense of a difficult journey fraught with sufferings, the intense yearning for a distant goal – are encapsulated in what became a classic text for the ancient Greeks and Romans. In later antiquity, the tale of Odysseus was taken as a religious allegory of man's renunciation of material pleasures in favour of the transcendent – that sacred 'place from which we came', in the words of the philosopher Plotinus.[1] Like pilgrimage, the voyage of Odysseus became in the ancient allegorical tradition (both pagan and Christian) a potent symbol for the inner spiritual journey to one's authentic home.[2]

The image of Odysseus travelling throughout the known world, suffering spiritual trials and temptations and striving for years in search of his place of origin, represents the prime image of quest in antiquity's epic tradition. It stands as a mighty symbol of certain elements which would become part of the pilgrimage tradition: the single individual, the traveller who loses all his companions, the hero who finds himself. But much pilgrimage, in many traditions, involves groups of people, social interaction, a communal search for a joint ideal. This chapter explores both these themes, looking at the importance of civic and pan-Hellenic identity in the communal context of Greek pilgrimage, and at the surviving writings of Pausanias, a single pilgrim who has left us a vivid account of his travels to sacred centres in Greece under the Roman empire.

PILGRIMAGE AND CIVIC IDENTITY IN GREECE

The Parthenon frieze is one of the most remarkable sculptures to survive from antiquity. It was created as part of the decoration with which the

people of fifth-century Athens adorned their spectacular new temple on the Acropolis. Begun in 447 BC, the Parthenon was one of the monuments rebuilt by the Athenians to assert the pre-eminence of their city after the long struggle against the Persians in the early part of the century. It celebrates not only the new spirit of democratic Athens and the defeat of the Persians (who had actually sacked the Acropolis and destroyed its temples in 479 BC), but also the power of the new Athenian empire in the Aegean. The Parthenon housed not just a great sacred image of the goddess Athena made by the artist Phidias, but also, significantly, the treasury of the so-called Delian League, the group of states which formed the Athenian empire.[3]

The Parthenon frieze represents and idealises the rituals of one of the principal festivals of Attica, the Great Panathenaea, celebrated every four years.[4] Whether the Great Panathenaea was in the strictest terms a pilgrimage or not, it was nonetheless a festival of the greatest religious and civic importance for the city of Athens. Its very name implies a union of all the Athenians, and its key event was the offering of a new robe to the holy statue of Athena Polias,[5] housed from about 404 BC in the Erechtheum, another important temple on the Acropolis which was also rebuilt in the fifth century. The significance of this festival is implied in

2 The Acropolis, Athens, from the south-west. The principal buildings still standing on the site are those of the great 5th-century BC construction programme; from left to right these are the cluster of buildings making up the Propylaea or entrance way and the small temple of Athena Nike, the Erechtheum and the Parthenon.

3 The Parthenon, view from the north-west.

Aristophanes' play *The Birds* (produced in 414 BC) when one of his heroes, planning to build a new city in the sky ('Cloud-Cuckoo Land'), remarks:

Oh what a splendid city it'll be! Who's going to be the guardian deity? For whom do we weave the sacred robe?　　　　　　　　　　　　(*The Birds*, 827f.)

That a mock Panathenaea should feature in Attic comedy as an activity which helped define the nature of Aristophanes' ideal city, indicates the prestige of the real event.

As a celebration so deeply connected with the civic nature of Athens, the Great Panathenaea was a complex interrelationship between what to us are the very differentiated spheres of the sacred and the secular. In ancient culture, there was no demarcation between the secular world and that of religious ritual. The sacred – consisting primarily of rituals and observances – pervaded most activities in everyday life as well as important festivals. Although festivals served to celebrate the gods, they also brought people into the city for trade and business. In some ways they united the community, but in other respects they emphasised social differences by enshrining them in ritual. For instance, a number of Athenian festivals, such as the Thesmophoria, the Stenia and the Skira were reserved exclusively for women.[6] By giving Athenian women a free rein and secret rites, these festivals in one sense allowed a possibility for creative religious expression usually denied by a male hierarchic society. But in doing so, and in excluding men, they were exceptions which proved the rule, merely inverting the usual civic structure (whereby the women stayed at home) and so essentially upholding it.

The Great Panathenaea brought together citizens both from within the city and from the countryside of Attica, as well as many of Athens' allies from abroad, to celebrate not only the birthday of their goddess but also their very identity as Athenians. The Parthenon frieze shows the Panathenaic procession of horsemen and chariots, bearers of offerings, sacrificial animals and women carrying ritual objects. The procession moves around the Parthenon from its west façade along both the north and south sides, and culminates in the representation of the major Olympian deities at the east. In the central scene of the east face, above the entrance through which a worshipper would step in order to approach Phidias' famous cult statue of Athena Parthenos, the frieze depicts a child offering to a priest the robe specially woven for the Great Panathenaea.

The sculptures of the frieze thus not only represent an ideal version of the festival, but in a sense enact the Panathenaic procession itself. However, the actual procession did not in fact go to Phidias' statue in the Parthenon, but to the ancient olive-wood image of Athena Polias (also housed on the Acropolis). In effect, the Parthenon sculptures represent and reflect a sacred event away from but on the same site as the sacred procession itself. To view the frieze, spectators would have to walk alongside it from the west face of the building (the side closest to the Acropolis entrance) towards the east, and would therefore themselves become participants in it. Through this visual participation, a viewer would join the collaborative religious ritual of the festival and the sacred journey which took a pilgrim to the cult image of Athena, which in ancient religious custom was identified with the goddess herself.[7] At those times when a visitor came to the Acropolis and no Panathenaic procession was taking place, the spectator's journey alongside the Parthenon sculptures to Phidias' statue constituted a kind of proxy pilgrimage, a vicarious participation in a sacred event scheduled for a different time.

While the Athena Parthenos was a static colossal image made of ivory and gold, the statue of Athena Polias, to which the Panathenaic procession was directed, was made of wood. Athena Polias, which the second-century AD traveller Pausanias tells us was the 'most holy thing' in Athens, was dressed, undressed and even washed at different events in the ritual year. Like the statue of Aphrodite Pandemos in the festival known as the Aphrodisia, Athena Polias even travelled out of the city for her ritual bath by the sea at the festival of Plynteria. On her return to Athens, she was accompanied by a torch-lit procession.[8]

The Parthenon frieze points to a key characteristic of ancient Greek religion, one deeply implicated in the fifth-century political structure of independent and often conflicting city-states like Athens, Argos and Sparta. Civic religion, including festivals of pilgrimage to and within one's mother city, was a profound way of evoking and establishing identity. To be an Athenian meant, at least in part, to be a participant of such civic festivals as the Panathenaea, Plynteria or Dionysia (during the course of which the masterpieces of fifth-century Attic drama were performed).[9] Like the pilgrimage to Guadalupe in modern Mexico, such religious celebrations and processions not only provided a focus for worship but also fulfilled the explicitly political purpose of binding the participant populace of citizens together as Athenians (or in the case of Mexicans, as 'Guadalupanos') in a common identity through their relations to a shared deity. Of course, just as they bound citizens together, so such rituals excluded non-citizens, foreigners and the lower classes (for instance, slaves) from full membership. Other city-states had similar

4 The Parthenon frieze, 5th century BC, British Museum. Detail of a young attendant handing over the *peplos* to the Basileus Archon, the priest of Athena. This image, from the centre of the east frieze, was placed directly over the entrance into the *cella*, where Phidias' cult statue of Athena Parthenos stood. To the right sit the gods Athena and Hephaestus.

public festivals which fulfilled a similar function. These would celebrate the principal deities worshipped by those cities, just as the Athenians focused on Athena. In Argos, for example, Hera was the chief local goddess, as was Artemis at Ephesus or Zeus at Olympia. And like the festivals of Athens, these festivals occasioned journeys – pilgrimages home – by citizens, colonists living in other parts of the Greek world (such as Sicily or Asia Minor) and allies.

This pattern of pilgrimage – travelling home to a ritual which marked home as sacred – was itself only one aspect of pilgrimage in classical Greek antiquity. It was a public or official model of pilgrimage, an activity performed as part of a citizen body. More significantly, this kind of civic festival celebrated *difference* – an Athenian's being Athenian rather than, and by opposition to, being Theban, Corinthian or Argive. By defining identity in this way, such festivals contributed to the intense sense of rivalry and competition between the fiercely independent Greek states.

We can evoke something of the flavour of a civic festival like the Panathenaea from this remarkable dialogue preserved in the *Life of Apollonius of Tyana*, written by Philostratus in the third century AD. Apollonius was a holy man and philosopher of the latter part of the first century AD whose miracles were celebrated throughout pagan antiquity and even occasioned a Christian refutation from Eusebius, the bishop and biographer of Constantine. While staying at Olympia (another notable centre of festival and pilgrimage throughout antiquity), Apollonius asks (VIII,18):

Tell me, Isagoras, is there such a thing as a religious festival? . . . and what material is it composed of?

He then answers his own question:

A most important material . . . and most varied in character; for there are sacred games in it, and shrines and race-courses and, of course, a theatre, and tribes of men, some of them from neighbouring countries, and others from over the borders, and even from across the sea. Moreover . . . many arts go to make up a festival, and many designs, and much true genius, both of poets and of civil counsellors, and of those who deliver harangues on philosophical topics, and contests between naked athletes, and contests of musicians, as is the custom of the Pythian festival.

This remarkable range of activities, from sport to drama, from art to philosophy, from competitions to foreign visits, is further evidence of the lack of separation of secular and sacred. A whole world of what we might define as secular activities is regarded by Apollonius as germane to a *'religious* festival'.

While not all festivals may have contained all these 'materials', this is nevertheless a vivid summary of what by the first centuries AD had come to be expected of a festival centre.[10] All these elements had their origins in archaic times and were already established by the fifth century BC. But Apollonius goes on to make a still more important point about pilgrimage to a festival:

I consider a festival to be not only the meeting of human beings, but also the place itself in which they have to meet. . . .

He illustrates this emphasis on the special nature of places sanctified as sacred centres with this foundation myth:

Because Herakles admired the natural advantages of Olympia, he found the place worthy of the festival and games which are still held there.

All ancient pilgrimage not only celebrated identity, but did so by linking it with a special place. The identity of the Athenians was inextricably linked with the site, the holy associations and the myths of Athens. The Acropolis, where the Great Panathenaea had its climax, was not only the highest part of Athens and the site of the original city, as Pausanias tells us (1,26,6), but it was the setting for many important Athenian myths. On the site of the Erechtheum, Erichthonius, the king of Athens who instituted worship of Athena, was brought up by order of the goddess after being born from the Earth of the seed of the god Hephaestus. One reason why pilgrims returned to their homeland in the civic festivals of ancient Greece was to strengthen the umbilical cord that linked them through their home city to their ancestors and their mythical origins.

PAN-HELLENIC PILGRIMAGE

In contrast with this city-based model of a journey home, pilgrimage also took place to pan-Hellenic sanctuaries which were sacred not just to one state or people, but to all those who considered themselves Greek. The supreme example of public pan-Hellenic pilgrimage was the great festival of Zeus, celebrated at Olympia in Elis every four years from the eighth century BC, where the Olympic Games took place.[11] As Pindar, the great early fifth-century lyric poet, wrote:

> Nor shall we name any gathering
> Greater than the Olympian.
> The glorious song of it is clothed by the wits of the wise.
>> (*Olympian Odes*, 1, 7–9)

The festival, which according to myth had been founded by Herakles, was the occasion for a truce (all too often broken, it must be said) between all the Greek states, which were to cease military action against each other for the duration of the celebrations. Hundreds, and perhaps thousands, of pilgrims would flock to Olympia for the festival, which, however, was very different from a city festival like the Panathenaea. It did in some sense assert a pan-Hellenic ideology whereby all the Greeks competed together and thus celebrated their equality and kinship as Greeks, in opposition to barbarians and foreigners like Persians or Egyptians. However, as the odes of Pindar make plain, victors in the Games were invariably celebrated as citizens of their own particular city or state. Even as the ideology of pan-Hellenic competition and pilgrimage asserted cultural and symbolic unity among the Greeks, so its practice played out the rivalries of the Greek states in the triumph of individual cities on the arena rather than the battlefield. In this, the modern Olympics, despite their entire lack of religious overtones, display a remarkable similarity to their ancient ancestors!

The Olympic Games, like the Pythian Games (held every four years at Delphi) and the bi-annual Nemean and Isthmian Games (all of which are hymned in Pindar's Epinicean Odes) were very public and official examples of pan-Hellenic gatherings. The ancient Greeks even measured time in terms of how many Olympiads (periods of four years between Olympic festivals) had elapsed from one historical occasion to another. But equally important was pilgrimage to sacred centres famous throughout the Greek world for divination, prophecy and healing.[12] Such pilgrimage might be official, on behalf of a state or monarch – as when, in Sophocles' play *Oedipus the King*, the Thebans send to Delphi to find out what to do with Oedipus – or it could be devotional and private. Even non-Greeks consulted the famous oracular temples: according to Herodotus (*Histories*, 1, 46), Croesus, the king of Lydia, consulted not only Delphi but also the oracles of Abae in Phocia, Dodona, Amphiaraus, Trophonius, Branchidae and even the shrine of Ammon in Libya.

In his play *Ion*, which tells the story of the mythical founder of Ionia, son of the Athenian princess Creusa and Apollo, Euripides (writing in the late fifth century) dramatises the experience of pilgrimage to the temple of Apollo at Delphi. The chorus, a group of slave-women attendant on Creusa, admire the statues and reliefs which adorn the courtyard in front of the temple, referring to the myths displayed there:

> Look
> Where the Lernaean monster falls!
> See how Herakles, son of Zeus, can ply
> his golden scimitar!
> Oh my dear, look there!
>
> I see! And there's another close beside
> who lifts a sparkling torch –
> I know the tale, we sing it at our looms! –
> it's the warrior Iolaus who
> chose to labour and to dare
> beside the son of Zeus.
>
> (*Ion*, 190–200)

As they discuss these images at some length, Ion, the temple attendant, comes upon them. They ask:

You sir, by the altar there, may we take off our shoes and go into the sanctuary?

Ion replies:

That is not permitted here . . .
If you have offered barley and would consult the god you may approach the hearth, but no one is to cross the temple sill unless he means to place a smoking sheep upon the sacred stone.

The chorus responds:

I understand. We only want to do what is allowed. We like looking round outside.

And Ion agrees:

Yes, look around at everything that is open to the public.

This dialogue evokes many of the circumstances of temple pilgrimage in the ancient world. Works of art were an essential decoration for all sacred centres (as on the Parthenon). The works of art Euripides evokes in the words of the chorus may have been votive offerings or dedications, part of the temple's programme of sculptural decoration (whether reliefs or pedimental sculptures) or sacred images with supernatural powers (although these are more likely perhaps to have been inside the temple). Any ancient pilgrim would have been confronted with many images: some were used in ritual, some commemorated donors or famous men, all were decorations. After admiring the images, the chorus naturally wants to enter the temple. But this is forbidden without the necessary ritual preparations, which in this case include the worshipper's need to ask a question of the god as well as the offering of barley-cakes and the sacrifice of a sheep. Since the slave-women do not have such a question (unlike their royal masters Xuthus and Creusa), they do not attempt to enter.

Euripides dramatises not only the visual environment of Delphi, but also the taboos and liturgical niceties surrounding any great shrine (including the Athenian Acropolis). Moreover, he focuses specifically (perhaps even ironically) on the Athenian origins of his chorus. The first thing the women notice as they enter is that Delphi is not as different from Athens as they had imagined:

> So holy Athens is not the only place
> where the gods have pillared courtyards
> and are honoured as guardians of the streets.
> Apollo's temple too has twin pediments
> like brows on a smiling face.

And later they say with joy, when they recognise Athena:

I see her, my own Pallas Athena!

It may be that there is a certain irony in depicting the slave population of Attica as incapable of imagining that any other city might have facilities like those of Athens. But in pointing to the parochial and deeply city-

5 Olympia, ruins of the palaestra, 3rd century BC. This colonnaded Doric building was the wrestling and boxing school.

based outlook of these Athenian pilgrims, Euripides is hinting at the great importance of the political frame of independent and competitive states even in the context of pan-Hellenic travel. It was this frame, above all, which would change when Philip of Macedon united Greece under the sway of the Macedonians in the fourth century BC and when his son Alexander put Greece at the centre of a vast empire of conquests. For the remaining centuries of antiquity, the world would be divided into much larger units than the single city (and its limited territory) envisaged here by the chorus. Instead, a new world picture of imperial provinces, governors and viceroys would make the intensely parochial vision presented by Euripides a thing of the remote past. While many of the patterns and modes of pilgrimage established in the period of Greek independence would continue throughout antiquity (from the civic festival to the visit to an oracular or miracle shrine), the political and cultural frame wherein such practices flourished would change radically.

One of the long-term religious changes which took place as a result of the rise of monarchy was in the conception of the priesthood.[13] In the city-states of Greece and Italy, priests might be drawn from particular kin-groups (for example from an aristocratic family, as was the case with the priests of Athena Polias in Athens) or from the city itself. In Athens, which was a democracy in the fifth century, the priestess of Athena Nike was elected by lot from all the Athenian women. In Athens and Republican Rome, the most important religious body was the government itself – the *demos* and the Senate. By and large, priests received modest fees and a special portion of the sacrificial meat. They tended to be isolated, devoted to the ritual and administrative duties which their sanctuary demanded.

They had little institutional power or prestige, and so pilgrimage tended not to involve a hierarchic sacred establishment.

With the conquest of Persia and Egypt, Oriental models of priesthood – including huge hierarchies of priests and temples dependent on a powerful high priest – became important in the Hellenistic world. Alexander's successors in Egypt, the Ptolemies, were crowned Pharaoh by the high priests of Ptah in Memphis. The power, prestige and influence of such a sacred hierarchy came to be appropriated by the monarch himself: Augustus and all subsequent Roman emperors were also Pontifex Maximus, or chief priest, in Rome. As long as pilgrimage to centres administered according to pre-Hellenistic models continued, it did not necessarily involve collusion with a priestly establishment. But when Christian pilgrimage began, the new religious establishment of Church and monasteries soon appropriated it as part of an accepted system which ultimately owed its origins to non Graeco-Roman models of priesthood.

The new political unity of Greece with Asia Minor, Syria and Egypt which came about after Alexander's conquests gave rise to a common 'Hellenistic' culture. This was centred not in old Greece but in the capitals of the Hellenistic monarchs, Alexander's successors, such as Pergamon and above all Alexandria. The establishment of Greek monarchies in the eastern Mediterranean – including the Ptolemies in Egypt, the Seleucids in Syria, the Antigonids at Macedon and the Attalids at Pergamon – led to profound changes in the religious system. Not only did Greek religious forms gradually adapt to their new environment, but foreign deities and cults spread into the Greek world. Particularly influential throughout later antiquity would be Isis (among whose devotees was Lucius, hero of

6 Ruins of the Temple of Apollo at Delphi, 4th century BC. The interior of the Temple contained the hearth of Hestia burning with eternal fire, a lavish collection of votive offerings, and the Adyton or inner sanctum, with the Omphalos (navel stone), the tripod of Pythia, Apollo's prophetess, and the oracle.

19

the second-century novel *The Golden Ass* by Apuleius) as well as Sarapis from Egypt and Cybele, the Great Mother, whose worship spread from Phrygia. The syncretism of Greek cults and Syrian or Egyptian religions developed into an amazingly complex system of numerous combined deities, shrines and rituals (at both local and national levels) as well as other important religious projects such as the Septuagint translation of the Hebrew Bible into Greek at Alexandria in the third century BC.[14] The changed political, cultural and social context gave rise to a new international dialect of Greek, the *koine*, common to all parts of the Hellenistic world; to a new cosmological, historical and philosophical understanding of the place of human beings in the world; and, perhaps above all, in terms of pilgrimage, to a transformation of the way in which individuals saw their identity. In a world where political power became increasingly remote, and where one's home city came to signify little more than the place of one's birth, pilgrimage may have affirmed a deeper and more personal identity than nationality.

Visitors to oracular temples such as Delphi or healing shrines like that of Asclepius in Epidaurus often came in need. If that need was fulfilled or a request was granted, pilgrims left votive offerings, statues and tablets to commemorate the god's miraculous response.[15] In Epidaurus archaeologists have found a number of inscriptions dating back to the fourth century BC and recording miracle cures by Apollo and Asclepius. Pilgrims to this temple (and we know that they continued to come until the end of pagan antiquity) made their offering and then slept inside the shrine. Often they would be cured in a vision during or after this period of sleep:

Cleo was with child for five years. After she had been pregnant for five years she came as a suppliant to the god and slept in the Abaton. As soon as she left it and got outside the temple precincts she bore a son who, immediately after his birth, washed himself at the fountain and walked about with his mother. In return for this favour she inscribed on her offering: 'Admirable is not the greatness of this tablet, but the Divinity, in that Cleo carried this burden in her womb for five years until she slept in the Temple and He made her sound'.[16]

Pilgrims came with all sorts of ailments. In the following inscription (as in several others) the miracle cure heals the protagonist not only of her illness but also of her doubts about the efficacy and miraculous powers of the god:

Ambrosia of Athens, blind of one eye. She came as a suppliant to the god. As she walked about in the Temple she laughed at some of the cures as incredible and impossible that the lame and the blind should be healed by merely seeing a dream. In her sleep she had a vision. The god stood by her and said that he would cure her, but that in payment he would ask her to dedicate a silver pig to the Temple as a memorial of her ignorance. After saying this, he cut the diseased eyeball and poured in some drug. When day came she walked out sound.[17]

Men, as well as women, came in search of healing. In this case the miracle was vouchsafed without even the post-sacrificial sleep:

A voiceless boy. He came as a suppliant to the Temple for his voice. When he had performed the preliminary sacrifice and fulfilled the usual rites, thereupon the temple servant who brings the fire for the god, looking at the boy's father, demanded that he should bring within a year the thank-offering for the cure, if he obtained that for which he had come. But the boy suddenly said, 'I promise'. His father was startled at this and asked him to repeat it. The boy repeated the words and after that became well.[18]

Such inscriptions take us deep into the world of the ancient pilgrim. They emphasise the many offerings associated with temples – offerings asking for a cure or prediction or good luck, and thank-offerings in return for the gifts of the gods. They evoke something of the ritual complexity surrounding such pilgrimage temples. This was a world of preliminary rites, of sacrifices, of dreams and purifications which frequently involved fasting or abstinence from certain foods. We will meet more of these rituals, described with remarkable precision and interest in ancient pilgrim accounts, when we look at pilgrimage during the Roman empire. But perhaps the most significant element of such pilgrim inscriptions and tablets is the world of folklore in which they thrived. Visiting a temple such as that at Epidaurus offered access to the supernatural through dreams and visions, through miracles and cures, and through inscriptions which recounted histories of previous encounters with the god.

Of course such inscriptions were propaganda, left in the vicinity of the temple by those (perhaps relatively few?) pilgrims who had been helped. They were erected where they would be seen by all newcomers, with the active collusion and encouragement of the temple authorities, who wished to advertise the superiority of their shrine. As in the notes left in pilgrimage centres such as Walsingham or in Mexican churches today, thanking God for some aid or miracle, it is rare to find complaints about the god's failure amidst the litany of cures and consolations. . . . But it was partly to read such texts and offerings that pilgrims came to the temple, as much perhaps as to seek a miracle for themselves. For these inscriptions, votive statues and commemorative plaques marked a history of the active presence of the god, breaking through the barriers of the natural world with his or her miraculous activity.[19]

PILGRIMAGE IN THE ROMAN WORLD

Graecia capta ferum victorem cepit et artes intulit agresti Latio.

Conquered Greece defeated her savage conqueror and brought the arts to rustic Italy. (Horace, *Epistles*, II,1,157–8)

In the last two centuries BC, and especially after the Roman conquests of Corinth and Carthage in 146 BC, the whole Mediterranean basin gradually came under the dominion of Rome. In 133 King Attalus III of Pergamon, who had no heir, left Asia Minor to the Roman people in his will. In subsequent years, Roman generals conquered Numidia, Pontus on the Black Sea, Egypt and the pirates of the Mediterranean. The fate of the Greek-speaking East was finally sealed when Octavian defeated Antony and Cleopatra – the last of the Ptolemies – at Actium in 31 BC, and returned to Rome to become Augustus, the first emperor. Yet, as Augustus' poet-laureate Horace noted, in cultural terms it was the Greek captive who conquered her savage conqueror and brought the arts to

7 Augustus' Tomb, Rome. Completed in 28 BC the Mausoleum of Augustus was the burial complex of the first imperial dynasty in Rome. Near the Mausoleum was the Ustrinum, or pyre for burning corpses, where the body of a deceased emperor was cremated prior to his becoming a god. The Mausoleum thus housed the remains of both an imperial family and a series of gods.

Rome. And not only the arts. In the new unified civilisation of the Roman empire, remarkable numbers of gods, rituals and cults spread through the Mediterranean area, especially from the east. By the later years of the empire, in the late third and fourth centuries AD, images and sanctuaries of originally eastern deities such as Mithras or Sarapis were to be found in such northern outposts of the Roman world as Britain. Indeed, no evidence is so convincing for the spread and diffusion of religions in the empire as the triumph of Christianity itself. For Christianity had been originally an obscure, peculiar and tiny Palestinian cult.

The patterns of pilgrimage which developed in the Roman world owed much to their Greek and Hellenistic inheritance.[20] Countless local cults, special syncretisms and notable shrines with more or less international significance made the religious profile of the empire not unlike that of Hindu India today. In principle, all gods were tolerated – the exceptions being only those whose followers (such as Jews, Christians and Manichaeans) were intolerant of other deities. There was an official religion, the imperial cult, in which the emperor (and his predecessors) were worshipped throughout the empire in temples dedicated to the imperial family or to Rome.[21] But for a more intense, direct and personal expression of piety, individuals might be devotees of specific cults – like Lucius to that of Isis in *The Golden Ass* or the second-century orator Aelius Aristides to the healing god Asclepius – or initiates in one of the mystery religions, such as the ancient rites of Eleusis or the more recent mysteries of Mithras.

Writing at the turn of the first and second centuries AD, the distinguished orator Pliny described the shrine of the river god Clitumnus near Spoletum in Umbria, north of Rome.[22] Near the source of the river

is an ancient and holy temple, in which stands Clitumnus himself clothed in a purple-bordered robe. The written oracles lying here prove the presence and prophetic powers of his divinity. All around are a number of small shrines, each containing its god and having its own name and cult, and some of them also their

own springs. . . . Everything in fact will delight you, and you can also find something to read. You can study the numerous inscriptions in honour of the spring and of the god which many hands have written on every pillar and wall. Most of them you will admire, but some will make you laugh – though I know you are really too good-natured to laugh at any of them.

(*Epistles*, VIII,8,7, letter to Voconius Romanus)

This passage describes a very Roman temple in the centre of Italy. We find here many of the same patterns of religious practice as in Greece. The god is identified with his statue (this was often but not always how ancient viewers approached cult images); he offers divination and oracular prediction to his visitors; his worshippers – like those at Epidaurus – leave inscriptions, whether formal plaques or informal graffiti or both. Pliny, the urban sophisticate, finds some of these inscriptions naïve – but they are all, as he recognises, expressions of the piety of pilgrims who have come to honour the god. One might see Pliny's rather self-conscious and even supercilious response to this activity of popular piety as a sign that the upper classes abstained from such occupations. But, in fact, not so much later in the second century AD, we find members of the élite, such as the orator Aristides, involved not only in sacred travel to temples but also in recording their pilgrimages. Like other ancient writers who describe sacred rites, Pliny remarks on the specificity of the different shrines set up around the main centre, with their own gods and their own particular rituals and worship.

8 Relief from the exterior wall at the west front of the Ara Pacis Augustae, Rome, dedicated in 9 BC. The Ara Pacis, or altar of Augustan Peace, celebrates the successful return of the emperor after campaigns in Gaul and Spain. The relief stood at the main entrance to the enclosure containing the altar, and its imagery – Aeneas pouring a libation to the gods prior to sacrificing a sow – presages the sacred activity which took place within.

9 Marble relief of Mithras slaying the bull, the cult image from the Walbrook Mithraeum in London. The image would have stood at the far end of the small and enclosed temple. The inscription records the dedicator, one Ulpius Silvanus, who served in the Second Augustan legion and was initiated into the mysteries of Mithras at Orange. Mithraism was particularly popular with members of the Roman military and seems to have been spread by them throughout the empire in the second and third centuries AD.

At Talmis on the southern frontiers of Egypt there survive the ruins of a temple dedicated to the god Mandulis.[23] Here were inscribed a large number of votive graffiti such as those Pliny describes. A man called Sansnos wrote a series of maxims into the wall:

Revere the divine. Sacrifice to all the gods. Travel in homage to each temple. Believe above all in your ancestral gods and revere Isis and Sarapis, the greatest of the gods, saviours, good, kindly, benefactors.[24]

Whatever the motives of this character in recording for posterity not only his own name but those of the deities to whom he was most committed, his inscription enshrines pilgrimage as the process of 'travelling in homage to each temple' beside religious awe and sacrifice as a prime signal of piety. Sansnos' willingness to praise Isis and Sarapis in the temple of another god to which he was a pilgrim, hints again at the syncretism and lack of exclusion that characterised religion in antiquity.

To go to Talmis one had to travel far. What awaited one at the end of this pilgrimage is hinted at in another, longer and stranger, inscription. It records an anonymous devotee's vision of the god:

I made myself a stranger to all vice and all godlessness, was chaste for a considerable period, and offered the due incense offering in holy piety. I had a vision and found rest for my soul. For thou didst grant my prayer and show me thyself through the heavenly vault; then washing thyself in the holy water of immortality thou appeardst again. Thou didst come in due season to thy shrine. . . .[25]

The vision of Mandulis, like the miracle of Asclepius to the voiceless boy at Epidaurus, is vouchsafed after a complex series of rituals. These include not only specific offerings (incense) given with the appropriate mental attitude (holy piety), but also abstinence both from evil-doing and from some of the normal activities of everyday life – in this case sex, though in some other cases certain kinds of food as well. The result of such specific rituals at the temple, in addition to the rituals enacted en route (such as abstinence from sexual conduct) and to the long ritual of travel to Talmis, was – for this devotee – a vision of his god. Clearly the ritual observances which surrounded the experience of pilgrimage in antiquity were of vital importance to its success.

Perhaps the finest ancient account of purification rituals in Graeco-Roman religion is to be found in the treatise *On the Syrian Goddess* ascribed to Lucian, an essayist of the second century AD, but possibly written a century later.[26] This is a first-hand description of the temple and rites at Hierapolis, or Mabbug, in Phoenicia. The author, himself a pilgrim, is particularly sensitive not only to the myths and rites of the temple itself but also to the rituals enjoined on the pilgrim in coming there. It is not beyond the bounds of possibility that this text is a sophisticated spoof of the 'loony fringe' of ancient religion, but – even if that were the case – it is still testimony for what went on (and was believed to go on) at the extremes of religious enthusiasm. The author writes:

10 A votive offering dedicated to the god Vulcan. Hammered silver leaf, 2nd–3rd century AD, British Museum. Found in Barkway, Herefordshire, the image shows the god dressed in cap and tunic. God of the forge, he stands by an anvil, holding the hammer and tongs of his craft.

I will tell what each of the pilgrims does. Whenever someone is about to come to the holy city, he shaves his head and eyebrows. Then after sacrificing a sheep, he carves it and dines on the parts. The fleece, however, he lays on the ground and kneels upon it, and the feet and head of the animal he puts on his own head. When he prays, he asks that the present sacrifice be accepted and promises a larger one for the next time. After finishing these activities he puts a garland on his head and those of everyone making the same pilgrimage. Then he sets out from his own country and makes the journey, using cold water for bathing as well as drinking, and he always sleeps on the ground, for it is a sacrilege for him to touch a bed before he completes the journey and returns to his own country. . . .

(Section 56)

These complex rituals, involving sacralising marks (the shaved head and eyebrows – marks used also by Theravada Buddhist monks), preliminary sacrifices and abstinence from home comforts such as hot water or a bed, are merely the initial or purification rites prior to the actual approach to the sanctuary or participation in a festival. They mark the special character of this particular journey, undergone under unusual circumstances, by which all who met the traveller would know that he was a pilgrim. They make the journey itself into a ritual.

On the pilgrim's arrival, other rituals and activities mark the occasion and place. At section 16 the author comes across two large phalli set up by the god Dionysus at the gate of the temple:

A man climbs up one of these phalli twice a year and lives on the tip of the phallus for a period of seven days. This reason is given for the ascent. The populace believes he communes with the gods on high and asks for blessings on all Syria, and the gods hear the prayers from nearby. (Section 28)

Pilgrims come and offer tokens (mainly money), in return for which the climber says prayers for each supplicant.

Among the sights in the temple, the writer describes a number of statues which combine Phoenician with Graeco-Roman deities, an oracle that speaks through a sweating cult-image of Apollo and, above all, the *galli*, or self-castrated priests. Putting it down to ancient custom and a rather convoluted myth of origin, the author tells how

each year in the sanctuary many castrate themselves and become womanish. . . . These people no longer wear male clothing. Instead they don feminine garments and do the work of women. (Section 27)

In a hyperbolic passage, he embroiders on the circumstances of this, presenting a radical picture of the reversal and inversion of everyday identity as well as the mixing of male and female sexuality:

While the rest are playing flutes and performing the rites, frenzy comes upon many, and many who have come simply to watch subsequently perform this act. I will describe what they do. The youth for whom these things lie in store throws off his clothes, rushes to the centre with a great shout and takes up a sword which, I believe, has stood there for many years for this purpose. He grabs it and immediately castrates himself. Then he rushes through the city holding in his hands the parts he has cut off. He takes female clothing and women's adornment from whatever house he throws these parts into. (Section 51)

Whatever the factual accuracy of this passage, it evokes the violence, danger and passion of religion in the ancient world. This was not an institutionalised series of state observances, but rather a dynamic and dangerous focus of rituals which defined and transformed the identities of participants.

The emphasis on ritual – particularly on the precision, specificity and order of details in ritual practice – which we find in all these accounts is perhaps most pointed in the great description of Greece written by the traveller Pausanias in the second century AD.[27] Pausanias, a Greek from Ionia in Asia Minor, went as a pilgrim not only to the most famous temples in Greece but also to many of the more remote and less celebrated shrines. Remarkable for his accuracy in recording the topography of the places he visited (archaeologists still use his text to help in the imaginative reconstruction of sites), Pausanias was even more precise and careful in describing the details of ritual. For instance, he described the altars of Zeus at Olympia not in the order in which they stood, but in the order in which sacrifice was made at them (v, 14, 4 and 10). For him such a liturgical or ritual order was more meaningful than a mere topographical catalogue or guidebook.

Immediately before exploring the Parthenon, in his first book on Attica, Pausanias describes the rites at the altar of Zeus Polieus (Zeus, god of the City):

Upon the altar of Zeus Polieus they place barley mixed with wheat and leave it unguarded. The ox which they keep already prepared for sacrifice goes to the altar and partakes of the grain. One of the priests they call the ox-slayer, who kills the ox and then, casting aside the axe here according to the ritual, runs away. The others bring the axe to trial, as though they know not the man who did the deed. (I, 24, 4)

Just as early Christian pilgrims to Palestine were very full and precise in their accounts of services and liturgy in the holy places, so here Pausanias recounts in analytic detail all the procedures of this strange rite, down even to the mixture of grains on the altar. He does not answer all the questions we might ask today, such as how often this ritual was performed, but he makes a point of finding out answers to a series of specific questions, *which mattered to him*, about sacrificial procedures and practices. What may initially seem his strange choice of what to tell us is in fact the most profound clue offered by his text to the way in which the ancients conceived of and thought about their religion.

Later in the same book, Pausanias comes to the altar of Zeus the Most High in front of the Erechtheum (1,36,5). Again he is painstaking in informing us that the Athenians never sacrifice a living creature here, nor do they offer wine (both such offerings being part of the normal pattern of sacrifice in the ancient world). On the other hand, they do offer cakes. Such rituals were special and specific to a particular god or shrine. Zeus Polieus on one part of the Acropolis was not the same as Zeus the Most High in another part. Pausanias' account as a whole presents a wonderfully rich ethnography of these rites, each of which was unique. One of the pilgrim's lessons in going to a temple was to learn how the locals worshipped, and to worship as the locals did. This is why Pausanias is so insistent on recording the altars at Olympia according to the ritual order in which they were used. A pilgrim like Pausanias – one might almost say a professional pilgrim, since he travelled to so many different holy centres – could become quite a connoisseur of such different local practices.

But such rites, which any pilgrim could see and record, were of a different order from the great mysteries of initiation in the ancient world. These secret rites – such as the Eleusinian Mysteries, to which pilgrims had been coming since archaic times and continued to come until the end of the pagan world – constituted a central aspect of religion. Among the many initiation mysteries which spread through the Roman empire in its later years (including Mithraism and Manichaeism), not least was Christianity. Pausanias refuses to describe the rituals (or even the images and architecture) of the sacred complex at Eleusis, the most famous of the mystery centres, holy to Demeter.[28] He explains that a dream (itself the result of a ritual vision, like the healing dreams at Epidaurus)

forbade the description of the things within the wall of the sanctuary; the uninitiated are of course not permitted to learn that which they are prevented from seeing. (1,38,7)

The ritual taboo of secrecy kept Pausanias' (perhaps uninitiated) readers from knowing the heart of a cult into which he was an initiate and which he himself recognises as one of the most wonderful sights of Greece (v,10,1). This taboo shows that, as an initiate, he saw the initiation cults as qualitatively different from the other rites and festivals (such as worship at the Acropolis or Olympian altars of Zeus) that he describes. It is not merely that Eleusis served a different group of people from Pausanias' main readership. While civic religion was inclusive of all citizens, the mysteries excluded non-initiates. They were in that sense élitist, although

11 Marble relief from Eleusis showing Demeter, Triptolemus and Persephone, second half of the 5th century BC. Demeter hands Triptolemus, represented as a youth, an ear of grain. According to the myth, the mission of Triptolemus was to disperse the grain to mankind and to teach human beings how to cultivate the land. His cult was one of the mysteries celebrated at Eleusis.

the exclusion was not based on belief or dogma, as in Christianity, but on ritual experience. As the Homeric *Hymn to Demeter* had already said in archaic times, the Eleusinian rites were 'awful mysteries which no one may in any way transgress or pry into or utter, for deep awe of the gods checks the voice' (476–9).

Despite, or perhaps because of, its secrecy and the dire consequences visited by the gods on anyone who broke the taboo, Eleusis attracted significant numbers of pilgrims throughout antiquity. Among the emperors initiated at Eleusis in Roman times were Hadrian, Lucius Verus, Marcus Aurelius and his son Commodus. It is a mark of the prestige of the cult, and of the importance of religion generally in the Roman world, that a small town, twelve miles from Athens, should have attracted such a distinguished string of Roman emperors in the second century AD. The last pagan emperor, Julian the Apostate (who ruled from 361 to 363 AD) was an initiate at Eleusis, and attempted to bolster the sanctuary with an imperial building programme as part of his battle against Christianity.

In some respects, pilgrimage in the ancient world was remarkably similar to pilgrimage in the world religions that began in the Near East – Judaism, Christianity and Islam. In many formal and social aspects, it was their historical ancestor. It emphasised ritualised travel, frequently modifying the normal activities of everyday life, to sacred centres often far away from where the pilgrim lived. It brought the pilgrim healing, miracles and contact with the divine forces of the other world. Like Christian and Muslim pilgrimage, it helped to build and reinforce the identity of devotees, initiates and believers through shared rituals and experience. In Olympia, the bones of the local hero Pelops (thought now to have been dinosaur bones) were one of the prime attractions, providing a cult of sacred relics centuries before the Middle Ages. Other shrines, from the tombs of mythical heroes such as Hippolytus, the chaste son of the Athenian king Theseus, to the Mausoleum of the deified emperor Augustus in Rome, were venerated like the tombs of Islamic and Christian saints. As in medieval Christianity, pilgrimages in antiquity focused around numerous holy, miracle-working and speaking statues, which attracted the veneration of multitudes and the protection of cities. Like Mecca and Jerusalem, ancient centres such as Delphi were regarded as the navel of the earth.

But there were also fundamental differences. Paganism was not a heavily theorised religion of the Book. Unlike the world religions, it had no theology, few written rules, few doctrines. Indeed it was not a single religion at all, but rather a clutch of practices, beliefs, rituals and superstitions of amazing variety and of very different intensities. In many ways this diversity, tolerated and indeed celebrated in its range of distinct and separate gods and practices, was more akin to the religions of South-East Asia than those of the Near East. Hinduism, especially, is a religion not of one Book but of many, not of one god but of countless gods, not of one series of beliefs and practices but of any number of divergent views and rites. It is this kind of rich diversity that ancient religion most resembles and that the practices of ancient pilgrimage bring to mind.

I. Viewer and Viewed: Images and Idols

a. *Colossal stone Buddhas from the Fenxian cave, the most magnificent of the caves at Longmen, to the south of Luoyang, China. Carved from the living rock in c. AD 672 during the reign of the Tang emperor Gaozhang, the statues represent Vairocana Buddha (centre) flanked by his disciples Kasyapa and Ananda and two Bodhisattvas.*

The culmination of most acts of pilgrimage is arrival at a sacredly charged space associated with a deity. The pilgrim knows that the spiritual summit of the journey has been reached because the sacred is not simply focused in a specially marked area, but more particularly is embodied by a specific object or set of objects. In the vast cave complex of Longmen near the city of Luoyang, Chinese Buddhists of the Tang dynasty (AD 618–907) carved out of the living rock approximately 100,000 sacred images in a total of 1,300 caves. This remarkable project, which is paralleled by similar Buddhist caves and mountain temples such as the spectacular caves of Ajanta and Ellora in India, culminates in a 55-foot high (16.7 m) image (Fig. Ia) of Vairocana, the Buddha of Ultimate Wisdom. By contrast, in a principally aniconic religion such as Islam, the pilgrim's ultimate goal is the Ka'ba or 'House of Allah' in the centre of the Mosque at Mecca, in which is housed the sacred black stone.

Often, as in Buddhist Longmen, though not in religions such as Islam or Judaism which proscribe the use of iconic representations of God, the pilgrim is confronted by an image of the deity. This sacred icon may be fixed, permanently marking out the sanctity of the place, or it may be moved in procession on festival days (which often coincide with times of special pilgrimage), as happened in the Plynteria or washing festival of Athena Polias in Classical Athens. But whether static or portable, the image is an object of worship whose specific qualities come to define the virtues of the place itself. Not only do pilgrims relate to the object through ritualised action (for example through touching and circumambulating the Ka'ba, or through prayer in front of the Wailing Wall in Jerusalem), but the

b. *Nandi Bull, the vehicle of Shiva. Colossal statue over 16 foot (5 m) high carved from the living rock at Chamundi Hill, near Mysore, India. Worshippers circumambulate the image; those in black are devotees of the Ayyappan pilgrimage cult.*

icon itself is frequently perceived as giving a direct response to worshippers. In the genre of the weeping Madonna or that of the miracle-working icon, an apparently inanimate image engages in physical activity. In Hinduism, the image is regarded as answering the worship of its devotees with a sacred and merit-bestowing gaze, technically called a *darshan*. The effort of the pilgrim in coming to the temple in order to view the god is rewarded by the deity, gaze for gaze.

The theme of the miraculous response of sacred images raises the central and potentially contentious question of the extent to which a deity is contained within and constrained by its image. Different religions and points of view within each religion have radically divergent ideas on this issue. In the world religions, which are defined as those based on sacred scriptures, the problem is compounded by debates as to whether divine power is best embodied within text, utterance or image. In general, pilgrimage is a central manifestation of popular devotion in these religions, emphasising as it does immediate contact with the divine rather than a theological intellectualising. Islam and Judaism conventionally deny the possibility of containing divinity within a humanly constructed artefact, while Hinduism, at the other extreme, tends to regard images or statues as vehicles of a sacred power which may be manifested through them and embodied in them but is not entirely or exclusively contained by them. The colossal statue of Nandi the bull (Fig. Ib), who is the divine vehicle of the god Shiva, at the temple of Chamundi near Mysore, is not only the figure of a bull but actually *is* Nandi as far as many of those who circumambulate the statue are concerned. The ritual action of such devotees, which includes bringing gifts of money and flowers as well as touching and circling the statue, has some resemblance with the actions of Buddhists circumambulating stupas (dome-shaped reliquaries) or of Muslims at the Ka'ba.

In all these cases, the act of encircling the sacred goal ritually defines a sacred space as well as marking the fact that the pilgrim has arrived there. The culmination of a spiritual journey is thus physically embodied by an action which is remarkably similar in form across very different religions. The circumambulation continues the theme of the pilgrim's movement but rather than involving a directional, linear striving to reach

c. *Artemis of Ephesus. Roman copy of the principal cult icon, which is now lost.*

the goal now encapsulates the sacred centre in a circular embrace. Nonetheless, the implications of such ritual actions, however similar their forms, have radically different meanings depending on different attitudes towards the very possibility of embodying the sacred.

Activities such as circumambulation may be prescribed by a religious tradition: some sacred images take such prescription further by incorporating the very act of worshipping them in the image itself. The fourteenth-century Byzantine icon representing the *Triumph of Orthodoxy* (Fig. 45) shows the famous Hodegetria icon from Constantinople displayed in triumph by angels amidst a procession of saints, monks, bishops and royalty, several of whom themselves hold icons. A later Christian example of such 'reflexive' representation, in which the image shows its own viewers worshipping it, is provided by Caravaggio's *Madonna of the Pilgrims* (Fig. Id). Here, the visitor to the church sees not only the Virgin and Child but also a pair of pilgrims who have come to worship them. The Virgin and Child, who emerge towards the pilgrims (and the viewer of the image) from an old, shabby, doorway that would have been an immediately familiar aspect of the lives of the pilgrims themselves, reply to the pilgrims' gaze with a gesture which acknowledges and blesses their presence. In her unremarkable dress and bare feet, this Virgin further resembles her worshippers.

One way of heightening the importance of a famous icon or statue, and thus the temple complex of which it is the cult image, is to make many reproductions of it so that pilgrims gain a sense of intimate contact with a sacred iconography. In modern culture, photography may fulfil this role. In antiquity, many copies of an archetypal cult statue, such as the famous image of Artemis at Ephesus in Asia Minor (Fig. Ic) were diffused throughout the Graeco-Roman world. Today, the original statue is no longer extant, but we have some intimations of its very complex symbolic form from replicas, of which a large number survive. The meanings of its highly unusual iconography are no longer recoverable, but it is noteworthy that this iconographic complexity was precisely one of the key features highlighted by the reproductions. The geographical spread of the replicas of Artemis of Ephesus made it possible for worshippers scattered over the whole Graeco-Roman world to relate directly to the original cult statue at Ephesus. A parallel is

d. *Caravaggio,* Madonna of the Pilgrims *(1603–4). Painted for the Cavalletti Chapel in the Church of Sant'Agostino, Rome, where it still hangs. The image depicts the Madonna of Loreto, the chapel's patron, brought to life before the pilgrims who worship her.*

evident here with the iconography of Hindu deities, which allows believers to recognise and venerate a god in a particular manifestation over a huge cultural and geographic area.

2

Exile and Return: Jewish Pilgrimage

'Three times in a year shall all thy males appear before the Lord thy God
in the place which he shall choose; in the feast of unleavened bread, and
in the feast of weeks and in the feast of tabernacles: and they shall not
appear before the Lord empty. Every man shall give as he is able,
according to the blessing of the Lord thy God which he hath given thee.'
DEUTERONOMY 16:16–17

Unlike the religions and religious practices of pagan antiquity,
ancient Judaism was distinctive in its belief in a single God. The
Jewish God was accessible not only through altars, oracles and
prophecies, but – perhaps above all – through texts. He made his
presence manifest to the prophets, but also wrote his creed on the tablets
of stone which Moses received at Sinai. Those tablets, preserved and
reverenced in the Ark of the Covenant, were perhaps the single most
sacred object in Judaism. In the kingdom established by David, the Ark
was brought to Jerusalem, the royal city, and housed in a special temple
built by David's son, Solomon. In this way Judaism would form a deeply
influential paradigm for the later Middle Eastern religions Islam and
Christianity, both of which traced their descent from Israel. For the
Judaism of David and Solomon's Temple brought together the kinds of
pilgrimage practices recognisable from Graeco-Roman and Canaanite
religions (such as the rituals described by the author of the *Syrian Goddess*)
with monotheism and a theology enshrined in texts.

As in other world religions (notably Islam), the sacred texts of Judaism
prescribe the act of pilgrimage as one of the obligations of the believer.
One of the injunctions given Moses at Sinai specifically refers to the
people of God appearing before the Lord three times a year.[1] In this way,
even before Judaism had a specific place in which to establish the
dwelling of the Lord, it had a prescriptive injunction for the performance
of pilgrimage. The activity of pilgrimage was conceived as an approach to
the presence of God, which was embodied not in *any* holy scriptures but
in the specific text which God himself had written on Sinai and which was
kept in the Ark. This was a profound departure from other ancient
religious practice, certainly from that of the Greeks.

However, just as Judaism began as the nomadic religion of a group of
tribes who (after Moses) carried the Ark of the Covenant with them as
they travelled, so its later history has been a story of displacement from

the Promised Land. The earliest Judaism had no fixed religious domain, but – according to Jewish myth – an original nomadism was converted into an enforced wandering. The Exodus from Egypt (which preceded the arrival in the Promised Land as it is presented in the Bible) is a sacred journey to the land of milk and honey. In the sixth century BC, after Solomon's Temple was destroyed by Nebuchadnezzar in 586, the Jews were exiled to Babylon. After the first century, following the destruction of the last Temple by Titus in AD 70, the Jews were exiled again in a Diaspora lasting nearly twenty centuries. During these periods of exile – much longer in total than the periods in which Jews occupied Palestine – it has often proved extremely difficult for Jews to visit the Holy Land. If pilgrimage is an act of returning the displaced self to a sacred centre, then the history of Judaism has been a virtually continuous displacement.

The motifs of exile and return have become central to Jewish tradition, experience and identity. Biblical narratives of wandering have become incorporated into Jewish ritual in such key festivals as Passover (celebrating the beginning of the Exodus) or Sukkot (the Feast of Tabernacles, which, according to some interpretations, recalls the temporary dwellings of the Israelites in the wilderness of Sinai). Exile and the lamentation for the lost centre became a fundamental theme of Jewish poetic writing. As it is memorably put in Psalm 137:1–6, which refers to the condition of the Jews after the destruction of the First Temple in the sixth century BC:

By the rivers of Babylon, there we sat down, yea, we wept, when we remembered Zion. . . . How shall we sing the Lord's song in a strange land? If I forget thee, O Jerusalem, let my right hand forget her cunning. If I do not remember thee, let my tongue cleave to the roof of my mouth: if I prefer not Jerusalem above my chief joy.

Exile became associated with iniquity. In the lamentations of Jeremiah, this evoked a repeated image:

Jerusalem hath grievously sinned; therefore she is removed: all that honoured her despise her, because they have seen her nakedness: yea, she sigheth, and turneth backward. (1:8)

The Lord hath cast off his altar, he hath abhorred his sanctuary, he hath given up into the hand of the enemy the walls of her palaces. . . . (2:7)

The punishment of thine iniquity is accomplished, O daughter of Zion. . . .
(4:22)

In turn, the return to Zion became associated with redemption. Particularly in Isaiah, the restoration of Jerusalem was used as a metaphor for the restoration of the people.

For Zion's sake will I not hold my peace, and for Jersualem's sake I will not rest, until the righteousness thereof go forth as brightness, and the salvation thereof as a lamp that burneth. And the Gentiles shall see thy righteousness, and all the kings thy glory. . . . (Isaiah 62:1–2)

Even the conquerors of Israel were envisaged as participating in the restored city and its faith:

The sons also of them that afflicted thee shall come bending unto thee; and all they that despised thee shall bow themselves down at the soles of thy feet; and they shall call thee, The City of the Lord, the Zion of the Holy One of Israel. . . . Violence shall no more be heard in thy land, wasting nor destruction within thy borders; but thou shalt call thy walls Salvation, and thy gates Praise.

(Isaiah 60:14,18)

In these prophecies, we see the association of three crucial concepts: redemption, return and a universalising attempt to bring other nations into the orbit of the Temple's powers. Return to the sacred centre is perceived as an act not merely of movement but also of restitution in moral and spiritual terms.

A DISPLACED PEOPLE

In the years after the destruction of the Temple by Titus, Jews remained in Palestine and may even have continued pilgrimage to the shattered remains of Jerusalem. A story associated with Rabbi Akiba, the great Talmudic scholar of the late first and early second century AD, tells of him gazing at the ruined Temple and seeing a glimmer of hope in its future restoration:

Therefore do I smile. The Prophets foretold both the destruction of Jerusalem and its restoration to glory. Now I have seen the first prophecy come to pass, and I know that the second will also be fulfilled.[2]

However, such hopes – which culminated in the rebellion of Bar Kochba in the mid second century AD – were dashed when Hadrian crushed the insurrection and utterly destroyed the remains of Jerusalem in AD 135. He refounded the town as the Roman colony of Aelia Capitolina and built a temple of Jupiter on the site of Solomon's Temple. Until the fourth century AD, Jews were forbidden even to enter this Roman city.

In the centuries of Christian and Islamic dominion, Jews were allowed to settle in Jerusalem and to visit Palestine from the diaspora communities abroad. However, we possess very little evidence of Jewish pilgrimage in this period. A particularly interesting account from the Middle Ages is provided by Rabbi Benjamin of Tudela, who travelled to Palestine from his home in Spain in the 1160s. His journey took him via Italy, Greece, Constantinople and the Middle East to the Holy Land and then onwards to Baghdad and Persia before his return via Egypt, Sicily and Germany. Benjamin's main aim was to visit the Jewish communities scattered through the Christian and Islamic dominions. However, he also had a particular interest in Jewish sacred sites and objects in the countries he visited. Here, for instance, are his comments on a major pilgrimage church in Rome:

Another remarkable object is San Giovanni in Porta Latina in which place of worship there are two copper pillars constructed by King Solomon of blessed memory, whose name, 'Solomon, son of David', is engraved upon each. The Jews in Rome told Benjamin that every year, about the time of the ninth of Ab, these pillars sweat so much that the water runs down from them. You see also there the cave in which Titus, the son of Vespasian, hid the vessels of the Temple, which he brought from Jerusalem; and in another cave on the banks of the Tiber, you find the sepulchres of those holy men of blessed memory, the ten martyrs of the kingdom.[3]

Here we find fascinating testimony to a diaspora Jewish tradition of martyred saints in Rome. Further, instead of seeing Rome full of Christian memorabilia, Benjamin (and his Jewish guides) interpret the monuments they see in Jewish terms. Rome becomes the burial ground for the dismembered fragments of the Temple – both of the Temple destroyed by Titus and also of its Solomonic predecessor. The significance of the ninth of Ab was not only that it commemorated the anniversary of the destruction of the Temple, but it was also the date when Jewish pilgrims were allowed to visit the Temple site from the fourth century AD.[4] To lament this tragedy, the pillars of Solomon in a Christian church in Rome produced a miracle for the Jews of the city.

When he comes to Palestine, Benjamin consistently scripturalises the Holy Land, associating contemporary towns with their Biblical origins. While this process is in many ways analogous to what Christian pilgrims did, Benjamin's scriptural base is of course the Old Testament in the days of Jewish monarchy rather than the New Testament's geography of Christ's ministry. On arrival, Benjamin comments:

It is one day hence to Acre, the Acco of scripture, on the confines of the Tribe of Asher. It is the frontier town of Palestine; and, in consequence of its situation, on the shore of the Mediterranean and of its large port, it is the principal place of disembarkation of all pilgrims who visit Jerusalem by sea.[5]

He locates the sites specifically associated with the great prophets of the Old Testament:

Mount Carmel. Under the mountain are many Jewish sepulchres, and near the summit is the cavern of Elijah, upon whom be peace. Two Christians have built a place of worship near this site, which they call St Elias. On the summit of the hill you may still trace the site of the altar which was rebuilt by Elijah of blessed memory, in the time of king Ahab, and the circumference of which is about four yards.[6]

Benjamin is keen to specify the exact details of the altar site and its measurements. He mentions Christian places of worship connected with what he sees as primarily a Jewish holy spot, but concentrates on what he believes to be the really sacred places, Elijah's cave and altar. By implication the Christian church, near but not at the actual spot of the prophet's holy action, is in some sense degenerate.

At times Benjamin's account reveals even more explicitly his distaste for the monuments of Christianity. In describing the newer religion's holiest site in Jerusalem he writes:

The large place of worship, called Sepulchre, and containing the sepulchre of that man, is visited by all pilgrims.[7]

Benjamin's circumlocution, 'that man', reveals his reluctance even to mention the name of Jesus. When he comes to Bethlehem, he notes the grave of Rachel, the place where several roads meet, even the small number of Jews in the town (twelve, all dyers by profession), but at no stage mentions the Church of the Nativity.[8]

Benjamin's Jewish interpretation of the landscape is reinforced by his recounting of Jewish legend and his repopulation of the landscape with

12 Capernaum, ruins of the synagogue. This impressive basilican building dates from between the late 2nd and the 4th centuries AD. Its main façade, with three entrances, faced towards Jerusalem. Despite the scriptural injunction of the second commandment ('Thou shalt not make unto thee any graven image'), many synagogues in Palestine and Syria were highly decorated in late antiquity, some with frescoes and many with mosaics.

remains of Jewish heroes. At Mount Zion, he tells the story of how two labourers found a cavern which led to a large hall supported by pillars of marble and encrusted with gold and silver. Within the hall were apparently contained the sepulchres of the kings of Judah, including David and Solomon. According to the legend, the workmen remained in the hall until frightened by a voice instructing them to 'get up, and go forth from this place'. Once they had recounted their experiences to the Patriarch of the city, the latter is said to have ordered the cavern to be walled up, thus hiding it from the gaze of future generations.[9]

The landscape of Palestine is also mythologised and made holy by specifically Jewish miracles:

Two parasangs from the (Dead) sea stands the salt pillar into which Lot's wife was metamorphosed; and although the sheep continually lick it, the pillar grows again and retains its original state.[10]

Anticipating Jewish pilgrims of today, Benjamin describes the Jews of Jerusalem going to the Western Wall to pay their devotions. He writes of

. . . the Western Wall, one of the walls which formed the Holy of Holies of the ancient Temple; it is called the Gate of Mercy, and all Jews resort thither to say their prayers near the wall of the courtyard.[11]

In the experience of diaspora Jewry, the very difficulty, even inability, to make the pilgrimage to Jerusalem became meaningful. The founder of the Hassidic sect, Rabbi Israel ben Eliezer, known as the Baal Shem Tov (Master of God's Name) is said to have attempted to visit Jerusalem in the eighteenth century:

He stretched himself upward and cried to God, 'Give me leave, Lord, and respite. Unloose that with which you hold me bound here in order that I may go into your land which calls me'. But God spoke powerfully to him and answered, 'Israel, it is my judgment over you that you remain in your place and do not appear in my land'.[12]

After much torment and against God's injunction, the Baal Shem decided to go. His trials on the journey and his sense that God had abandoned him eventually convinced him not to pursue his voyage but to return home. As his disciple Dov Baer of Mezritch, known as the Great Maggid, is reported to have said:

Now in exile the holy spirit comes upon us more easily than at the time the Temple was still standing.[13]

Some exiled Jewish communities engaged in pilgrimages far removed from the Holy Land itself. In late medieval times, for instance, Persian Jews appear to have echoed the practices of their Muslim rulers in revering tombs attributed to religious heroes.[14] The grave associated with Ezekiel, located at Dhu'l-Kifl, was actually sacred not only to Jews but also to Muslims, for whom the prophet was a saint. The tombs of Mordecai and Esther in the city of Hamadan, meanwhile, acted as pilgrimage centres during celebrations of Purim, when a scroll was read recounting the dangers that had faced previous generations of Jews.

In the absence of the Temple, and among those Jews during the Diaspora who could not make pilgrimage to its ruined site, a sense of continuity with an ancient tradition could nevertheless be maintained.

13 Jewish family celebrating Hanukkah, London.

14 Orthodox Jews at prayer by the Western Wall of the Temple, Jerusalem.

Synagogues were more than meeting places: they housed the Law (Torah) which, in embodying Jewish tradition, provided a distant echo of the Ark itself. The Passover service, not only a ritual embodiment of exile and return, but also one of the biblical pilgrimage-feasts, became a remembrance of Jersualem. It was an occasion on which Jews affirmed their future return to the Promised Land with the phrase 'next year in Jerusalem'. Thus, even without the Temple, prime qualities of Jewish pilgrimage – sin, atonement, diaspora, redemption and veneration for the dead – were preserved and relived in the rituals of the tradition. Many such features can be found in the post-Holocaust impulse to visit both the places of massacre, such as Auschwitz, and their memorials, such as the museum of Yad Veshem in contemporary Israel.

That desire for atonement and redemption was never separate, throughout the Diaspora, from a yearning for the reunification of the people and a myth of return to Palestine. The potent dream of uniting the scattered people of the Lord is well expressed by Benjamin of Tudela, at the very end of his travelogue:

May the Lord in his mercy be full of compassion towards them [the communities of diaspora Jews] and us, and may he fulfil towards both the words of his Holy Scripture: 'The Lord thy God will turn thy captivity, and have compassion upon thee, and will return and gather thee from all the nations, whither the Lord thy God hath scattered thee.' – Amen, Amen, Amen.[15]

CITY OF DAVID, TEMPLE OF SOLOMON

The experiences of scattering and exile found their expiation in the yearning for the Promised Land. In both cases the sense of dispersal apparently gave rise to a desire for unity which was expressed in spatial and spiritual terms by homing in on the holy city, its Temple and the Ark within. Perhaps central to the continuous aspiration for Zion as the ultimate holy place in Judaism was the claim that Yahweh himself chose the Holy Land as the dwelling of Israel (Joshua 1:2–6). However, even during the Exodus, Yahweh was considered to be accessible not in a fixed place in the Promised Land but in the portable Ark of the Covenant which God had instructed Moses to make.[16] The Ark was a wooden chest covered with gold plates, in which Moses placed the tablets of the Law which God had given him at Sinai.[17] In Palestine, the injunction to go on pilgrimage three times a year on the feasts of unleavened bread (Passover), weeks (Shavu'ot) and tabernacles (Sukkot) could be fulfilled by fixing the location of the holy in a single centre. This was Shiloh, the central sanctuary of the Israelites (where the Ark of the Covenant was kept) and the object of pilgrimage for the tribes of Israel until David moved it to Jerusalem.

Pilgrimage to Shiloh, at least in the ideal form described in the Bible, included women as well as men (despite the original injunction which only mentioned males), petitions to the Lord and sacrifices.[18] The sacrificial ritual is described in the Book of Samuel:

And the priests' custom with the people was, that, when any man offered sacrifice, the priest's servant came, while the flesh was in seething, with a fleshhook of three teeth in his hand; and he struck it into the pan, or kettle, or cauldron, or pot; all that the fleshhook brought up the priest took for himself. So they did in Shiloh unto all the Israelites that came thither. . . . (I Sam. 2:13–14)

The term for pilgrimage-feasts in Hebrew is *hag*, the etymological ancestor of *hajj*, which is still the Arabic term for the Muslim pilgrimage to Mecca. The word *hag* implies turning around and dancing – evoking some of the activities that came to be associated with pilgrimage in the Jewish tradition.[19]

The reasons why David moved the holy centre to Jerusalem are not entirely clear. What is certain, however, is he bolstered the significance of his new royal capital by creating a new permanent location for the Ark of the Lord, recovered from Shiloh which had been sacked by the Philistines. Politically, David seemed to be appropriating the holy embodiment of Jewish faith to establish a kingship which unified the tribes not merely through might but also through sacred authority. He was able to move the Ark with the support of the Prophet Nathan and in this way to establish his dynasty with divine approval. David's act of transferring the Ark is several times celebrated in the Bible and became embodied in repeated ceremonial in Jerusalem thereafter.[20] Such ceremonies themselves became objects of pilgrimage and helped to consolidate the House of David.[21]

However, the fixing of the Ark in Jerusalem was not without contradiction. In wishing to house the Ark in a permanent temple, David was introducing a radical innovation in Jewish religious history. As he said to Nathan:

See now, I dwell in an house of cedar, but the Ark of God dwelleth within curtains.[22]

While Nathan was initially favourable to David's plan, on divine injunction he forbade David to build the temple itself:

Thus saith the Lord, thou shalt not build me an house to dwell in; for I have not dwelt in an house since the day that I brought up Israel unto this day; but have gone from tent to tent, and from one tabernacle to another.[23]

David was thus allowed to authorise his new dynasty by bringing the Ark to his new capital, but the fixing of the Ark in a permanent place – representing the further institutionalisation of its cult – was denied to him. It has been argued that Nathan's pronouncement reflects the position of a conservative religious faction which sought to preserve the nomadic quality of worship inherited from the wandering desert origins of the Israelites.[24]

In the event, the building of the Temple was left to David's heir, Solomon, as foretold by Nathan to David:

And when thy days be fulfilled, and thou shalt sleep with thy fathers, I will set up thy seed after thee, which shall proceed out of thy bowels, and I will establish his kingdom. He shall build an house for my name, and I will stablish the throne of his kingdom for ever.[25]

With Solomon, the unity of God's house and sacredly ordained kingship was finally confirmed.

Solomon built the Temple on Mount Moriah in Jerusalem. It was, according to the Bible, a perfect cube in shape, 20 cubits each way, and consisted of a porch leading into a series of ever more sacred rooms. The form of the Temple itself echoed that of the Ark, especially in its use of gold overlay and its imagery of cherubim.[26] An object designed to be portable (rings were attached to the Ark through which poles could be passed) was housed in a building whose appearance was designed to recapitulate, make permanent and monumental its sacred presence.[27] Beyond the porch was a chamber called the Holy Place and beyond this a small inner shrine called the Holy of Holies, a dark windowless room in which the Ark was placed. Two courtyards, in which sacrifice was offered, separated the Temple from the outside world.[28] This building acted not only as a religious space, but was a legal centre for judgments.[29] The siting of the Temple on a hill in the city of David thus had fundamental symbolic significance. In social terms, the establishment of Jerusalem demonstrated clearly a shift from the nomadic culture of the early Israelites to a more sedentary life under the monarchy. In political terms, it implied the concentration of authority in a single divinely appointed dynasty. In religious terms, it involved the centralisation of worship.

This range of significance and the power of Jerusalem to act as a focus for the people of Israel were emphasised in the scriptural account of Solomon's dedication ceremony:

Then Solomon assembled the elders of Israel, and all the heads of the tribes, the chief of the fathers of the children of Israel unto king Solomon in Jerusalem. . . .[30]

In response to Solomon's summoning of the people and the sacrifices performed, God granted a theophany in which His presence filled the new Temple:

And it came to pass, when the priests were come out of the holy place, that the cloud filled the house of the Lord. So that the priests could not stand to minister because of the cloud: for the glory of the Lord had filled the house of the Lord.[31]

This sign was taken as a sanctification of the Temple, as God's approval of Solomon's action in placing the Ark inside it, and of Solomon's kingship. As David's dynasty was ratified, so the placement of the Ark was confirmed:

Then spake Solomon, The Lord said that he would dwell in the thick darkness. I have surely built thee an house to dwell in, a settled place for thee to abide in for ever.[32]

In this initial ceremony, in addition to affirming the Temple's spiritual authority, Solomon was seen as tying the Temple's meanings to the moral restitution of the people:

When thy people Israel be smitten down before the enemy because they have sinned against thee, and shall turn again to thee and confess thy name, and pray, and make supplication unto thee in this house: then hear thou in heaven, and forgive the sin of thy people Israel, and bring them again unto the land which thou gavest unto their fathers.[33]

The pilgrim who visited Jerusalem on one of the great pilgrimage-feasts would have come to the focus of royal power. Pilgrimage to the Temple was associated with the ultimate place of arbitration in legal terms as well as those of moral self-examination and penitence. Pilgrims would have ascended the Temple mount, symbolically coming ever closer to God, who was believed to be both present in the Temple and yet was also far above it. The sanctuary was seen in one sense as the highest point on earth, the quintessential meeting place of humanity and Yahweh.[34] Yet the Temple compound itself consisted of a series of boundaries which ultimately could not be penetrated by anyone save a limited group of priests.

Over time the Temple became an extraordinary nexus for mythical and symbolic meanings. In later Judaism, it was the place where the waters of the Deep were blocked off on the first day of creation; it was the first place and so the centre of the world; it was the site from which the dust was gathered in order to make Adam; it was the location of Adam's first sacrifice and the site of Adam's grave; it was the place where Cain and Abel offered sacrifice (and thus the site of Abel's death). The Flood was caused by lifting the Temple's foundation stone and releasing the waters of the Deep; the Temple was the site of Noah's first sacrifice after the Flood, of Abraham's circumcision and Melchizedek's altar in Salem.[35] The Temple thus became a material commemoration of the whole sacred history of the Jewish people.

The yearning for the Temple is wonderfully expressed in Psalm 84: 1–2, 10:

How amiable are thy tabernacles, O Lord God of Hosts! My soul longeth, yea, even fainteth for the courts of the Lord: My heart and my flesh crieth out for the living God. . . . For a day in thy courts is better than a thousand. I had rather be a doorkeeper in the house of my God, than to dwell in the tents of wickedness.

Yet this was a theological conundrum. The Temple had to accommodate both the transcendence and the immanence of God. Implying that God was only present in the Temple (or the Ark) would confine his potential omnipresence. Solomon himself, in dedicating the Temple, expresses this apparent contradiction:

But will God indeed dwell on the earth? Behold the heaven and heaven of heavens cannot contain thee; how much less this house that I have builded. Yet have thou respect unto the prayer of thy servant. . . . That thine eyes may be open toward this house night and day, even toward the place of which thou hast said, My name shall be there: that thou mayest hearken unto the prayer which thy servant shall make toward this place.[36]

The Temple and the Ark could thus be said to mediate the presence of Yahweh with the people in a special way. But this caused problems in exile, when the Temple had been destroyed by the Babylonians, since religious meetings could occur only in places where God had clearly made his presence known. The incompatibility between the need for the presence of God and the exile of the Jews was in the Bible only resolved by revelation, when God appeared in a theophany to prophets such as Ezekiel and Daniel. In this way, God's presence could be mediated not merely through a fixed place and object (embodied in the Temple and the Ark) but also through the living charismatic authority of a prophet in exile.

On the return of the Jews from exile in Babylon (in the sixth century BC), the destroyed Temple of Solomon was rebuilt as the Second Temple, partly at the behest of the prophets Haggai and Zechariah, although it is likely that the Ark itself had been lost in Nebuchadnezzar's sacking of Jerusalem. Subsequently the Temple was reconstructed in a still more grandiose manner by Herod the Great. Herod's Temple (the Third Temple) was the one from which Christ is said to have expelled the money-changers and which Titus destroyed in AD 70. These latter Temples were still regarded as the dwelling place of the Lord, despite the loss of the Ark.[37]

Many of the implications and meanings of pilgrimage to the Temple for Jews in the period just before its final destruction are well summarised by this passage from Philo Judaeus, a Hellenised Jew from Alexandria writing in the first half of the first century AD:

The highest, and in the truest sense the holy, temple of God is, as we must believe, the whole universe. . . . But he provided that there should not be temples built either in many places or many in the same place, for he judged that since God is one, there should be also only one temple. Further he does not consent to those who wish to perform the sacred rites in their houses, but bids them rise up from the ends of the earth and come to this temple. . . . One who is not going to sacrifice in a religious spirit would never bring himself to leave his country and friends and kinsfolk and sojourn in a strange land, but clearly it must be the stronger attraction of piety which leads him to endure separation from his most familiar and dearest friends who form as it were a single whole with himself.[38]

If Philo even partially expressed the feelings of most first-century Jews, one can see how catastrophic was Titus' destruction of the Third Temple.

ISRAEL REGAINED

If the fall of the Temple were not to imply the end of Jewish religious practice, some new means of worship and an alternative mode of articulating religious community had to be evolved. Among the new forms developed by diaspora Judaism (which may themselves echo religious adaptations instigated in earlier periods of exile) were the establishment of synagogues, the ending of animal sacrifice at an altar and the exploration of a whole new topography of Jewish pilgrimage. Just as when Christianity lost the Holy Land in the early Middle Ages and used this opportunity to develop new sites of pilgrimage in Europe, so Jews in Palestine sought out places associated with their own holy figures. The earliest Christian pilgrims to Palestine also frequented many of these Jewish sites – indeed, a majority of the early Christian sacred places in the Holy Land referred to Old Testament events.[39]

In more recent times, the desire for return was to become more than a spiritual aspiration: it took the form of a political project which finally crystallised in the late nineteenth and early twentieth century into Zionism. This was a largely secular movement in which the sacred themes of return and redemption were translated into the political language of nationhood and minority civil rights. The Zionist cause, especially as propagated in the 1890s by Theodore Herzl, won many adherents among the oppressed Jews of central and eastern Europe: by 1914 the Jewish population of Palestine had more than trebled to 85,000 through immigration.[40] After the Holocaust, the international community helped to create the state of Israel in 1948. Just as the original kingdom of Israel acted to centralise dispersed Jewish tribes, so the contemporary nation-state is built on the premise of uniting Jews who have been dispersed around the globe.

The Temple has not been rebuilt, although the Wailing Wall (the Western Wall of the Temple) and Jerusalem itself have retained their focal significance for Jews. This significance has become imbued with a series of political implications which assert a modern myth of unity through nationhood.[41] Many of the immigrant Jewish communities have, however, attempted to preserve some aspects of their ethnic identity against the strong impulse to merge into the new nation. In the case of many Moroccan Jews, who, ironically, have felt discriminated against in Israel, the revival of pilgrimage practices has taken on a new religious and political significance which emerges directly out of the current political situation. Rather than incorporating them into a secular state bound by a nominal Judaism, pilgrimage has helped to assert their distinctiveness in opposition to other Israelis. These Moroccans have reinscribed the ritual landscape of the Holy Land with a series of their own saints, such as Rabbi David u' Moshe, whose body is believed to have been mysteriously transported from his tomb in the Moroccan Atlas to a new shrine in northern Israel. Many of the Moroccan shrines lie in peripheral areas,

15 Synagogue at the Hadassah Medical Centre, Jerusalem. The stained glass windows, designed by Marc Chagall, represent the twelve tribes of Israel. In this view (from left to right) the windows of Naphthali, Joseph, Benjamin, Reuben and Symeon are shown.

especially those with high Moroccan Jewish populations. Not only do the Moroccans seek their saints' intercession for help in everyday existence, but some pilgrimages explicitly associate mystical religion with political advocacy. Rabbis and politicians appear together on such occasions, and the images of shrines are even used to support political campaigns in television programmes.[42]

In the Diaspora, the Promised Land was a mythical ideal for Jews. The people saw their identity in terms of a land from which they were in exile. Ritual practice in the Diaspora, such as the orientation towards Jerusalem, encouraged the notion of a common Judaism transcending spatial, temporal and linguistic differences, much like the practices of prayer and sacrifice in Islam. However, the creation of an apparently unified (at least for Jews) nation-state has forced members of a common religious faith to confront significant cultural divergences. When the return to Jerusalem ceases to be a myth, the realities of social and political existence have the potential to create exile within the Promised Land itself.[43]

16 The old Jewish cemetery, Prague. One of the oldest ghettos of the Diaspora to have survived into the 20th century, Prague boasts a number of ancient synagogues, a Jewish Town Hall, and the cemetery (*left*), which was founded in the later 15th century.

II. The Sacred Site: Contestation and Co-operation

a. *Exterior of the Dome of the Rock, Jerusalem, 7th century* AD. *Located on top of the Jewish Temple Mount, the octagonal building has side porches facing in the cardinal directions. Marble and tilework in blue, white, yellow and black cover the outer walls. The central dome is 115 foot (35 m) in height and coated with gold leaf.*

No event is more traumatic in ancient Jewish tradition than the razing of the Second Temple by the Roman emperor Titus in AD 70. This brutal act of iconoclasm, coupled with Hadrian's destruction and re-founding of the city in AD 135, is an ironic testimony to the sacred significance of the city and the Temple, not only in the Jewish imagination but also in that of those who felt compelled to demolish a nexus of such evident power. The charisma of the site was only reinforced subsequently when other religions (tracing their origins back to, yet also in opposition to, Judaism) sought to construct their own sacred spaces in the city.

Such competitive use of a single sacred space by multiple religions has led to highly charged forms of contestation on the levels of architecture, tradition and, not least, politics. One

reason for this is that the obliteration of architecture or sacred objects by no means achieves an obliteration of their memory or cultural significance. On the contrary, the destruction of the Jerusalem Temple only served to reinforce the religious identity of those who had once worshipped there and their descendants.

The landscape of pilgrimage (and of sacred worship more generally) consists of much more than mere geography or architecture. It is a landscape of memory, myth and tradition in which monuments play as much a symbolic as an actual role. This symbolic significance of the lost can lead to the restoration of a destroyed centre centuries after the act of destruction. At the Marian shrine of Walsingham, which was brutally suppressed by Henry VIII during the English Reformation, a vibrant tradition of pilgrimage has re-emerged in the twentieth century. In the seventeenth century, the Muslim emperor Aurangzeb attempted to suppress the Hindu holy city of Benares, not only by destroying its sacred monuments and replacing them with mosques but also by changing its very name to Mohammedabad. The attempt failed, but its legacy was a city of post-seventeenth-century Hindu architecture and a number of highly contested mosques (see Fig. IIb).

In other cases, the potent memory of a violated site may lead to the destruction of its replacement. Recently, Hindu extremists tore down the mosque constructed by the Mughals at Ayodhya, a site which they venerate as the birthplace of the god Rama. Jerusalem is still more complex: currently Jews have access to the remains of the Temple in the form of the Wailing Wall (Fig. IIc), yet the very act of approach and worship there is also a reminder of contested history. The pilgrim's view of the Wall is surmounted by eloquent testimony to Islam's appropriation of the site in the form of the magnificent Dome of the Rock.

The Dome of the Rock itself (Fig. IIa), built by the caliph Abd al-Malik in AD 691–2, was deliberately placed on the site of the Temple to express Islam's continuity with its Jewish origins, as well as to mark Judaism's disinheritance from its spatial centre. The site has been given a further layer of significance beyond its Jewish mythological associations with such critical biblical events as the sacrifice of Isaac by Abraham, since it is seen by Muslims as the point from which the Prophet Muhammad ascended into Heaven. A principal motivation for building the Dome was that Mecca was at the time in the hands of a rival caliph, so that political competition became translated into sacred space and mythology. The architectural form of the Dome appropriates that of Byzantine octagonal churches and in particular the circular form of the main Christian shrine in Jerusalem, the Holy Sepulchre, thus marking a visual link with the Christian presence in the city. And yet, just as the Dome's situation denies the ultimate title of Judaism to the site of the Temple, so the Koranic inscription in its interior denies Christian doctrine by asserting the oneness of God in

b. *Panorama of Benares, seen from across the Ganges, showing the Hindu holy city with a Mogul mosque dominating the sky-line. Early 19th century.*

c. *The Wailing Wall and Temple Mount, Jerusalem.*

opposition to the Holy Trinity. The building is not by any means a pure elimination of earlier traditions, but rather is given shape by its opposition to and replacement of them.

Jerusalem therefore provides one spatial model of the close juxtaposition of religious faiths. It is the supreme example of a place where monotheistic religions, each one with a single exclusive scripture, contest the sacred ground (although there are others, such as Mount Sinai,

d. *Worshippers (Hindu and Buddhist) queuing to pay devotions to the main deity, Chamundi Temple, near Mysore, Karnataka, India.*

which all three religions venerate as the site where God gave Moses the Law). Yet Jerusalem does not demonstrate the only possible outcome for a juxtaposition of faiths. While monotheism and exclusivity often (though by no means always) lead to competition between religions, a more polytheistic and inclusive kind of religion such as Hinduism, despite the example of Ayodhya, need not generate such conflicts. Take the case of the Temple of Chamundi near Mysore, which is venerated both by Hindus and by Tibetan Buddhists (Fig. IId). Rather than attempting to appropriate the space sacred to another religion, here devotees of both faiths worship the same cult image in the same temple. In this case, because the name of the Hindu goddess Chamundi is the same as that of the Tibetan consort of the deity Heruka, Tibetans come on pilgrimage to the site. Another example is Mount Kailas in the Himalayas, where Hindus, Buddhists and local Shamanistic worshippers (Bons) venerate different deities in the same place.

Whatever members of different religions may feel about worshipping what is apparently the same image, even adherents of the same religion can exhibit radically different responses. In Christianity, belonging to what is apparently the same faith does not preclude and may even reinforce controversy. Protestants, Catholics and Orthodox visit a number of different sites in Jerusalem, and even in visiting the same sites perceive and interpret their experience of sacred space very differently. Within the walls of a single building, the Church of the Holy Sepulchre (Fig. 25), different Christian factions (such as Roman Catholics and the Orthodox) look after separate parts of the church and have different places for exercising their liturgy. Other confessions (for instance Evangelical Protestants and Ethiopians) have their main sites of worship outside the building. While some believers recognise Jesus's tomb to be that inside the Holy Sepulchre, others regard as authentic a tomb in a garden outside the current city walls. One lesson to be drawn from the complex series of attitudes around the Holy Sepulchre is that co-operation may itself embody a form of contestation.

3

The Centre in the Desert: Muslim Pilgrimage to Mecca

'Surely, the first House established for the benefit of all mankind is
the one at Mecca, abounding in blessings and a means of guidance for
all peoples.'
KORAN, 3:97

Even in the secular West, the idea of 'Mecca' provides a powerful metaphor for the fulfilment of aspirations. For Muslims, however, Mecca implies much more than an image of desire. It is a sacred space reserved purely for the *umma* (the Islamic community of faith), a physical centre towards which all believers should turn – not only in belief but also in bodily worship. Yet it is not located in any of the great political strongholds of the Islamic world. It lies in the Hijaz, a strip of land lying along the east coast of the Red Sea that the Koran itself calls an 'unfruitful valley'.

Islam is the youngest of the world religions, and its tenets both incorporate and reinterpret the teachings of earlier faiths. Moses and Jesus are regarded as early prophets, but their religions are said to have distorted the will of God. In the seventh century AD the Prophet Muhammad was apparently given a final revelation from God while he lived in Mecca and nearby Medina. The divine message came to be recorded in the Koran, 'the Perfect Book'. Written in Arabic, this text helped to define the identity of a new religion anxious to distinguish itself from the other great faiths of the Near East. It also served to establish patterns of belief and practice that would be followed far into the future. As one Islamic scholar has noted: 'The Prophet departed, the Revelation remained.'[1]

Muslim descriptions of the origins of Mecca also reflect the idea of a faith emerging out of and indeed appropriating the myths and practices of older traditions. Allah is said to have chosen the Arabian peninsula as the location of the origin of the world, and to have created the rest of the earth in a series of concentric circles leading away from what became, literally, 'the navel of the earth'. Adam, the first prophet, then lived on the site before being expelled from Paradise. Later, following Allah's command to leave the fertile land of Syria, the prophet Abraham built a shrine in the 'unfruitful valley' which echoed the divine residence of God in heaven. This earthly House of Allah came to be known as the *Ka'ba*, or 'cube'.

The Prophet Muhammad was born in Mecca around AD 570. Within seventy years he had not only restored the sacred shrine to Allah, but also established the foundations of the Islamic faith. The practice of the Prophet – embodied in the 'tradition', or *sunna*, and recorded in textual materials called *hadiths* – has become a model for all Muslims. Five central pillars of faith are mentioned in the Koran. Four of these specify actions which are to be repeated at steady intervals, reminding the believer constantly of his or her identity as a Muslim. Allah is to be proclaimed God, and Muhammad his Prophet. Fasting should be practised during the holy month of Ramadan. Alms are to be given, and prayers said five times a day. It is the last of the great pillars of faith, however, which confirms the believer's identity in a way that is exceptional because its performance is necessary only once in a lifetime. This is the *hajj*, or pilgrimage to the holy city of Mecca in what is now Saudi Arabia. Alone among all of the contemporary world religions, therefore, Islam actually requires its followers to go on pilgrimage, provided health and funds permit. As the Koran states: 'Pilgrimage to the House is a duty laid upon people which they owe to Allah, those of them that can afford the journey thither' (3:98). The *hajj* signifies proper devotion to the will of God, and literally means 'an effort'. Even though perhaps only ten per cent of the world's 600–700 million Muslims manage to undertake the journey before they die, the thoughts of the entire *umma* are likely to be with the one or two million who reach Mecca each year.

For some Muslims, the injunction contained in the fifth pillar of Islam provides a key to the unity of peoples professing the Islamic faith. Pilgrims to the House of Allah are required to strip themselves of all marks of identity except those which indicate their allegiance to Islam. One *hajji*, conversing with the famous North American Muslim and black activist Malcolm X, expressed this ideal of cultural diversity submerged within a common religious identity in the following way:[2]

This would be an anthropologist's paradise. . . . Every specimen of humanity is brought together at Mecca during this pilgrimage. It's probably the only incident and the only time and the only place on earth where you can find every specimen of humanity – all cultures, all races . . . all of everything.

Yet we would be foolish to assume that a world religion such as Islam, whose tenets are designed to span and transcend both historical change and cultural variation, is a faith which reflects the perfect unity enjoined in its holy book. 'Islam' means 'submission' to the divine will, but such submission can take many forms.[3] Thus, it is a religion of conflicts and contradictions, made sharper because many believers strive towards incompatible conceptions of orthodoxy and truth. Differences of interpretation and practice fracture the faith along many fault-lines – between urban and rural practice, scripturalist and mystic notions of authority, the politically powerful and the politically weak. . . . No study of Islamic pilgrimage can avoid these issues of conflict and divergence, even as it describes the *hajj* – the one occasion when a large part of the *umma* comes together, synchronising movements in time and space to converge on the central point of faith.

17 Mecca, Saudi Arabia. Pilgrims gather in concentric circles around the Ka'ba, shown here draped with the *kiswah*, or black cloth. The Ka'ba dates largely from the 7th century AD, though it has been much restored. The foundations of the present construction contain fragments from the building known to Muhammad.

18 Persian calligraphic motto, 17th century. The figure is a basmala, or form of writing moulded into a figurative representation to read 'In the Name of God, the Compassionate, the Merciful'.

ORIGINS OF THE HAJJ: FAITH, TRADE AND CONQUEST

Call to mind the time, when the disbelievers plotted against thee that they might confine thee, or kill thee, or expel thee. They planned and Allah also planned, and Allah is the best of planners. . . .   (*Koran*, 8:31)

Around AD 400 pastoral nomads of the Koreish tribe established a permanent settlement in the valley of Mecca. The bedouin way of life in the area was characterised by constant feuds, but common religious and judicial customs required the declaration of periods of truce – times of sacred peace during which pilgrimage to local gods as well as trade could take place. Around religious sites there existed a protected or holy area (*haram*), in which the spilling of blood was not permitted. The trading centre at Mecca benefited from these rules, since it was located on the incense route along the east coast of the Red Sea. Pagan tribes would come to worship at the Ka'ba, exchange goods at great fairs and compete in recitals of poetry. As the settlement developed into an economic and political power, it also encouraged the centralisation of worship in Mecca. The Ka'ba became a pre-eminent shrine, surrounded by the idols of visiting tribal groups. Gradually, as one shrine gained in importance, so did a single deity – Allah, the God in whose name people fulfilled contracts, honoured relatives and fed their guests (*al-ilah* means 'the God'). Thus, peaceful commerce and worship, trade and religion, reinforced each other. One writer has attempted to provide a vivid evocation of the scene, as if it were occurring before our eyes:[4]

Within the tumultuous confusion which fills the desert, the festivities at the beginning of each season represent the only enjoyable periods of rest. A peace of God at this time interrupts the continuous feuds for a fair period of time. The most diverse tribes which otherwise did not trust each other at all, make common pilgrimage to the same holy places without fear, through the land of friend and foe. Trade raises its head, and general and lively exchange results. . . .

Muhammad was born into a poor but respectable branch of the Koreish clan. His great-grandfather, Hashim, had previously played an important part in consolidating much of the Meccan commercial empire. He himself was a trader and married the widow of a rich merchant: he did not begin to preach until he had reached the age of 40 or so. At first, he attracted little attention from fellow Meccans, but as he began to appeal to a wider public his strong opposition to polytheism and the worship of idols proved unpopular among the Koreish. These rulers of Mecca may have been afraid that their trading links would be threatened if pagan religious festivals were curtailed. They were also puzzled as to why Muhammad should have been the one chosen by God to receive a revelation, and are reputed to have asked: 'Why could God not choose a bigger man with better means (and a bank balance) at his disposal to be the Prophet . . .?'[5]

In 622, Muhammad and his followers were forced to flee the city, and it is from the year of this flight and exile, or *hijra*, that the Muslim era is dated. The Muslim refugees sought refuge in Medina (*Medinat-un-Nabi*, or 'city of the Prophet'), where Muhammad found military and spiritual support for his aims and assumed an important role as arbiter of disputes.

The Prophet was a skilful politician and military leader, and began to combine raids on the caravans of the Koreish with the exertion of economic pressure on Mecca. Trade links between Mecca and Medina also helped to increase the influence of Islamic ideas, and in 629 some 2,000 Muslims even managed to undertake a lesser pilgrimage (*umra*) to the city.

By 630 the city of his birth had given in to Muhammad's military and political pressure, and such success was codified in ritual and doctrine. Islam's enemies were treated with mercy, but the idols of Mecca were destroyed and the Ka'ba purified. A traditional story from the time of the Prophet, recorded in the eighth century by Ibn Ishaq of Medina, provides an interpretation of these developments offered by a Muslim defending his faith to the King of Abyssinia:[6]

. . . O King, we were plunged in the depth of ignorance and barbarism; we adored idols, we lived in unchastity; we ate dead animals, and we spoke abominations; we disregarded every feeling of humanity, and the duties of hospitality and neighbourhood; we knew no law but that of the strong, when God raised among us a man, of whose birth, truthfulness, honesty and purity we were aware, and he called us to the unity of God, and taught us not to associate anything with Him, he forbade us the worship of idols; and enjoined us to speak the truth. . . .

Thus, non-believers were prevented from entering the Ka'ba, and in the spring of the tenth year after his flight to Medina the Prophet performed another pilgrimage to Mecca. These actions, accomplished shortly before his death in June 632, confirmed Mecca as the holiest city in Islam, with the Ka'ba as its most sacred point. Muhammad's last pilgrimage was also to prove a model for future Muslim practice. To perform the *hajj* was to follow in the footsteps of Adam, Abraham and, above all, the Prophet himself.

Under Muhammad's successors the Arab tribes conquered large parts of North Africa, the Holy Roman Empire, Turkey, Persia and Afghanistan. United for the first time, they were able to penetrate frontiers that the Roman and Persian empires had grown too weak to defend. In the words of one commentator, Islam became 'a composite civilisation, as well as a religion and social order'.[7] Key to such success was the creation of an Arab consciousness based on common faith rather than tribal loyalties.

In AD 660 the political capital of the Muslims was shifted from Medina to Damascus, and Mecca itself remained a town of relatively modest proportions. It was prevented from expanding too far because it was surrounded by mountains, and never saw the construction of great buildings – perhaps because these would have been seen as too much of a challenge to the predominance of the Ka'ba. Yet, as the following quotation indicates, its significance as a site of worship was to prove decisive:[8]

Mecca was a frontier town, raw and unfinished, a commercial boom town that would likely have soon become an urban ghost had it not found a new and extraordinarily successful export item of its own manufacture.

The history of the Hijaz has seen numerous generations of Muslims (and European Crusaders) attempting to appropriate Mecca's economic wealth, use its religious status to bolster their political authority, or even redefine its spiritual significance. From the earliest days of Islam, local political leaders were eager to exploit the profitable pilgrim trade, and some were even prepared to claim descent from the Prophet to bolster their authority. In 1201 the sherif, or ruler, of the port of Yanbu, situated to the north, sent his son to attack Mecca, and took the town easily since the Amir of the city had, with a lamentable sense of timing, taken all his men away on a minor pilgrimage. The descendants of this sherif, who could claim descent from the Prophet himself, reigned as nominal rulers of Mecca until the Treaty of Versailles in 1919. Such apparent authority did not prevent them from being subject to the 'protection' of rulers in Cairo, including the sultans of the Ottoman empire from the sixteenth century until the beginning of the twentieth.

More subtle ways of obtaining political and religious status from association with Mecca and Medina have been available to ambitious Muslims. The Malaysian government has recently decided to take over the organisation of the *hajj* on behalf of its citizens – a way of identifying the nation-state with Islam. Other forms of patronage have enabled the powerful to cement a reputation for generosity, piety and influence. The 'Mosque of the Footprints' at Damascus lay along the highway leading to the Hijaz, Jerusalem and Egypt, and became the recipient of many gifts, including endowments for people to take up the route to Mecca on behalf of those who could not go themselves. In the thirteenth century an Egyptian sultan made a pilgrimage to Mecca bringing with him a *kiswah* (a silk covering for the Ka'ba) embroidered in gold with verses from the Koran.[9] This action indicated not only reverence for the building but also the sultan's authority within the city, and the covering was subsequently replaced by Egyptian rulers every year. Status could also be gained by having one's name mentioned in the Friday prayers delivered at Mecca, and this fact provided a useful source of funds for local sherifs, who could be persuaded to adapt their spiritual inclinations for monetary gain. It is easy to understand the origin of the Meccan saying: 'We do not need any agriculture – God has given us the pilgrims as our annual crop.'

Mecca has also provided an important arena for competing definitions of proper Islamic practice. In the eighteenth century, uncompromising Sunni Muslims known as Wahhabis succeeded in forcing much of the interior of the Arabian peninsula to adopt their version of the faith through a combination of proselytisation and conquest. They did their best to restore the piety of pilgrimage by banning musicians and prostitutes from caravans, and made their presence felt in the Holy City itself, as the following historical account indicates:[10]

At the hajj . . . of 1800 Mecca saw hordes of Wahhabi warriors, accompanied by their women and children, swarming through its streets like streams from the hills following rain and praying with unaccustomed fervour at the Holy Places.

The doctrines of the Wahhabis have been compared with those of Calvinist Puritanism in Christianity because of their asceticism and suspicion of all forms of idolatry. Indeed, these Muslim puritans took on the role of iconoclasts and destroyed the graves of the Shi'ite saints in the holy town of Karbala (Iraq) – an action shocking to much of the Muslim community. In 1802 they actually blockaded Mecca. The commander of their forces had had a dream in which the Prophet appeared and warned him that he would die within days if he took so much as a single grain from the Holy City by force. Thus, instead of attacking directly, he simply cut off the water supplies from Arafat, literally severing Mecca's lifeline. Subsequently, the sherif of the city was obliged to obey Wahhabi codes of dress and behaviour, and the Meccans themselves – outwardly at least – adopted more ascetic practices, even setting their tobacco on fire to satisfy the new invaders. In response, Mehmet Ali, Pasha of Egypt, spent much of the subsequent two decades directing military campaigns against the Wahhabis. In victory, he proved relentless. A bounty was declared for every Wahhabi head brought to him, and their impaled bodies were placed before the gates of Mecca.

However, after the fall of the Ottoman empire, control of the Hijaz was finally surrendered by the Turks. They had thrown in their lot with the German army during the First World War, and met resistance from the British (including T. E. Lawrence), allied with bedouins and local Arabs. Such developments ironically created a new opportunity for Wahhabis to spread over the Hijaz during the 1920s.

Since the Second World War, the nature of the pilgrimage to Mecca has changed enormously, not least because the number of pilgrims today constitutes perhaps up to five or ten times that of a century ago. The discovery of oil in the region during the 1930s has turned the Saudi Arabian state into a world economic power. Yet pilgrims are still expected to respect 'puritan' standards of behaviour, avoiding alcohol and all unseemly forms of dress. Despite the efforts of Mehmet Ali, the Wahhabi legacy is still evident in the performance of the *hajj*.

PILGRIMAGE IN PRACTICE: THE RITES OF THE HAJJ

The *hajj* is carried out between the eighth and the thirteenth days of the twelfth month of the Muslim year. Thus, it occurs at the zenith of the annual calendar, bringing it to a close. Like Christian pilgrimage to Rome or Jerusalem at Easter, it draws the community of believers together not only in a single place but during a single, sacredly charged time. A journey to Mecca undertaken at some other time is seen as a 'lesser' pilgrimage (an *umra*, or 'visitation'). As a practice enshrined in the Koran, but also influenced by earlier, pre-Islamic traditions, the pilgrimage is made up of a series of formal rites, with specific injunctions for each of its stages.

First, the Muslim identity of the traveller must be established. Nowadays, pilgrims run a gauntlet of walkie-talkies wielded by Saudi guards, as well as producing identity cards and special passports. Such secular safeguards of the sanctity of Mecca are reinforced by religious practice. Before pilgrims even pass the boundary stones that mark the edge of the holy territory of Mecca, they prepare themselves by vowing to abstain from worldly actions during the pilgrimage, including the development of emotional or sexual ties. Men put on robes made of two plain white

19 Pilgrims circumambulating the Ka'ba at Mecca.

sheets, while women wear plain dresses, and it is frequently believed that pilgrims will present themselves at the Last Judgment dressed in the clothes they have worn at Mecca. All personal adornment, including signs of wealth, is forbidden.

Rites of purification include ritual washing and the cutting of hair and nails, actions which will not be repeated until the end of the pilgrimage. Since many pilgrims now come to Mecca by plane, such preparations may actually take place before they board the aircraft. On arrival, pilgrims are entrusted to guides whose task is to see that the appropriate rites are carried out correctly. The central point of Mecca for the pilgrim is the Ka'ba. However, this building is only some 43 feet (13 m) high and 36 feet (11 m) square. It is thus much too small to allow collective worship within its walls, and rites are therefore carried out around its exterior – a vast and enlarged courtyard of about 180 by 120 yards (164 × 110 m). Even in their daily lives at Mecca, pilgrims may wish to be near this area, and rent is high for accommodation near the mosque, even if it is of inferior quality by comparison with apartments located further away.

The *hajji* soon acquires a sense of the sacred geography of Mecca: he or she traverses the boundary of purity that surrounds the city itself, before reaching the courtyard and finally encountering the House of Allah, and it is as though different zones of sacredness lead in concentric circles towards the Ka'ba. Objects that touch the latter are imbued with some of its sacred power – whether they are the black cloth that covers it, the rainwater that falls from its walls, or the whisks of brooms used to sweep its floors. John Lewis Burckhardt, a traveller in the eighteenth century, noted that holy men of his day were said to settle near the Ka'ba, and some went on the *umra* twice daily, as well as performing a sevenfold circumambulation of the shrine seventy times a day. The Ka'ba even held attractions for those who could not sleep:[11]

Men are seen, in the middle of the night, running to the mosque in their sleeping-clothes; here they perform the walk round the Kaba, kiss the black stone, utter a short prayer, drink the water of Zemzem, and then return to their beds.

The present Ka'ba has been restored from the original seventh-century building, and incorporates the famous black stone (a meteorite), embedded in a wall about two feet (0.6 m) from the ground. This may originally have been a *betyl* – a sacred rock embodying the deity which, before the birth of Muhammad, was moved around according to the movements of the bedouin (rather like the Ark of the Covenant of the Israelites). The fixing of this stone in the Ka'ba reflects a 'sedentising' of the faith, and is a firm statement of the close and permanent association between Islam and Mecca. In the tenth century, a Shi'ite sect called the Carmathians actually attempted to assert their authority by carrying the stone away and keeping it for twenty years as a form of ransom. Despite its probable pre-Islamic connections, the stone has been redefined to accommodate Muslim beliefs. According to some traditions, it is a relic from Adam or Abraham, and was kissed by the Prophet himself. There are also Muslims who say that it was sent by an angel of Allah to record deeds which will be examined on the Day of Judgment. One theory states that it was originally white but has been darkened by the sins of humanity.

During the *hajj* itself, after arriving at the courtyard, the pilgrim kisses the black stone; indeed, over the centuries part of the stone has been worn down by the kisses of these pilgrims, eager to copy the action of the Prophet. If, however, it cannot be reached in the mass of bodies, pilgrims call out a salutation to it from afar. They also swirl in a continuously moving circle round the Ka'ba. The ritual of walking round it seven times is said to have been invented in imitation of the angels who circle the throne of Allah. Then, the pilgrims must run between two hillocks, in commemoration of the actions of Hagar (wife of Abraham), searching for water for her child, Ishmael. Water is still present in the courtyard in the shape of the well of Zam Zam, believed to have been miraculously created, which has no formal place in the rites but provides bottled souvenirs to take home after the pilgrimage. Pilgrims also try to drink its bitter water after completion of the rites, and – according to some accounts – a sprinkling of it is believed to make the sins of pilgrims 'fall away like dust'.[12]

Then follows one of the most important parts of the *hajj*. This is a journey to the Mount of Mercy at Arafat, situated some twelve miles to the east. Here Muhammad is said to have addressed his followers for the last time, and a whole day of sermons and prayer is devoted to this site, called the 'day of standing'. At sunset, however, as soon as the ceremonies are over, such relative calm is transformed into great activity, as pilgrims go as quickly as possible to gather materials for the next day's event, the stoning of the pillars at a place called Mina. Speed on this occasion is often a matter of some pride, and in the past fights might break out between caravans, anxious to move faster than other pilgrims. Burckhardt noted, for instance, that '. . . two hundred lives have on some occasions been lost in supporting what was thought the honour of the respective caravans'.[13] The stoning itself is not mentioned in any text of the Koran, but stems from a popular tradition that tells how Abraham hurled stones at the devil when tempted to disobey God's command to sacrifice his son. Each pilgrim throws forty-one stones over a period of three days at three pillars, which are taken to represent Satan.

Even today, carrying out the pilgrimage can entail considerable sacrifice for the believer, who may have had to endure great economic costs and physical hardship to come to Mecca. The next part of the pilgrimage symbolises such self-abnegation, as well as invoking Abraham's willingness to sacrifice his son on God's command. A sheep or other animal is ritually slaughtered, and even if the meat itself does not reach Allah, it is hoped that the righteousness thus expressed by the believer will do so. Chapter 22 of the Koran states:

For every people We appointed rites of sacrifice, that they might pronounce the name of Allah over the quadrupeds of the class of cattle that He has provided for them. Remember then that your God is One God, and submit yourselves, therefore, wholly to Him . . . eat thereof yourselves and feed the needy, those who are content and those who are distressed. . . .

Finally, pilgrims have their hair cut and return to Mecca, possibly also visiting Medina and the Prophet's mosque there. In the latter town, the second holiest in the Muslim world, notices forbid visitors to prostrate themselves before the tombs of the Prophet and his successors. The presence of such signs hints at the difficult balance the *hajj* must strike between the abstract piety expressed in the Koran and the tangible, physical reminders of faith expressed in rites associated with pilgrimage. The former runs the risk of losing its appeal in the real world of feeling, sensation and need; the latter, however, can come dangerously close to idolatry.[14]

20 OPPOSITE Illustration of
pilgrims at the Ka'ba, from a
Miscellany prepared in AD
1411 for Iskandar, Governor
of Fars, modern-day western
Iran. The pilgrims are
wearing ritual costume,
made of two pieces of white
cloth. One touches the black
stone.

21 Interior of the Great
Mosque of Sidi Okba in
Kairouan, Tunisia, showing
the *mihrab* (concave niche
placed in the qiblah wall,
which points the worshipper
in the direction of Mecca)
and *minbar* (high seat or
pulpit from which orations
are delivered). The same site
has been used for a
succession of mosques ever
since the city was founded in
the 7th century AD. One of
the holiest cities of Islam,
Kairouan was a major centre
of medieval Islamic culture.

The *hajj* is likely to be a unique act in the life of the believer. Even as it
brings followers of Islam into a centripetal process, converging on the
Ka'ba in body as well as mind, it has implications that are far more
centrifugal in character. The notion of union with others beyond the Holy
City is expressed most powerfully at the time of sacrifice, since it is not
only Muslims participating in the *hajj* who kill an animal, but ideally all
Muslims in the whole of the *umma* at exactly the same time. Thus all
believers, no matter how distant, can share vicariously in the actions of
the pilgrimage. However, the process of reaching the object of religious
longing, embodied in the Ka'ba, also contains a curious irony that is
keenly felt by some believers. Once they have reached the House of God
itself they are denied, for once in their lives, an orientation for their
worship. Pilgrims can no longer look towards a distant city, an object of
desire that up to that moment had always been located far beyond the

horizon. They have, in a very real sense, achieved their highest goal on earth, but in doing so have deprived themselves of a fixed direction for their prayers.

TRANSFORMATIONS AND TRANSITIONS

I set out alone, finding no companion to cheer the way with friendly inter-course. . . . Swayed by an over-mastering impulse within me, and a long-cherished desire to visit those glorious sanctuaries, I resolved to quit all my friends and tear myself away from my home. As my parents were still alive, it weighed grievously upon me to part from them, and both they and I were afflicted with sorrow.

These are the words of Ibn Battuta,[15] a theologian born in Tangier in 1304, who devoted so much of his life to journeying through Asia and Africa, tracing the contours of the Muslim world, that he became known as the 'Traveller of Islam'. However, again and again, he was to return to Mecca, making pilgrimage after pilgrimage to the Holy City. His description of his first *hajj* introduces us to the theme of this section: a discussion of the perceptions and reflections of pilgrims as they journey to Mecca.

Any account of the *form* of the *hajj* – its activities and rituals – reveals little of the way it is *experienced* by its participants. If the pilgrimage is supposed to be an expression of the unity of the *umma*, how does this work in practice? Do pilgrims feel a sense of communion with those of the same faith but another nationality? To what extent do they 'see' Mecca through radically different cultural spectacles? And what about the experience of the journey as a whole? After all, arrival at Mecca is only the centre-point of a process that can take weeks, even years, for the traveller to fulfil. The examples below attempt to explore some of these questions. They cannot be 'typical' of the *hajj*, since no standard pilgrimage can exist, but they examine the experiences of people whose thoughts are oriented in some way towards Mecca, even though they come from societies that are worlds apart in perception and motivation.

The 'hac' among Turkish villagers: pilgrimage as an image of return

Villagers who live on the Central Anatolian plateau do not live lives of exceptional piety or devotion. Yet their assumptions, their ways of understanding the world, are nevertheless pervaded by Islam. Further-more, the pilgrimage is an important part of their experience of faith. It offers a glimpse of the future world that will be their final home after death. Carol Delaney, an anthropologist who has studied these villagers for many years, writes:[16]

Unlike notions of pilgrimage that have influenced the Christian West, notions in which the movement is perceived primarily as a 'going forth', so that even life itself can be construed as a pilgrimage, the Muslim notion embodies an image of return, a return to place of origin.

The image of Mecca is a constant presence throughout the lives of these villagers, and the famous *ezzan*, the call to prayer, beckons them not only to pray, but also to turn to the Holy City itself:[17]

. . . the call is inescapable . . . that sound, repeated five times a day every day, every year, all of one's life, makes inroads on the brain. One begins to adjust one's own rhythm to the call and not the clock, adjusting also to the intervals between calls . . .

and the object is Mecca:

. . . that point on the horizon that speaks so eloquently of things unseen and organized orientation in space as well as time. . . .

The *hajj* is usually performed by older villagers, who see the journey as an important part of their life-cycle, a conclusion to lives of activity and effort. Trips are organised by local travel-agents who gather people from the same area and take them directly from Turkey to Mecca. This means that the same group of fellow villagers can be guided round the Holy City together, having taken provisions from their village as well as the prayers and petitions of those who have remained in Turkey. Just as the ties to home are maintained by pilgrims as they walk together through the streets of Mecca, so those left in Turkey maintain vivid memories of their absent friends and kin. Delaney notes that 'our thoughts and prayers automatically travelled to the absent villagers'.[18]

On their return, the pilgrims act as channels for the blessings of Mecca. The myrrh, frankincense and jewellery that they bring home retain some of the lustre of their holy journey. Ever after, pilgrims are treated with deference by others. Men seem actually to enter a new stage in life, symbolised by the growing of a beard, not only echoing the unshaven state required in Mecca, but also as a sign of age and wisdom. They may also spend much of their time sitting in the precincts of the village mosque. Indeed, Delaney remarks: 'They seem to desire to transform their own space back home into an image of Mecca or the "other world".'[19]

The *hajj* is a kind of quintessential journey that orientates the lives of these villagers, even in Turkey. Indeed, it is striking that the metaphor of the pilgrimage pervades the way in which they perceive other journeys in their lives. Those villagers who have temporarily emigrated to rich European countries such as Belgium come to see their return to Turkey as a minor echo of the *hajj* – a return to a longed-for country, a vital centre far away. Yet the pilgrimage to Mecca also contains a surprise for villagers, and one that has the potential to alter the way they view their faith. They expect it will be the ultimate expression of Muslim unity; indeed, they presume they will be able to understand other pilgrims and share essential customs and practices. However, Delaney reports that, on reaching Mecca, they are confronted by myriad peoples speaking many different languages and actually feel shocked that they cannot understand fellow Muslims. Thus, we see how the juxtaposition of Muslims from around the world may not reinforce a sense of unity: rather, it may make it seem impossible ever to achieve. Such a conclusion is reinforced by past incidents in the Holy City, where conflicts between pilgrims of slightly different faiths or practices have occasionally led to violence and even death.

Admittedly, the consequences of cultural displacement are not as

22 Contemporary Egyptian wall painting of the Ka'ba and a man on a horse carrying a sunshade, indicating that the owner of the house on which it is painted has made the pilgrimage to Mecca.

serious for the Turkish villagers as such incidents would suggest. On returning home, they seem happy to tell stereotypical stories of the journey, designed to conform with and confirm fellow villagers' expectations. In this way, the conventional image of Mecca is maintained, and the experiences of the few not allowed to interfere with the aspirations of the many.

Malcolm X: pilgrimage and the transformation of the self

Malcolm X has a controversial place within the political mythology of the 1960s. Like John Kennedy or Martin Luther King, he is known as a man who fought for and ultimately was assassinated on account of his beliefs. Born in the United States, the son of a Baptist preacher, he spent much of his life in the Nation of Islam organisation as an advocate for black rights and the principle of separation from a white society seen as inherently racist. His pilgrimage to Mecca, unlike that of the Turkish villagers described above, was essentially that of an individual, travelling alone, to the holiest shrine of a religion that he had consciously embraced. He made his journey in 1964, and the experience is recorded in his autobiography and correspondence.

Malcolm made an unpromising start to his *hajj*, since he reports his discomfort at arriving in Jedda and being forced to wait as pilgrimage authorities examined and checked his unconventional history as a Muslim. He was, after all, an American, and on hearing of the presence of a pilgrim from the United States many of his fellow travellers at Jedda presumed he must be Muhammad Ali, the boxer. However, he finally managed to make his way to Mecca, and recorded the impact of the journey thus:[20]

I think that the pilgrimage to Mecca broadened my scope probably more in twelve days than my previous experience during my thirty-nine years on this earth.

For Malcolm X, leader of a struggle for black autonomy in the United States, the pilgrimage raised the issue of identity, and more especially race. In a context where all appeared to be reduced to the same level – eating, sleeping and praying together – he found himself living with people who in his own country would have been considered white. By voluntarily undertaking the *hajj*, he had to face the fact that the faith made no distinction between people other than that between believer and non-believer. He wrote on a postcard:[21]

I have just visited the Holy City of Mecca and witnessed pilgrims *of all colors*, from every part of this earth, displaying a spirit of unity and brotherhood like I've never witnessed during my entire life in America. It is truly a wonderful gift to behold.

White people could no longer be seen as irredeemably racist. It was as though the experience of Islam and the *hajj* not only stripped 'the white' from their minds, but also forced Malcolm X to rethink the assumptions on which his life had been based.

What is striking about the juxtaposition of Malcolm X's journey with that of villagers from the Anatolian plateau is that they appear to see two entirely different Meccas. For Malcolm X, accustomed to living as an outsider in a country of conflict and fractured identities, the rites of the *hajj* provided a brief experience of unity, expressed through common allegiance to Islam. For villagers whose everyday lives are characterised by the assumption of common belief and practice, both in their home and in the Muslim community as a whole, an encounter with others of the same faith but other cultures is disturbing in a radically different way – one in which the unity of the *umma* is not affirmed, but begins to be questioned.

Permanent pilgrimage: the journey that never ends
For both Malcolm X and the Turkish villagers, the *hajj* provides a temporary interlude in lives devoted to many other concerns. The situation is very different for the final group of Islamic pilgrims we shall consider – West African Muslims, who often devote their whole lives to the pilgrimage.[22] Muslim pilgrims have come from this part of Africa since the arrival of Islam around the eleventh century. Members of royal families could combine pilgrimage, trade and diplomacy as they moved between courts and palaces along the North African coast. Indeed, at times, residence in the more advanced centres of learning appeared to be almost

as important as the *hajj* itself in enhancing the status of the returning pilgrim. By at least the nineteenth century, more humble Muslims began to undertake the journey. So bad were the conditions in pre-colonial times that pilgrims were not expected to return home: even if they were not enslaved, they might succumb to combinations of disease, thirst or violence. (However, it was and still is considered by many Muslims to be a sign of grace to die in or near the Holy City. Suffering on the journey itself may also increase the spiritual merit gained.)

Most West African pilgrims can now take the train across the continent to Mecca, but others follow the long tradition of overland travel, with whole families making the journey in lorries, on camels or perhaps on foot. At times this has truly constituted a society on the move, and even the efforts of the Sudanese government in the 1960s to close its borders to them did not prevent the illegal movement of thousands of people. Conditions of travel are not helped by the habit of some lorry drivers of stopping repeatedly and demanding extra money before restarting. It has even been known for local inhabitants to erect tables at arbitrary points on the route, intercept parties of pilgrims and charge for bogus entry certificates into the Sudan. As one writer has put it:[23]

To travel with the pilgrims is to experience a paradoxical world with the ascetic, aesthetic and religious intermingled with the secular, pragmatic and immoral. Some of the most pious behaviour and exacting religious practice exist alongside appalling squalor . . . such are the compromises of the pilgrim road.

The colonial period in West Africa saw an improvement in the infrastructure of the area, making travel easier. However many inhabitants of Nigeria fled their own country, embarking on a form of exodus to be free from the colonial powers and nearer to the home of the Prophet. These migrants of the early part of this century have formed the nucleus of the West African population that is still located in the Sudan and Chad, having found large areas of agricultural land available to them. The result of these developments has been a cultural phenomenon that appears, to the outsider, to be extraordinary. Many Muslims now live lives of permanent transition, half-way between their countries of origin and Mecca itself. Northern Nigerians may remain for generations in seemingly temporary pilgrimage camps in the Sudan without ever going to Mecca. They give many reasons for having stopped, ranging from the pragmatic (the demands of family, or debts) to the spiritual (such as the unpropitious nature of the time, or the will of God).

Such 'pilgrims' deny that they have settled, and see themselves as being permanently on the road. Thus, they may work for years as farm labourers for Arabic-speakers without ever learning much Arabic. Although they earn money, they do not invest in local banks since they see such funds as devoted ultimately to travel to Mecca. Their villages, frequently set apart from surrounding communities, are constructed from ephemeral mud and straw, rather than the traditional brick of the Sudanese. They are frequently viewed with considerable suspicion by local populations in the Sudan, and may be seen, like so many immigrant populations, as criminal and threatening. However, their lives of devotion to a religious ideal and separation from mundane existence can also give them an air of sanctity. Some choose to become a fakir, a holy figure believed to have special powers and knowledge because of a life-long devotion to the Koran. It is believed that people who give alms to such a person gain *baraka* or blessing from God.

Despite their somewhat ambiguous reputation, these pilgrims regard themselves as superior to indigenous Sudanese since they are 'purer' Muslims. Their lives are made up of work and prayer, and devotion to holy men. Children are educated in Koranic schools, which help keep them away from the Sudanese, who are materially more successful but seen as a corrupting influence. They are taught to see pilgrimage as the ultimate virtue, frequently learning this from people who themselves have never been on the *hajj*. The finest greeting one can offer is 'May God send you to Mecca'. Occasionally, a village leader will actually make a return trip to the Holy City, and this will be the cause of considerable celebration, as though the *hajji* has acquired grace on behalf of the community as a whole. The majority of these West Africans may never, unlike Malcolm X or the Turkish villagers, reach the Holy City, and yet it casts a shadow over their lives that is just as powerful as its influence in the lives of the true *hajji*.

SAINT AND SUFI: ALTERNATIVE ROUTES TO THE SACRED

All the world religions face common problems in the distribution of religious authority. Is it to be concentrated in particular places or texts, or regarded as omnipresent? What role can special functionaries play in defining or even embodying the sacred authority that comes, ultimately, from God? Islam is a faith that, in its 'scripturalist' forms, mistrusts all forms of worship that detract from the centrality of the Koran in defining the relationship between the believer and an infinitely powerful God. Unlike the Christian doctrine of the Incarnation, the divine attributes of God are held to be remote from human nature, so that according to orthodox teaching no person can be closer to God than any other. Mecca and Medina are, ideally, revered not because they represent the birth- and dwelling-places of the Prophet, but because they are reminders of the original revelation granted to him.

Yet for many Muslims, both Allah and Mecca are very remote vehicles for divinity. Traditions have therefore emerged which attempt to mediate between the high points of faith and the concerns of the ordinary believer by locating spiritual power in more tangible or localised forms. Indeed, the sacred topography of Islam consists of pathways which lead to places other than Mecca or Medina, and numerous forms of travel apart from that of the *hajj* have emerged, ranging from journeying for scholarly purposes to visiting local shrines of important holy figures.[24] The Prophet himself saw Jerusalem as a holy place, and during the first years of his influence he and his followers actually prayed towards this city. However, after he quarrelled with the Jews of Medina, the object of prayer (or *qibla*) was changed to Mecca. Even today, many Muslims rank

Jerusalem as a pilgrimage centre second only to Mecca and Medina in importance. Muhammad is even said to have ascended to heaven via a ladder leading from the sacred stone in the Dome of the Rock in Jerusalem, a mosque dating from the end of the seventh century. Ibn Battuta describes his visit to the city thus:[25]

We then reached Jerusalem (may God ennoble her!), third in excellence after the two holy shrines of Mecca and Madina, and the place whence the Prophet was caught up into heaven. . . .

Shi'ism has provided a powerful sectarian movement within Islam for centuries, and one which has also had some effect in moving the emphasis of worship away from Mecca and Medina. In the early days of Islam, a number of disputes emerged as to the location of religious authority. Some insisted that the political and religious leader of Islam had to be a descendant of Ali, the son-in-law and cousin of the Prophet himself. Ali was said to have been directly nominated by the Prophet as his successor, and to have received secret knowledge which was in turn handed on to his male descendants, known as Imams. This doctrine originally provided a powerful means of protest against the Ummayad dynasty of Caliphs who had assumed authority in the Muslim world. It has continued to be influential in Islam, not least by maintaining the notion of allegiance to a divinely appointed and sinless spiritual leader – even if at present such a leader is apparently invisible to the material world. Shi'ites believe that the Mahdi, or 'Guided one of God', will return, restore true Islam and bring their perceived oppression to an end.

The visiting and worshipping of tombs of the Imams and other holy places occupies a central place in Shi'ite religious practice. These are seen almost as extensions of Mecca and Medina, so that visits to them are considered almost as meritorious as going on the *hajj* itself. Indeed, shrines at Najaf and Karbala, the location of tombs of important Shi'ite martyrs, have considerable political importance in so far as they represent alternatives to Mecca (and Sunni domination) as sources of sacred power.

Islam has provided still other means of locating spiritual power within specific holy figures. Muhammad al-Kittani, a scholar writing in the late nineteenth century, argued that a devotion to Muslim 'saints' accorded well with the letter of Islam. *Baraka*, or grace, could be seen as legitimately transmitted to earth through them:[26]

Without [saints] the sky would not send rain, the earth would not cause its plants to grow, and calamity would pour upon the inhabitants of the earth.

Sufism has for many centuries represented a powerful alternative source of such power. Originally, it was a reaction against over-legalistic formulations of Islam, and stressed the importance of developing a powerful inner conviction of faith, a personal religious experience that could even lead to ecstasy. Sufis themselves have tended to be mystic ascetics who try to come closer to God through spiritual exercises and contemplation. (The word *suf* possibly refers to the coarse, woollen material worn by early adherents as a sign of renunciation.) They claim a deeper knowledge of the Koran than can be obtained from accepting its

23 OPPOSITE Interior of the Dome of the Rock, Jerusalem, completed for Abd al-Malik in AD 691–2.

external meanings at face value, and some have evolved the notion of an 'inner way' or 'spiritual itinerary' to God made up of stages of development. The sufi Abu Sa'id, born in AD 967, actually recommended that his followers avoid the *hajj*, on the grounds that they should concentrate on mystical experiences rather than mere devotional exercises. When asked why he had not been to Mecca, Abu Sa'id is said to have replied:[27]

Why have I not performed the Pilgrimage? It is no great matter that thou shouldst tread under thy feet a thousand miles of ground in order to visit a stone house. The true man of God sits where he is, and the Bayt al-Ma'Mur [celestial archetype of the Ka'ba] comes several times in a day and night to visit him and performs the circumambulation above his head. Look and see!

According to the story, all those present could indeed see the vision of the Ka'ba described by the sufi ascetic.

This dramatic emphasis on the notion of 'internally inspired' pilgrimage is echoed by the following lines, originally in Persian, taken from the work of an eleventh-century sufi poet called 'Abdallah al-Ansari:

> Know that God Most High has built an outward
>   Ka'ba out of mud and stone,
> And fashioned an inward Ka'ba of heart and soul alone.
> The outward Ka'ba, Abraham did build,
> The inward Ka'ba was as the Lord Almighty willed.

Although often in tension with orthodox Islam, sufism has proved attractive within more 'popular' versions of the faith. By developing elaborate spiritual concepts as well as introducing music, dancing and seances into worship, it has sometimes even threatened the position of the mosque as the centre of religious life. Its mystical figures have also provided alternative locations for pilgrimage, since they have come to be seen as mediators between the divine and everyday worlds, and their tombs have become tangible objects of reverence after their deaths. It is as though the charismatic authority they embodied during their lives can be retained in material form after their demise.

The story of Sidi 'Abd al-Rahman illustrates this phenomenon in a remarkable way.[28] He was a *hajji* and sufi scholar who was born in the early part of the eighteenth century and educated in Algiers and Egypt. The expanding sufi order which grew around him in Algeria aroused the enmity of local Islamic authorities, not least because he drew rural clients away from their patronage. When he died in 1793 or 1794, government employees were instructed to steal his body from its tomb and take it to the capital, to safeguard against the possibility of the corpse becoming the object of pilgrimages which could resist centralised political control. However, local people claimed that, by divine miracle, his corpse actually remained within its original tomb. Thus, the *baraka* of the saint was, in effect, appropriated by rival locations simultaneously, and his followers bestowed on him the title of Abu Qabrayn, 'the man with two tombs'.

As this story indicates, figures who are granted great spiritual power may combine it with authority in more mundane matters. In North Africa generally, holy persons called *marabouts* often performed key religious and political roles, and thus came to be viewed with some ambivalence by sultans, who perceived them as alternative sources of authority. *Baraka* has often been seen as transmitted along chains of marabouts, leading in a sacred genealogy from Muhammad himself. One scholar who has worked in Morocco reports a conversation with a man who attempted to explain to him the role of the marabout as mediator between humans and God:[29]

If you need a paper from the government office, which is better? Do you go straight to the official and ask for it? You might wait a long time and never receive it. Or do you go to someone who knows you and knows the official? Of course, you go to the friend, who presents the case to the official. Same thing with baraka. If you want something from God, you go to [the marabout].

In considering this example, we are perhaps reminded indirectly of the potential significance of the *hajj*. We see how a pilgrimage for all believers can represent a powerful principle of universal allegiance and practice within a religion whose impulses can so easily be diverted into localised and parochial expressions of the faith.

III. Images of the Orient

a. *Burton's tomb, in the form of an Arab tent, Mortlake Cemetery, London. On her husband's death, Isabel Burton had requested of the Dean of Westminster that her husband be given an Abbey burial, as had been granted to Livingstone. When she was refused such permission, Isabel followed Burton's wish to be buried with his wife in a Bedouin tent by having the tomb constructed in Mortlake. She herself was placed alongside her husband after her death in 1896.*

One of the problems for westerners studying pilgrimage is the persistent difficulty of discarding Judaeo-Christian assumptions. This problem is acute in the study of eastern religions such as Hinduism and Buddhism, because they are not necessarily based on a single sacred scripture or a single God. Colonial powers attempted to understand the manifestations of Hindu belief which they encountered in eighteenth- and nineteenth-century India as comprising an internally consistent system on the model of an ideal Christianity. They castigated what they saw as the excesses of Hinduism according to the criteria developed for identifying heresy, idolatry and heterodoxy in Christianity. Islam, on the other hand, has many affinities – historical and theological – with the Judaeo-Christian world. It too is a monotheistic and prophetic religion of the Book. However, Arab societies were also subject to the colonial encounter and therefore to forms of definition and classification which elevated the western model of society and religion.

Mecca's streets are denied to non-Muslims. Yet they too became subject to the colonial gaze as the history of the *hajj* witnessed a number of clandestine visits from westerners. Entry to the city was usually undertaken in disguise, since an unbeliever risked his life if discovered violating the city by his presence. Although hardly deserving commendation for their decision to ignore Islamic taboos, these 'Christian *hajjis*' have often left invaluable accounts of their experiences, even if some descriptions stretch the credibility of the modern reader. Ludovico Bartema, who visited Mecca at the beginning of the sixteenth century, stated that he had seen unicorns in the mosque, a claim that reinforced European beliefs that distant and largely unknown lands were the source of physical prodigies.

One and a half centuries later, in 1679, a 15-year-old cabin boy from Exeter called Joseph Pitts was returning home from a voyage to the West Indies and Newfoundland when he was captured by Algerian pirates and sold into slavery. This unfortunate event was to turn him into a somewhat reluctant *hajji*, since he was forced by his master to convert to Islam. Pitts claims in *A Faithful Account of the Religion and Manners of the Mahometans* to have hated his new religion heartily. While admiring of the zeal of people who would willingly drink rainwater as it ran off the Ka'ba, he found the Muslims idolatrous, and expressed his rebellion against his fate by secretly eating pork and deliberately saying prayers in a state of impurity.

The earliest truly scholarly account of the pilgrimage was written by John Burckhardt, drawing on his travels of 1814–15. In Arabia, he managed to avert suspicions that he was an English spy, and adopted the persona of 'a private gentleman from Egypt'. By living in the Holy City for some months he managed to collect information about Meccan society as well as the *hajj* itself. Confident in his western upbringing, he commented that 'learning and science cannot

be expected to flourish in a place where every mind is occupied in the search of gain, or of paradise . . .' (*Travels in Arabia*, London, 1829, p. 211). Yet Burckhardt, even as he noted that the experience of the *hajj* could be disillusioning to some pilgrims, commented that similar criticisms could be made of 'our Christian holy-land'.

Sir Richard Burton (Fig. IIIb) became probably the best known of all 'Christians' at Mecca. He obtained a commission in the Bombay Army (East India Company), and was used by Sir Charles Napier, his commanding officer, as an interpreter and useful source of information. On leaving the army, Burton devised a project that would involve the penetration of Mecca, the 'forbidden city' of the Muslims. He also received funds from the Royal Geographical Society, on the grounds that he would be providing information on a little-known area.

Burton was well aware of and indeed admired Burckhardt's account of Mecca; he even made a point of visiting the latter's grave in Cairo. Like the Swiss scholar, he adopted a disguise, and his preparations for the role were meticulous, even involving an examination of the Indian Muslim's way of drinking a glass of water. In a book on *Falconry in the Valley of the Indus* (1852), Burton describes the pose he adopted, with a characteristically boastful reference to his sexual attractiveness:

With hair falling upon his shoulders, a long beard, face and hands, arms and feet, stained with a thin coat of henna, Mirza Abdullah [Burton's pseudonym] . . . – your humble servant, gentle reader – set out upon many and many a trip. . . . Thus he could walk in to most men's houses quite without ceremony; – even if the master dreamed of kicking him out, the mistress was sure to oppose such measure. . . .

(Quoted in G. S. Burne, *Richard F. Burton*, Boston, 1985, p. 37.)

Burton found himself on the road to Mecca in 1853 and described his first sight of the city:

About one a.m. I was aroused by general excitement. 'Mecca! Mecca!' cried some voices; 'The Sanctuary! O the Sanctuary!' exclaimed others. . . . I looked out from my litter, and saw by the light of the Southern stars the dim outlines of a large city, a shade darker than the surrounding plain.

(*A Pilgrimage to Mecca and Medinah*, London, 1937, p. 285.)

The visit to the Ka'ba represents another important stage in the journey:

I may truly say that, of all the worshippers who clung weeping to the curtain, or who pressed their beating hearts to the stone, none felt for the moment a deeper emotion than did the Hajji from the far-north. . . . But, to confess humbling truth, theirs was the high feeling of religious enthusiasm, mine was the ecstasy of gratified pride. (Ibid., p. 288)

Burton managed to take notes at night in microscopic script, and claims to have drawn diagrams on the inside of his pilgrim's garb. In a leather pouch normally used to contain the Koran he carried a watch, compass, money, and pencils and paper. Participation in the rituals of the *hajj* was combined with general observations of the city, which he found to be a flourishing, bustling place (unlike the Mecca, still suffering from Wahhabi attacks, that Burckhardt had encountered). Burton then returned to Cairo to write up his experiences, and published his three-volume *Pilgrimage to Meccah and Al-Medinah* in Bombay. This was to become a classic text of exploration, but also a fine example of Burton's idiosyncratic style. About a quarter of the entire work is in footnotes (as if Burton needed to prove his academic credentials in an extravagant display of the tools of scholarship) and the text is punctuated by phrases in Arabic, French and Italian. Anecdotes and personal observations are juxtaposed with learned discourses on geography, archaeology, anthropology and etymology. Passages in Latin and Greek are used to draw a discreet veil over some of the more salacious observations on Arab life.

Throughout his life, Burton prided himself on his satanic looks, displayed a scorn for Victorian sexual hypocrisy, and revelled in his ability to pass himself off as a Muslim. However, on his deathbed he was administered the Holy Sacrament by a Catholic priest at the insistence of his wife, Isabel. Burton had kept two sets of diaries on his travels: notes on social and cultural observations, and also a personal record of rather more intimate events in his life. The latter was destroyed by Isabel, who then wrote a biography of her husband which described him as 'pure' and 'refined'. It is as though even in death Burton could not help but adopt one final, deceptive persona. His tomb (Fig. IIIa), although situated in the decidedly British ground of a Catholic cemetery in Mortlake, West London, was constructed on the model of an Arabian tent.

It is clear that Burton constructed a vision of the East that conformed with his expectations as much as it did with his experience. His writings reinforced a European literary tradition, labelled by some writers 'Orientalism', that revelled in imagining an exotic and primitive East in contrast to the urban and rational western world. Those at Mecca are said by Burton to have a veneer of 'austerity' and 'ceremoniousness' which soon broke down under provocation so that 'the screaming Arab voice, the voluble, copious, and emphatic abuse, and the mania for gesticulation, return in all their deformity'. Like Burckhardt, Burton retained the notion that different peoples exhibited essentially different characters, and he even went so far as to divide Arabs into three races according to skull shape and temperament. The text is designed not only to describe Mecca, but also to present the image of an adventurous Englishman encountering, as Burton put it, a people at a lower 'stage' of society.

On one level, Burton conforms to the view that nineteenth-century explorers provided Victorian Britain with apparently scientific evidence to fuel its prejudices. The fierce individualism of such travellers combined with a strong sense of nationally self-interested – indeed imperialist – ambition. Burton refers to Egypt, for instance, as 'a treasure to be won'. However, such a view presents too crude a picture of a man whose relationship with his own culture was ambivalent. Burton was a British soldier who could still publish a poem called *Stone Talk*, satirising British heroes in war. Although a willing agent of imperialism, he also embraced the virtues of Islam and disapproved of the activities of Christian missionaries. Like Sir James Frazer, an early anthropologist and author of the hugely successful *Golden Bough* (1890), Burton presented an image of a world beyond that of Victorian morality, whose alluring yet seemingly primitive practices could be enjoyed vicariously. It is perhaps not surprising that Burton was never quite acceptable to the authorities of empire, even as he never quite accepted them.

b. *Sir Richard Burton, dressed as a Mecca pilgrim.*

4

The Gospels Embodied: Christian Pilgrimage to the Holy Land

'. . . behold a man clothed with Rags, standing in a certain place, with his face from his own house, a Book in his hand, and a great Burden on his back. . . .'

JOHN BUNYAN, *THE PILGRIM'S PROGRESS*, LONDON, 1678

John Bunyan's classic Protestant allegory *The Pilgrim's Progress* opens with the memorable image of Christian turning away from his own house to go on a journey, carrying a burden and a book. These two elements – the burden and the book – were radically to transform the nature of the pilgrimage traditions which Christianity inherited from the ancient world. The burden was original sin, from which God had redeemed man through Christ. The book was the Bible. The burden of sin would drive Christians to seek redemption through spiritual practices such as pilgrimage. The Bible, the book revealed to the Prophets and Evangelists by God, would define not only the path to salvation through Christ, but also the map of the Holy Land in which Christ had lived and to which his followers would come. As Christian memorably puts it on a later page of *The Pilgrim's Progress*,

Here is a poor burdened sinner. I come from the City of Destruction, but am going to Mount Zion, that I may be delivered from the Wrath to come. . . .

Of course, *The Pilgrim's Progress* belongs to a very different period and context of Christianity from the time of Constantine's conversion. But within a few years of the legalisation of Christianity by Constantine in AD 312, the first Christian pilgrim of whom an account has survived was on her way to Palestine under this twin impulse of 'the burden and the book'. Constantine's mother, the empress Helena, visited the Holy Land in 326–7.[1] As Eusebius, bishop of Caesaria in Palestine and the imperial biographer, portrayed her:

Though advanced in years, yet gifted with no common degree of wisdom, she hastened with youthful alacrity to survey this venerable land.

(*Life of Constantine*, 3,42)

In part Helena went to discover the actual holy places where, as a still earlier Christian traveller, Melito of Sardis, had written, 'the deeds were accomplished and proclaimed'.[2] In part also she went to expiate the sins of the imperial family, which had led in 326 to Constantine's execution of

24 The sarcophagus of St Helena, 4th century AD, Vatican Museums. Carved in porphyry, this sarcophagus was found in the mausoleum of St Helena on the Via Labicana in Rome. It represents a battle of Romans and barbarians, with cupids holding garlands on the lid. The sarcophagus has no overt Christian imagery or symbolism. With such military subject-matter it seems likely that it was intended for a male member of the Constantinian dynasty, but was used instead for the body of Helena, the emperor's mother.

his eldest son, Crispus, for adultery, and the subsequent suicide of his own wife, Fausta.

Whatever other motives there may have been for this journey, which followed an age-old form of imperial travel, Helena's trip was to have fundamental consequences for the history of Holy Land pilgrimage. For she would not only find the site and the very remains of the True Cross (according to the legend which swiftly became widespread in the fourth century), but would inaugurate the building of a series of great imperial basilicas in Jerusalem and Bethlehem.[3] Her voyage became the model for many.

CONTESTING THE VALUE OF PILGRIMAGE

The woman saith unto him, Sir, I perceive thou art a prophet. Our fathers worshipped in this mountain; and ye say that in Jerusalem is the place where men ought to worship.

Jesus saith unto her, Woman believe me, the hour cometh, when ye shall neither in this mountain, nor yet at Jerusalem, worship the Father. But the hour cometh, and now is, when the true worshippers shall worship the Father in spirit and in truth.   (John 4:19–21,23)

Unlike Muhammad or the Buddha, Jesus had not recommended or enjoined pilgrimage upon his followers. In the years of secrecy and persecution after his death, the practice of pilgrimage had hardly been possible for Christians, and before the conversion of Constantine there had been little in the way of Christian travel to Palestine for specifically sacred purposes. Indeed, some of Jesus's sayings, such as that quoted above, seem to militate firmly against contemporary Jewish traditions of venerating the tombs of the Prophets.[4] Later, however, other stories and sayings of Christ came to be associated with pilgrimage, not least his call to the apostles to 'follow me' (Matthew 4:19) and his journey with the travellers to Emmaus after the Resurrection (Luke 24:13–35).

Pilgrimage to the Holy Land began in earnest after the victory of Constantine over the pagan Licinius in the eastern half of the Roman empire (AD 324). This was a momentous event in the history of Christianity, for it united the eastern and western halves of the Mediterranean for the first time under a Christian monarch. Swiftly Constantine set about adapting Christianity to its future role as the dominant religion of the empire. In 325 he summoned the Council of Nicaea, the first Ecumenical Council of the whole Church. Its purpose was to resolve some of the doctrinal disputes which split Christians in the fourth century. It is not surprising that one of these concerned the activity of pilgrimage. Pilgrimage was one of many novelties in Christian ritual created by the sudden and remarkable translation of Christianity from a persecuted sect to an officially accepted and imperially fostered religion. Others included the building of large basilicas, the creation of a public liturgy and the use of art in worship and church decoration. Like the use of images, pilgrimage became a source of debate between theologians.[5]

In particular, Gregory of Nyssa, brother of St Basil and an influential writer on mystical and ascetic themes, wrote a powerful attack on the practice of pilgrimage in the late fourth century. In his second epistle (PG 46,1009–16), Gregory points out that

when the Lord invites the blest to their inheritance in the kingdom of Heaven, He does not include a pilgrimage to Jerusalem amongst their good deeds.

(1009, paragraphs BC)

He argues that travel to Palestine 'is found to inflict upon those who have begun to lead a stricter life a moral mischief', for the journey offered many temptations – not least the sinful ways of those who lived in the Holy City and the dangers to women pilgrims en route of sexual misconduct with their male escorts. More deeply, he suggests that 'change of place does not effect any drawing nearer to God' (1013, B). The altars of Gregory's native Cappadocia are no less holy than those of Jerusalem:

What advantage, moreover, is reaped by him who reaches those celebrated spots themselves? He cannot imagine that our Lord is living, in the body, there at the present day, but has gone away from us (who are not there); or that the Holy Spirit is in abundance in Jerusalem but unable to travel as far as us.　　(1012, C)

Gregory's case, theologically, was that what mattered in spiritual terms was the individual's heart and not the places he or she happened to visit.

25 Church of the Holy Sepulchre, Jerusalem, 12th-century crusader façade. Originally built under the patronage of Constantine the Great and his mother Helena in AD 325–6, the Holy Sepulchre encloses both the traditional site of Golgotha, where Christ was crucified, and that of his tomb, known as the Anastasis, or Resurrection. The church was burned by the Persians in 614 and then razed to the ground by the Muslim Caliph al-Hakim in 1009. In 1048, when Jerusalem was still under Muslim control, the efforts of the Byzantine emperor Constantine IX Monomachos resulted in a major rebuilding of the Anastasis rotunda. The Crusader conquest of Palestine in 1099 led to yet more extensive gothic reconstruction and refurbishment, of which this façade survives.

God could not be confined to Palestine. Other bishops agreed. St Augustine wrote (letter 78,3):

God is everywhere, it is true, and He that made all things is not contained or confined to dwell in any place.

St Jerome, one of the Church Fathers most in favour of pilgrimage, said in a sermon:

By the cross I mean not the wood, but the Passion. That cross is in Britain, in India, in the whole world. . . . Happy is he who carries in his own heart the cross, the Resurrection, the place of the Nativity of Christ and of his Ascension. Happy is he who carries Bethlehem in his own heart, in whose heart Christ is born every day.
(Homily on Psalm 95)

Throughout the Christian tradition, those who have most forcefully insisted on the spiritual have followed this argument, that, however useful holy sites, relics and images may be, they are not necessary for salvation. In nineteenth-century Russia, Leo Tolstoy wrote a story arguing precisely this case.[6]

Yet such theological meditations from the Church hierarchy failed to make any impression on those who wished to see and to worship at what Eusebius called 'the most marvellous place in the world' (*Life of Constantine* 3,31). From the imperial family (including not only Constantine's mother but also Eutropia, his mother-in-law, and a century later the empress Eudocia, wife of Theodosius II) to relatively humble men and women, from bishops and holy men to simple monks and nuns, from clergy to laity, a broad cross-section of the religious Christians of the empire were fired to make the arduous journey to Palestine.[7] Perhaps above all they wished to witness, as Eusebius put it, 'a clear and visible proof of the wonders of which that spot had once been the scene' (3,28). Constantine himself inaugurated the process, not only by sending Helena to Palestine, but also by building a number of impressive basilicas at the most important sites – the Holy Sepulchre, the Mount of Olives (where the Ascension had occurred), Bethlehem and Mamre (where Abraham had entertained the three angels). When describing the Holy Sepulchre, Eusebius explicitly tells us the emperor's motives in building it: to be 'an object of veneration and attraction to all' (3,25).

Despite their doubts, even many Fathers of the Church found themselves wishing to go on pilgrimage or encouraging their congregations to do so. Both Gregory of Nyssa and Jerome went to the Holy Land, and Jerome settled there. Augustine, in his role as Bishop of Hippo, tested a priest accused of a sexual scandal by sending him to the shrine of St Felix at Nola, 'a holy place, where the more awe-inspiring works of God might much more readily make evil manifest' (letter 78,3). John Chrysostom, Patriarch of Antioch and later of Constantinople, recommended the holy sites as a way of bringing home the Gospel's lessons. He suggested the merits of visiting Job's dunghill in his Homilies to the Antiochenes (5,1) and argued that nothing could so effectively create a desire for chastity as the 'spectacle of universal desolation' which engulfed the site of the city of Sodom.

Perhaps it was St Jerome, who lived in Palestine in the last years of the fourth century, who caught the spirit of Holy Land pilgrimage most acutely. His account of the travels of Paula, a noblewoman from Rome, captures some of the extraordinarily powerful pull – almost a physical force – which came to be associated with the holy places:[8]

With a zeal and courage unbelievable in a woman she forgot her sex and her physical weakness, and longed to make there, amongst those thousands of monks, a dwelling for herself. . . . And she might have done so, if she had not been summoned away by a still greater longing for the holy places. . . .

(letter 108,14,3)

This longing, which elsewhere he describes as a 'burning enthusiasm' (letter 108,9,2), led pilgrims like Paula to prostrate themselves, kiss the holy spots and see visions. At Bethlehem

she solemnly declared in my own hearing that, with the eye of faith, she saw a child wrapped in swaddling clothes, weeping in the Lord's manger, the Magi worshipping, the star shining above, the Virgin Mother, the attentive foster-father; and the shepherds coming by night to see. . . .   (letter 108,10,2)

In Paula's vision, the whole sacred narrative comes alive in its proper, authentic place. For the more contemplative Fathers, Bethlehem may have been a place in the heart, the birth of Christ a daily event in the spirit; but for Paula such things had a tangible, verifiable, existence by being located and experienced in their original settings.

'VISIBLE PROOFS': THE BIBLE AS LANDSCAPE AND RELIC

Climbing Sion you can see the place where once the house of Caiaphas used to stand, and the column at which they fell on Christ and scourged him still remains there.

  Inside Sion, within the wall, you can see where David had his palace. Seven synagogues were there, but only one is left – the rest have been 'ploughed and sown' as was said by the prophet Isaiah. As you leave and pass through the wall of Sion, towards the Gate of Neapolis, down in the valley on your right you have some walls where Pontius Pilate had his house, the Praetorium where the Lord's case was heard before he suffered. On your left is the hillock Golgotha where the Lord was crucified, and about a stone's throw from it the vault where they laid his body, and he rose again on the third day. By order of the Emperor Constantine there has now been built there a 'basilica' – I mean a 'place for the Lord' – which has beside it cisterns of remarkable beauty, and beside them a bath where children are baptised. . . .   (*The Journey of the Bordeaux Pilgrim* 592–4)

This quotation comes from the earliest surviving personal account by a Christian pilgrim to Jerusalem. Its author came to Palestine from Bordeaux in AD 333, less than a decade after St Helena.[9] The Bordeaux Pilgrim described the Holy Land at a time before most of the churches and monasteries which would later fill it were built. Indeed, he even felt the need to explain to his readers what the unfamiliar kind of building called a 'basilica' was. Writing only twenty years after the legalisation of Christianity, the Pilgrim could not be sure that knowledge of its new forms of art and architecture had reached his intended readers. His text reveals many of the trends in pilgrimage to Palestine which would become current in the following centuries. He shows an interest in Old Testament sites and stories as much as those connected with the lives of Jesus and the Apostles; he focuses on natural wonders and miracles such as the saltiness of the Dead Sea (section 597) or pools where people have been cured (589); and he remarks on the settings of liturgy (for example the place of baptism at the Holy Sepulchre).

  But above all, the Bordeaux Pilgrim anticipates those who were to follow him by seeing the landscape of Palestine as a physical manifestation of the Bible's text. In his account, and in those which came after it, Palestine became the Holy Land. He journeys through the city of Jerusalem not so much as it actually was in his time, but as it was recorded in the Bible, which described events at least 300 years before his trip. He maps scriptural events, such as Christ's scourging and trial, as well as biblical places, such as David's palace or the site of the Crucifixion, directly onto the topography through which he walks. The biblical event or place becomes synonymous with existing landmarks such as the column on Mount Sion identified as the column of the Flagellation or the vault identified with the Tomb. Quite insignificant objects such as the 'walls where Pilate had his house' (presumably pretty unremarkable walls in their own right) become imbued with the significance of the Passion story. Spots which simply had no landmark or association at all before the Christianisation of the city suddenly acquire a literary reference that makes them holy, such as 'the place where once the house of Caiaphas used to stand'. In effect the biblical story could now be told through topography, by means of a walking tour through the city, in utterly tangible and experiential terms.

It was this tangibility that proved so overwhelmingly attractive. In the words of Paulinus of Nola, a correspondent of Jerome,

the principal motive which draws people to Jerusalem is the desire to see and touch the places where Christ was present in the body.   (*Epistles* 49,402)

As Cyril of Jerusalem, who was bishop of the city for much of the second half of the fourth century, pointedly phrased it, 'others merely hear, but we see and touch' (*Catechetical Lecture*, 13,22). Repeatedly in his homilies, Cyril would refer to the place in which his congregation (many of them pilgrims) were standing, as proof of the facts of scripture. Likewise, Eusebius had seen the discovery of the Holy Sepulchre as 'a clear and visible proof of the wonders of which the spot had once been the scene' (*Life of Constantine* 3,25).[10] The holy places, some of whose association with biblical events had been invented so as to map scripture onto the landscape, now became the testimony and witness for the truth of scripture.

Even as the Bordeaux Pilgrim was visiting the Holy Land it was being transformed to accord with the text which he – and everyone else – was using as a guide book. He describes no basilica on Mount Sion, but by the mid-fourth century there was a church there, where the feast of Pentecost was celebrated. By the fifth century, the site had become the setting for the Last Supper and the institution of the Eucharist. Many important scriptural events changed their locations in this way: the Bordeaux Pilgrim encountered the site of the Transfiguration on the Mount of Olives in AD 333, but by the time of St Cyril's homilies in Jerusalem (about 348) the site had shifted to Mount Tabor. In Palestine as a whole, several pilgrimage sites (such as the tombs of Jonah and Joshua) were duplicated and existed in competition with each other. Literally the whole land, and in particular the city of Jerusalem, was being reshaped to accord with the Bible, and with the demands of pilgrims to see the places which bore the Bible witness.

The result of this process was remarkable. If one knew one's Bible, then one had a key to finding one's way around. In perhaps the most endearing and valuable of all the early pilgrim accounts, written in the 380s by a woman traveller from Gaul or Spain called Egeria, a group of pilgrims visit Melchizedek's palace at Salem.[11] 'Then,' Egeria writes (15,1), 'I remembered that according to the Bible it was near Salem that holy John baptised at Aenon. So I asked if it was far away. "There it is," the Presbyter said, "two hundred yards away. If you like we can walk over there."' All one had to do was to think of a text, and the authentic spot could be provided. Truly this was a world which one had but to 'see and touch'.

Just as the holy places became a collection of sacred texts criss-crossing the landscape, so they gathered within them objects and relics that were themselves key features of the Bible. A handbook to Jerusalem probably produced in the sixth century, called the *Breviarius* lists the more important relics in the great basilicas.[12] In the Holy Sepulchre was the True Cross, the lance 'with which they struck the Lord', the plate on which John the Baptist's severed head was carried and the horn with which David was anointed king. In the Sion basilica was the Crown of Thorns, the column of the Flagellation and the stones from the stoning of St Stephen. Many of these objects had their own clergy – the ninth-century *Commemoratorium* (a list of priests and monks attached to the Holy Land churches, compiled for the emperor Charlemagne) lists two priests for the Holy Cross and two for the Lord's Chalice (which had by then found its way into the collection at the Holy Sepulchre).[13] Such relics gathered the tangible witness to a whole number of sacred texts together in places which were themselves living proof of the great biblical events. The *Breviarius* notes that the Holy Sepulchre was the site not only of the Death and Resurrection, but also of the creation of Adam and Abraham's sacrifice of Isaac.

Such relics swiftly acquired complex rituals and miraculous properties. In the anonymous account of a pilgrim from Piacenza in Italy, written about AD 570, we can glimpse some of the circumstances of a first confrontation with the True Cross:[14]

In the courtyard of the basilica is a small room where they keep the Wood of the Cross. We venerated it with a kiss. . . . At the moment when the Cross is brought out of this small room for veneration, and arrives in the court to be venerated, a star appears in the sky, and comes over the place where they lay the Cross. It stops overhead whilst they are venerating the Cross, and they offer oil to be blessed in little flasks. When the mouth of one of the little flasks touches the Wood of the Cross, the oil instantly bubbles over, and unless it is closed very quickly it all spills out. When the Cross is put back into its place, the star also vanishes, and appears no more once the Cross has been put away.   (*Travels of the Piacenza Pilgrim*, 20)

The miraculous appearance of the star and the remarkable behaviour of the oil were themselves proofs of the Cross. By their association with the Cross, these vials of oil acquired a sanctity ultimately derived from the fact that the Cross and the Holy Sepulchre itself were the material embodiments of scripture, which was itself divine revelation.

Little flasks of oil like these, lead and clay ampullae filled with water from the Jordan, boxes with earth from a sacred tomb, became the standard souvenirs – or 'blessings', as they were known – which pilgrims brought back from the Holy Land. Often decorated with scenes of scripture, such objects became a tangible link with Palestine for those back home who had not made the trip. They became talismans for warding off demons, and standard articles in medieval healing and medicine.[15] In return for these, and for the blessing of pilgrimage itself, pilgrims left the holy places crammed with gifts. The Piacenza Pilgrim notes, at the Holy Sepulchre, that

there are ornaments in vast numbers which hang from iron rods: armlets, bracelets, necklaces, rings, tiaras, plaited girdles, belts, emperors' crowns of gold and precious stones and the insignia of an empress. (*Travels*, 22)

Many of the icons and treasures still in the monastery at Mount Sinai, already in the fourth century an important pilgrimage centre (which Egeria visited) were originally acquired by donation in this way.[16]

For visitors to the Holy Land one of the most impressive ways in which the living and contemporary presence of scripture could be evoked was through worship. Egeria, in particular, devoted a large section of her account to describing rituals and liturgy.[17] Scripture was continually recited, so that in every holy place Egeria visited the appropriate biblical passage was read aloud. She was particularly struck by the sensual vividness of the Jerusalem liturgy – churches 'ablaze with lamps' (24,9), the smell of incense (24,10), and the decorations 'really too marvellous for words' (25,8):

All you can see is gold and jewels and silk; the hangings are entirely silk with gold stripes, the curtains the same, and everything they use for the services at the festival is made of gold and jewels. You simply cannot imagine the number, and the sheer weight of the candles and the tapers and lamps and everything else they use for the services.

Particularly interesting is Egeria's account of the pattern of liturgical services. Worship was not contained in a single building, but moved through the churches of the city. Celebrants and congregation processed together through the holy places throughout the day, the bishop presi-

26 OPPOSITE Icon on the inside of the lid of a 6th-century Palestinian reliquary box, formerly in the Sancta Sanctorum Treasury, Vatican Museums. From bottom left to top right the scenes depicted are the Nativity, the Baptism, the Crucifixion, the women at the tomb and the Ascension. The image of the women at the tomb breaks from the narrative precedents in the Bible (which describe the tomb as a rock-hewn cave) and depicts the tomb as the *aediculum* built by Constantine's successors in the 4th century and visited by pilgrims.

27 Icon depicting Christ with the Abbot Menas, encaustic on wood, 6–7th century AD, Louvre. The inscriptions in Coptic identify the two haloed figures as Father Menas, Abbot, and the Saviour. Between the heads is a Christogram. Christ embraces the Abbot with his right arm in a gesture of protection. Menas holds a small scroll and with his right hand makes a gesture of blessing, which is sanctioned and supported by the presence of Christ. The icon thus offers its viewers a formal hierarchy of intercession, through the Abbot to Christ, who succours him.

ding at each church in turn. The topography of Jerusalem was experienced liturgically as a historical narrative of the Passion. In effect worship itself had become a kind of pilgrimage through the city as sacred territory, a pattern of liturgy that would become highly significant not only in Jerusalem but in Rome and Constantinople as well.[18]

'IMPELLED BY GOD': THE JOURNEY TO PALESTINE

Travelling about twenty miles a day, the Bordeaux Pilgrim must have taken about a year to complete his return trip. Of that year, perhaps no more than three months were actually spent in the Holy Land. These figures give some idea of the enormity of the undertaking involved in a pilgrimage to Palestine. It required money, courage and very hard work. And this was in the days of good Roman roads, a united empire patrolled and relatively well safeguarded by imperial troops and an established tradition of travel exemplified by the likes of Pausanias and Aelius Aristides in the second century AD.[19] In later years, after the fall of Rome to Alaric the Goth in 410 and that of the eastern provinces of the empire to the Arabs in the seventh century, travel became still more difficult.

In effect, much more time was spent going to and from the sacred goal than in the holy place itself. In pilgrimage the act of travel acquired an importance perhaps almost as great as that of the rituals and relics at the sacred centre. To travel safely pilgrims often went in convoy, as a group of fellow-seekers rather than separate individuals. Swiftly, Christianity bred an ideology of solidarity with other pilgrims, and even of equality, whereby, whatever one's social station, as a pilgrim one was the equal of others on the same path. Egeria evokes something of this solidarity when describing her journey to Job's tomb (13,2):

So I set off from Jerusalem with some holy men who were kind enough to keep me company on the journey and wanted to make the pilgrimage.

Moreover, the journey itself began to be seen as an act of worship. In a vivid passage, Gregory of Nyssa wrote:

Our carriage was, in fact, as good as a church or monastery to us, for all of us were singing psalms and fasting during the whole journey.   (*Letter* 2, PG 46,1013, B)

When pilgrims converged on the holy places, this spirit continued. Eusebius described St Helena 'in simple and modest dress, mingling with the crowds of worshippers and testifying her devotion to God by a uniform course of pious conduct' (*Life of Constantine*, 3,45). Seven centuries after Helena, a Cluniac monk called Rudolf Glaber, writing in the 1040s, evoked a similar sense of mass pilgrimage in which all the social classes mingled:[20]

At the same time from all over the world an innumerable crowd began to flock to the Sepulchre of the Saviour in Jerusalem – in greater numbers than anyone before had thought possible. Not only were there some of the common people and of the middle class, but there were also several very great kings, counts and noblemen . . . many noble ladies set out with the poor people.   (*History*, 680)

These pilgrims paint a very different picture from the descriptive accounts of Pausanias and the author of *On the Syrian Goddess* (see Chapter 1). They are much more aware of the collaborative enterprise they are on, and of those they travel with. Travel itself becomes part of the ritual of pilgrimage, a holy activity whose practices include psalms and fasting, whose society is the company of holy men, whose very means of transport has become the equivalent of a church. From its earliest beginnings such travel was regarded as a sacred activity which bred a mutual atmosphere of being outside the ordinary licences of secular life.

One way of fostering such a religious spirit during the long months of travel, as well as guarding against the temptations of which Gregory of Nyssa had warned, was to stay in monastic accommodation en route. The well-paved roads of the Roman empire were provided with official rest houses and post stables where travellers on imperial business could stay the night and change horses. More humble folk stayed at inns. But as pilgrimage grew, benefactors (from pilgrims like Paula to the emperor Justinian himself) provided hospices for the use of Christian pilgrims. A network of travel from monastery to monastery, from Christian community to Christian community, came into being throughout the empire and became an alternative to the official routes and hostels. This specifically sacred network of places to stay made a profound contribution to the non-secular nature of the journey. Egeria's account, for instance, reveals her desire to keep wholly away from the profane. In a journey which spans the distance from the Atlantic to the Euphrates, there is hardly any intrusion of the secular world at any stage.

GUIDANCE AND IDEOLOGY: THE CHARISMA OF HOLY MEN

Unlike the priests who looked after sacred centres in the classical world, the clergy who were the caretakers, guides and often the star attractions at the holy places of Christianity belonged to arguably the most coherent and formidable organisation the western world had yet known. Professing a single Creed, ruthlessly uprooting all heretical deviations from its doctrines, and basing its views on one sacred scripture, the Church was a force of powerful ideological and cultural cohesion. It established an ecclesiastical hierarchy of bishops and theologians which soon existed parallel with, and often replaced, the temporal hierarchy of the state. In the monasteries which rapidly came to span Christendom from Egypt to Britain, the Church trained an élite of active intellectuals and administrators who manifested all the energy of religious fervour and recent conversion. In its liturgy and sermons, the Church presented to its congregations a religion that was simultaneously personal and universal. In other words, by contrast with pagan antiquity the holy sites of Christendom were in the hands of a single, immensely powerful, organisation.[21]

In the Holy Land, the priests and monks who tended the sacred sites were the pilgrims' guides and interpreters. They provided not only knowledge but also liturgy. They turned Palestine into a religious

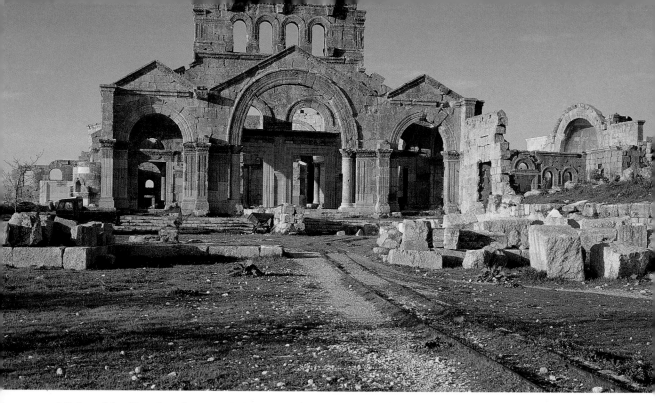

28 Ruins of the Church and Monastery of St Simeon Stylites, Qal'at Sim'an, Syria c. AD 475–500. One of the largest churches built in the eastern Mediterranean before the 6th century, this cruciform church celebrated the site where the Stylite lived atop three successively taller pillars. Pilgrims came from as far as Arabia and Gaul to hear him preach and to receive blessings.

experience, an experience whose meanings were coherent from site to site and with other holy places such as Rome. Throughout her account, Egeria repeatedly mentions the holy men, priests and bishops with whom she has talked. They are her guides at Sinai (1,2), her hosts in Arabia (9,1), her companions to the land of Uz (13,1). They give her mementos (19,19) and discuss the Bible (20,9). But perhaps most interestingly, they become part of the actual goal of pilgrimage. 'God also moved me with a desire to go to Syrian Mesopotamia', Egeria writes (17,1), for

the holy monks there are said to be numerous and of so indescribably excellent a life that I wanted to pay them a visit.

The sight of these monks is a high-point of her trip (20,6):

We had the unexpected pleasure of seeing there the holy and truly dedicated monks of Mesopotamia, including some of whose reputation and holy life we had heard long before we got there. I certainly never thought I would actually see them . . . these are of the kind who perform many miracles.

The holy men of Syria and Egypt were more than just the Church's representatives in the east.[22] They were living proof of the contemporaneity of miracles, of the charisma of the sacred. For Christians, these ascetics and 'athletes of Christ', as writers christened them, showed that the era of the apostles and the martyrs was by no means over: the power of the faith to control the forces of nature and to witness the presence of the Lord could be seen in the flesh. When a young pilgrim called Daniel went to Palestine, he got no further than the column of Simeon the Stylite at Telnesin near Antioch. St Daniel, as this young pilgrim was to become, never reached Jerusalem. The confrontation with Simeon, the living example of ascetic renunciation, in his element – 'the wilderness of the spot and the height of the pillar and the fiery heat of the scorching sun' (*Life of Daniel*, 7)[23] – was enough. Daniel was called, not only to the holy life but to that of the Stylite saint. He set up his pillar not in Palestine but in 'a second Jerusalem, namely Constantinople' (ibid. 10).

Such ascetics were much more than sacred paradigms of a renunciation which others could never achieve. They heard petitions, arbitrated in law-suits, gave blessings and sermons and performed miracles. Their prestige was so immense that they would be visited by patriarchs, generals and emperors. Although their way of life, perched at the tip of a pillar, and even some of their functions, relate them to the phallus-climbers at the temple of the Syrian Goddess several centuries earlier (see Chapter 1), their social status and cultural meaning was radically different. As the supreme exemplars of Christianity's teaching of monastic abstinence, their fame (in both decorated tokens and literary hagiographies) swiftly traversed Europe and they had extraordinary power. This was not confined to firing the religious imagination by their example; on the contrary, they were prime advisers to temporal authorities as well. While the phallus-climbers occupied their pillars for a week, the Stylites braved the elements on their columns for a lifetime. They were not famous by virtue of the temple where they lived, but in their own right, as physical, visible, tangible proofs of the amazing power of the Holy Spirit to tame the mortal flesh.

THE IMAGE OF PILGRIMAGE

We have seen that, as pilgrimage to the Holy Land grew, the holy places and relics were not the only goals sought by the early Christian pilgrim. Apart from the basilicas and splendours with which the cream of the pious nobility had endowed Palestine, there were also the monks, the liturgy and the holy men. In the sixth-century *Life of St Nicholas*,[24] Abbot of the monastery of Holy Sion in Lycia (Asia Minor), the saint visits Palestine twice (27),

to adore the venerable wood of the Cross and all the holy places and the venerable fathers.

By the sixth century, the sainted inhabitants of the Holy Land, living and deceased, were as much goals of pilgrimage as the relics of Christ himself. Soon the very act of pilgrimage itself became a paradigm for piety, for holiness. Someone who had been on pilgrimage could be held up – not only in his or her lifetime, but perhaps even more so after death – as an 'athlete of Christ'.

In the earliest hagiographies – the lives of the great founders of Egyptian monasticism such as St Anthony and St Pachomius – the image of Jerusalem (if it occurs at all) echoes as a quotation from biblical texts. Such saints did not need to go to the Holy Land. But soon, a pilgrimage to Palestine became a standard feature of a saint's life. Eastern saints such as Nicholas or Theodore of Sykeon, and westerners such as the English missionary St Willibald made the trip.[25] More to the point perhaps, their biographers were careful to record these journeys in their hagiographies. The pilgrimage to Palestine became in its own right a sign of the piety and religious fervour of the individual.

The most interesting instance of the record of a pilgrimage becoming sanctified is what happened to the account of Egeria. Her manuscript survived with the nuns to whom she sent it, probably in Spain. There, at the end of the seventh century, it was picked up by a monk called Valerius, who used it in a letter on the holy life to his brethren at Vierzo in Spain.[26] For Valerius, Egeria's account is a paradigm in spiritual virtue:

We revere the valorous achievements of the mighty saints who were men, but we are amazed when still more courageous deeds are achieved by weak womanhood, such deeds as are indeed described in the remarkable history of the most blessed Egeria, who by her courage outdid the men of any age.

(Letter in Praise of Egeria, 1)

By the seventh century, Egeria had become a saint.

Valerius recounts Egeria's travels at some length, emphasising her 'longing for God's grace', her 'greatest application', her 'unwearying thanks' and fearlessness. He remarks on the distances she travelled, the mountains she climbed (3):

Nothing could hold her back, whether it was the labour of travelling the whole world, the perils of seas and rivers, the dread crags and fearsome mountains, or the savage menaces of the heathen tribes, until with God's help and her own unconquerable bravery, she had fulfilled all her faithful desires.

For Egeria, the 'labours of pilgrimage' brought the rewards of sainthood 'in the choir of heavenly virgins with the glorious queen of heaven, Mary the Lord's mother'. As an 'exemplary woman' her model served to exhort the brethren not just to pilgrimage but to greater rigour and abstinence in their own monastic lives.

First-hand texts such as Egeria's became models for the compilations and travel books about the Holy Land that were so popular in the Middle Ages. As the Venerable Bede wrote (describing Adomnan's seventh-century account of Bishop Arculf's pilgrimage to Palestine), such works were 'very useful to many people, especially to those who live far away from the places where the Patriarchs and Apostles used to be, and can know the holy places only from what they learn from books' (*History of the English Church*, 5,15). Bede himself used Adomnan for his own compilation *On the Holy Places*,[27] while in the twelfth century Peter the Deacon, librarian of St Benedict's great monastery of Monte Cassino, used extracts from Egeria herself in his *Book on the Holy Places*.[28] Holy Land pilgrimage, though still practised vigorously by many, was not possible for the mass of the pious. It was something to be accessed through books; it had become a literary image, a religious paradigm, more than a fact.

In the twelfth century, the Russian abbot Daniel, who visited Palestine in about 1106, wrote:[29]

I have written this [account] for the faithful. For if anyone hearing about these places should grieve in his soul and in his thoughts for these holy places, he shall

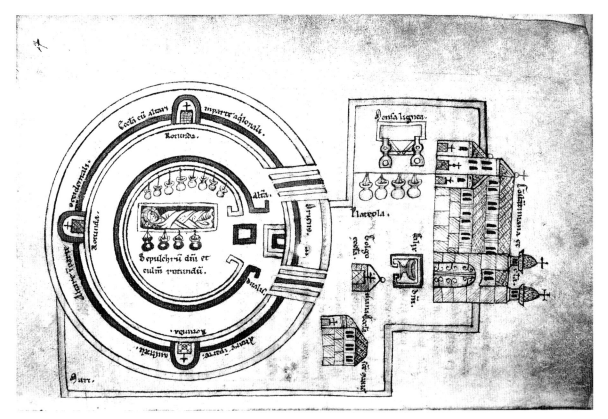

receive the same reward from God as those who shall have travelled to the holy places.

(Pilgrimage of Daniel, 1a)

In medieval thinking, even to read about pilgrimage – if it brought about the proper spirit of contrition – had become equivalent to making the trip oneself.

The way first-hand accounts, like Egeria's or Arculf's, were transformed into exemplary lives and distillations of sacred knowledge indicates something of the remarkable paradox in Christian pilgrimage to Palestine. On the one hand travel to the Holy Land was pilgrimage *par excellence*, the model for all sacred journeys in Christendom, the supreme site of martyrdom, the supreme treasure-house of relics beside which all the martyr-tombs, reliquaries and cathedrals of the world paled. Indeed, the great pilgrim centres of the east (such as Constantinople with its great collections of relics and churches) and the west (like Rome and Compostela) were to a large extent modelled on and related to the Holy Land. Many of their prime objects came from there. On the other hand, pilgrimage to the Holy Land was the great exception. It was travel to another world, where people by and large spoke a different language from Latin or Greek, and which was for much of the time under non-Christian domination. By the high Middle Ages in Europe, most Christian pilgrimage was local or national. The Holy Land was very far away. Its importance was as a model, as a paradigm for the superhuman effort involved in living a good life, as an example of how all people could – if

29 Arculf's plan of the Holy Sepulchre, Vienna Codex 609, fol. 4v., 13th century. Several manuscript copies survive of Adomnan's late 7th-century account of Bishop Arculf's pilgrimage to Palestine between AD 679 and 688. This 13th-century version elaborates upon its model by illustrating the tomb and other features of the church. This is not an accurate copy or plan, but rather a vivid insight into the way in which the Holy Sepulchre was imagined in western Europe in the later Middle Ages.

they had the dedication of Egeria in Valerius's eulogy – become one of the holy.

THE PILGRIM AND THE SWORD: THE CRUSADES

Take the helmet of salvation, and the sword of the Spirit.   (Ephesians 6:17)

Christian pilgrimage, as a religious activity, was peaceful in its origins. Unlike the Muslims with their concept of *Jihad*, or holy war, Christians had never seen war as an essential or even a laudable component of their piety. Early Christianity's many soldier saints, such as St Martin of Tours, were saints despite, not because of, their profession. Early Christian pilgrimage, which was established in the long peace of the *Pax Romana*, was practiced within a single empire by people who were citizens of that empire, whether they came from Rome or Bordeaux, from Spain or Constantinople.

But in AD 638, only sixteen years after the death of Muhammad, the caliph Omar entered Jerusalem, riding upon a white camel. After being in Christian hands for just over 300 years, Palestine had fallen to the Infidel. By 717, a little more than eighty years after the Prophet's death, the Arab empire stretched from the Pyrenees through the whole of North Africa and Syria as far as India in the east and the very walls of Constantinople to the north. It was a phenomenal military and religious achievement by any standards, and a terrible shock – both political and psychological – to Christendom.

The Arabs were in fact very tolerant of Christianity.[30] They allowed worship in the holy places, the continuity of monasteries and ecclesiastical structures, and the practice of pilgrimage. Unlike the Byzantines, they permitted a freedom of Christian worship in which sects that had been pronounced heretical by the Church could flourish in peace. Monophysites, Nestorians, Maronites, Jacobians and Copts continued their traditions alongside the Orthodox. In the eighth century, when Byzantium was in the grips of the Iconoclast controversy, the foremost apologist in the Orthodox iconophile party was John of Damascus, himself a monk based under Muslim domination in the Monastery of St Saba in the Holy Land. Just as the Church under Islam maintained its orthodoxy, so it also maintained its images. The few icons to have survived Iconoclasm in the east did so because they were in the collection of the great monastery of St Catherine at Mount Sinai – a monastery in Muslim territory (see Fig. 76).

But Christians were second-class citizens under Islam. They had, like Zoroastrians and Jews, to pay special taxes. Their holy places took second place behind the holy sites of Islam. For instance, the Muslims took over the great cathedral of St John at Damascus. Jerusalem was the third of the Muslim holy cities, the site of Muhammad's ascent to Paradise. On the Temple Mount, where Solomon's Temple and the Holy of Holies were believed to have stood, the Arab caliphs built the Dome of the Rock and the Al Aqsa mosque in the late seventh century. Christianity's most holy places were now surmounted by spectacular Muslim buildings, whose entry was barred to Christians.

Christian pilgrims still came to Palestine after the Arab conquest. But it was a much harder trip, fraught with many difficulties. St Willibald, who went to the Holy Land in the 720s, was arrested by the Muslim authorities on suspicion of spying. He was frequently ill, although the holy places did their work in this regard: simply entering the Holy Sepulchre cured him of temporary blindness (*Life of Willibald*, 24).[31] While the holy places themselves were kept in good repair, many Christian towns suffered. A pilgrim called Jacinthus, writing in the mid-eighth century, remarks that 'the city of Bethlehem is destroyed, even though there are still a few houses there' (*Pilgrimage of Jacinthus* 323,1).[32] And there were pirates and bandits to be avoided, many of whom were Muslims and saw Christians as fair game.

By the eleventh century, Christendom itself had been transformed. What had been ostensibly a single faith when Omar conquered Jerusalem was now a religion in schism. There was war between Pope and Emperor in the west, with generations of antipopes being nominated by the emperors and the papacy itself often having to flee Rome. Moreover, there was a deep doctrinal, liturgical and theological split between the Greek-speaking Orthodox Church in the east (comprising the Patriarchates of Constantinople, Antioch, Alexandria and Jerusalem) and the Latin-speaking Catholic Church based in Rome. This conflict led to mutual dislike, distrust and excommunication.

One of the effects of the deeply bellicose history of medieval Christendom, both in its relations with outsiders like the Arabs and in its internal disputes, was a transformed attitude to the relationship between religion and war. In the early Church, despite the concept of a just war, military activity was not seen as an important part of the Christian life. To 'put on the whole armour of God', as St Paul put it in the Epistle to the Ephesians (6:11), was seen in spiritual terms as waging a war against the sins of the

30 Krak des Chevaliers, Palestine, 13th century. View of the south and west fronts. One of the most impressive of all crusader castles, Krak des Chevaliers was built by the Knights of St John of the Hospital. It possessed a chapel, chapter-house and cloister in accordance with the rules of the Order, whose brethren took vows of poverty, chastity and obedience. The impressive concentric castles built by this and other orders were effectively the main line of defence for Christian Palestine.

flesh. But by the high Middle Ages such scriptural injunctions began to be interpreted literally. Ironically, the first religion to invent the notion of a holy war had been Islam, with its concept of the *Jihad*. But by the eleventh century in Christendom, 'the breastplate of righteousness' came to be perceived as the armour one wore in a military struggle blessed by the Church against the Infidel or even against another Christian group.

In 1095 Pope Urban II preached a Christian holy war against Islam.[33] His purpose was to rescue the Holy Land from its long captivity in the hands of the Arabs. In advocating a crusade, he united the spiritual paradigm of pilgrimage to Jerusalem (which Valerius so emphasised in his reading of Egeria) with the chivalrous ideals and opportunist potential of war. Not only was this a pious war, a war fought to rescue the holy city of Jerusalem, but it was a war sanctioned, blessed and advocated by the apostolic successor of St Peter himself. Many of those who went on crusade, in a mixture of piety and aggression, religion and opportunism, gained little save, perhaps, salvation itself. Others had the image of booty, and even of carving themselves a kingdom in the east. But politically, Palestine was relatively unimportant to Christendom beside those Muslim lands much closer to home: its significance was supremely as a symbol.

Yet this symbol brought together remarkable gatherings and alliances among the crowned heads of Europe, not to speak of lesser noblemen. The Second Crusade, preached by St Bernard himself, the leader of the Cistercian Order of monks, took King Louis of France and King Conrad of the Germans to Palestine. The Third Crusade, summoned to save Christian Palestine after Saladin had retaken Jerusalem for Islam, attracted Richard the Lionheart of England, Philip II of France and the Holy Roman Emperor Frederick Barbarossa. Other distinguished crusaders were the emperor Frederick II and St Louis of France, whose dying words (on crusade against the Infidel at Tunis in 1270) were 'Jerusalem, Jerusalem'. Such monarchs spent many months away from home, in alliance with potentates who were their worst enemies back in Europe. What they gained on crusade was a prestige that afforded a rare glory in the union of perhaps the two supreme ideals of medieval Europe – pilgrimage and chivalry.

To go on crusade was always seen as an act of pilgrimage, for which the Church granted remission of one's sins. Yet the Crusades involved carnage on a huge scale. Just over a hundred years after the conquest of Jerusalem from Islam in 1099, Byzantium itself became considered a fair target for a Christian holy war, when (in the disaster of the Fourth Crusade in 1204) the crusaders turned their arms on Christendom's greatest city to set up their own empire in Constantinople. The paradox in modern eyes of combining piety and war was already seen in the taking of Jerusalem by the First Crusade in July 1099. Before the final assault the crusaders fasted. They walked barefoot round the city following their priests, who carried holy relics and preached sermons on the Mount of Olives. On the day of the conquest, a week later, having stormed the city, they massacred the Muslim and Jewish population, man, woman and child.

Once conquered, Palestine was transformed into the Frankish kingdom of Outremer. Its pilgrims were always liable to enemy raids. Saewulf, who visited the Holy Land around 1101–3, just after the triumphs of the First Crusade, remarks of the road from Joppa to Jerusalem:[34]

It was very dangerous too, because the Saracens, who are continually plotting an ambush against Christians, were hiding in the caves of the hills and among rocky caverns. They were awake day and night, always keeping a look out for someone to attack, whether because he had not enough people with him, or was fatigued enough to leave a space between himself and his party. (*Travels*, 8)

The Latin-speaking crusaders set up their own ecclesiastical hierarchy, with their own clergy, bishops and patriarchs, often in direct competition with the established Orthodox priesthood. The local Christians of the east were both liberated by the Crusades and at the same time turned into second-class citizens, even in a Christian kingdom. In the long term, this exacerbated the split between the Churches in the east and the west. In the short term, it had liturgical repercussions. Abbot Daniel, a Russian pilgrim who visited Palestine in the early twelfth century, tells of the descent of the holy light at Easter by which 'the grace of God comes down unseen from heaven and lights the lamps in the Sepulchre of the Lord' (*Pilgrimage of Abbot Daniel*, 97). He himself placed a lamp in the Tomb, 'at the place where the most pure feet of Our Lord Jesus Christ lay', while 'at the head stood the lamp of the Greeks and at the breast the lamp of the monastery of St Saba'. Despite the presence of the crusader king Baldwin I of Jerusalem, 'by the grace of God these three lamps were lit, but of the Frankish lamps which had been hung higher up not one was lit'. This account reveals a certain pride in having participated in a miraculous act as well as the particular bias of a single pilgrim towards the Greek rite (later Abbot Daniel describes the Orthodox monks singing vespers, while 'the Latins on the great altar began mumbling after their own fashion'). It points to liturgical rivalries between the different Christian sects. The Latins may have occupied the high altar but the holy light still favoured the Greeks.

Nor were pilgrims during the period of the crusader kingdom always well served by Christians who had come to settle in Outremer. Burchard of Mount Sion, a Dominican friar of German origin, who came to Palestine in about 1280, was mordant about the kinds of people attracted to make a new life in Palestine.[35]

Whenever someone was a malefactor such as a murderer, a robber, a thief, or an adulterer, he used to cross the sea, either as a penitent, or else because he feared for his skin and therefore did not dare to stay in his own country; and so they came thither from all parts, such as Germany, Italy, France, England, Spain, Hungary and other parts of the world. And while they change the sky above them they do not change their minds. Once being here, after they have spent what they had brought with them, they have to acquire new (funds) and so, they return to their 'vomit', doing the worse of the worst. . . . (*Pilgrimage of Burchard*, 13.1)

31 The transference of the Holy Fire, outside the Holy Sepulchre, Jerusalem, Easter Saturday. The feast of the Holy Fire takes place as part of the Orthodox celebration of Easter. A candle is lit within the Holy Sepulchre on Easter Saturday, signifying the coming of the Resurrection. Thousands of pilgrims and locals throng outside the church, eager to receive the flame.

32 West façade of the crusader Cathedral of St Nicholas, Famagusta, Cyprus, 14th century. After the fall of Acre, Famagusta became the chief trading centre in the Christian Levant and its temporary opulence was marked by a number of magnificent churches reminiscent of the gothic architecture of mainland France. After the Turkish conquest of the island in the 16th century, the cathedral was converted to a mosque.

Burchard believed such settlers 'tread the holy places with polluted feet'. In the hands of such hosts, 'pilgrims who do not know how to take care of themselves, trust their hosts and lose their goods and their honour'.

CONVERTING THE HEATHEN: A LEGACY OF THE CRUSADES

Jerusalem remained in Christian hands for less than a hundred years. In 1187, Saladin reconquered it for Islam. Yet the image of a holy war, like the image of peaceful pilgrimage itself, became a formidable ideal in Christian culture. Throughout the Middle Ages, it was the dream of monarchs and churchmen, pious yeomen and even children, to liberate

33 Rotunda of the Temple Church, London, 12th century. The Templars built a number of circular churches as part of the tradition of architectural 'copies' of the Church of the Holy Sepulchre (and in particular the distinctive shape of the Anastasis rotunda) which survive from the Middle Ages throughout Europe.

the Holy Land by miracle or by war. Henry IV of England, on whose soul lay the heavy sin of murdering his anointed predecessor Richard II, dreamed that he might rescue Palestine in expiation and die in Jerusalem. In 1212, a boy visionary of about twelve years old, called Stephen of Cloyes, preached a children's crusade. Contemporary estimates that 30,000 children followed his preaching and gathered in a children's army at Marseilles are certainly exaggerated. But they give some idea of how strongly the image of liberating Jerusalem appealed to people of all ages, social classes and stations. The crusade was a disaster: the children were sold into slavery in North Africa by the ship owners who had offered them free passage to Palestine.

But those hundred years of a Christian Jerusalem were a potent inspiration to the cause of Christianisation. Pilgrimage itself was never the ancestor of missionary conversion, but crusade – military pilgrimage to the land of the Infidel – was the mother of missionary zeal. The Teutonic knights, the last of the military Orders set up to fight for Christendom in Palestine, conquered vast tracts near the Baltic and brought Catholicism to the Slavs. In 1219, during the Fifth Crusade, St Francis of Assisi went to Egypt in an attempt to convert the Sultan. He failed to persuade him, despite offering to undergo an ordeal by fire.

But the combination of conquest and conversion, whose paradigm was crusade against Islam, had a profound impact on the history of Europe. After the end of the Middle Ages, the great age of European expansion justified its conquest of the Indies and the Americas not as imperialism but as the bringing of Christian salvation to the heathen. It was this child of the Crusades, the aim of universal conversion, that was to inspire the missionaries who fostered and furthered the work of colonisation. The colonies – especially in Latin America – were not only conquered by European powers, but transformed into Christian countries by the missionary crusade of the Church.

IV. Containers of the Sacred: Ampullae, Souvenirs and Tokens

a. *Small silver container for a* linga *to be carried on the person, from Karnataka.*

b. *Buddhist plaque from Bodhgaya, found in South-East Asia.*

ilgrimage is as concerned with taking back some part of the charisma of a holy place as it is about actually going to the place. One of the most characteristic aspects of pilgrimage art in all the world religions is the proliferation of objects made available to pilgrims and brought home by them as reminders and even as tangible channels of connection with the sacred experience. In this way, the influence of the site can be retained in the domestic or mundane context to which a pilgrim has returned. Such souvenirs may themselves be collected into large accumulations of sacred mementos, such as the collections of sixth-century Byzantine lead ampullae from Palestine probably given by the Lombard queen Theodolinda to the cathedral treasuries at Monza and Bobbio in Italy in the first quarter of the seventh century. Like the relics of saints and the narratives written by

pilgrims, the souvenirs brought back from pilgrimage have an afterlife: they are reminders of pilgrimage; they may act as advertisements for the pilgrimage site, encouraging others to make the journey; they may even (as in the case of the ampullae) become relics in their own right.

Some souvenir boxes actually contain material from or even fragments of the pilgrimage site in the form of natural matter to be found there, such as water, earth and bits of wood or stone. Other kinds of reliquaries contain things produced at a pilgrimage site, such as holy oil or images. Such material may then be reincorporated into local ritual practices at home: holy oil or water was often used in medieval Christian healing and likewise the amulets blessed by Buddhist saints are used for cures in Thailand. Fragments can also be used to link special sites in a network of sacred geography, so that for

c. *Medieval lead pilgrimage token, depicting the head of
St Thomas of Canterbury.*

d. *Byzantine clay pilgrims' ampulla.*

instance the waters of the Ganges are dispersed
to other pilgrimage centres throughout the
whole of India, while relics such as the earth
from near St Martin's tomb in Tours were sent to
the major churches of France in the sixth and
seventh centuries AD

Containers of matter from a sacred place are
notable not just for what they hold, but because
they record its nature or origins. In a modern
example of a plastic ampulla from Palestine (Fig.
IVe), the body of the container indicates that it is
filled with 'holy water from Nazareth', while
the Crucifixion image on the lid is labelled
'Jerusalem'. Here, in a culture of high literacy,
texts are used to recall Palestine as a sacred unity.
In less literate cultures, such as that of most
Byzantine pilgrims in the seventh century AD,
images were used to evoke a story, a place or a
holy figure, as in the case of a clay ampulla with a

bearded saint holding a book (Fig. IVd). Whether
using labels or images to adorn the casket, such
ampullae condense within a single object not
only part of a sacred site but also a narrative
connected with that site. Moreover, unlike more
elevated forms of art, they are affordable by
pilgrims of almost every financial level. As is
evident within much pilgrimage practice, the use
of such objects acts to widen access to sacred
forces, to spread the imagery and the experience
of the holy to a broad constituency.

Souvenirs which contain fragments from a
place may be contrasted with those whose value
derives largely from the fact that they represent a
figure significant to the sacred centre where they
were bought. On sale at most Shiva temples in
India are small, affordable, clay or glass images
of the central icon of Shiva, the *linga*. Such
objects – other examples include the Christian

e. *Modern plastic ampulla, with water from Palestine.*

f. *Modern Buddhist pilgrims' souvenirs from Jiuhuashan, China.*

statuettes of Mary available at Walsingham (Fig. IVg) and the gaily painted images of Kuan Yin, the goddess of Compassion, for sale at the Buddhist sacred mountain of Jiuhuashan in contemporary China (Fig. IVf) – are above all portable. They may be taken home as gifts, or to adorn a shrine, and their value rests in their origins at a pilgrimage centre. However, rather than offering a portion of the site transferred to one's home, such objects act as metaphors stimulating the religious imagination to remember the experience, the statue or the place which the image recalls.

The memorabilia of pilgrimage are also a means of marking the pilgrim's identity as one who has made the journey. For instance the numerous kinds of lead amulets available at the tomb of St Thomas Becket in Canterbury throughout the Middle Ages (see, for instance, Fig. IVc) were worn by returning pilgrims as a sign of their penitential journey. Like ampullae containing water said to have been tinged with St Thomas's blood, the Canterbury badges and amulets, after being worn round a pilgrim's neck, were often dedicated in their local church as a kind of popular relic. Often tokens reproduced the miracle-working image at the centre of pilgrimage, such as the shrine of Becket or the Schöne Maria at Regensburg in Germany, where in one year (1520–1) over 100,000 clay and almost 10,000 silver pilgrimage badges were produced. This atmosphere of mass production can lead to an inflation of image-making, both democratising and diffusing the power of the image. Such production of souvenirs was often controlled by the religious élite at a given site, and certainly broadcast its fame. Yet by removing the image from its original context, pilgrims could more easily reinterpret the image in accordance with their own assumptions and needs.

g. *Modern Christian pilgrims' souvenirs from Walsingham.*

5

Geographies of Sainthood: Christian Pilgrimage from the Middle Ages to the Present Day

By the tenth century, Muslim tolerance of Jews and Christians in Jerusalem had given way to militancy and violence. The caliph al-Hakim even ordered the rock of the Church of the Holy Sepulchre to be destroyed, although his attempt at desecration was foiled by the hardness of the rock and the fragility of his workmen's chisels. Deprived of easy access to the Holy Land, Christian pilgrims were left to choose between two courses of action. One was to attempt to take back the sacred sites by force, as we saw in Chapter 4. However, the relief provided by military means was always to be intermittent, and Jerusalem remained largely under Muslim rule until the twentieth century. A different solution could be found in the creation of a sacred landscape in Europe. Sanctified sites could, in effect, duplicate the shrines of the Holy Land, either through imitation, the appropriation of relics from Palestine itself or the generation of indigenous local relics. Of course, many holy sites had existed in Europe for hundreds of years, such as the church of St Martin at Tours, an important pilgrimage site since the fifth century. Nevertheless, the great increase in pilgrimage centres, churches and shrines in eleventh- and twelfth-century Europe can be seen in part as a response to the loss of the Holy Land.

Rome claimed pre-eminence as a site of pilgrimage in the western Mediterranean, combining its status as a seat of empire with its access to spiritual authority. The city boasted not only the tombs of St Peter (the rock of the Church) and St Paul (apostle to the Gentiles), and indeed fragments of the True Cross, but also the presence of Peter's living embodiment, the Pope. The pious traveller could leave the city with a token depicting the keys of the apostle – a symbol which asserted the continuity of the Church. In addition to these prime attractions, Rome boasted numerous 'marvels' from the tombs of the martyrs, such as St Lawrence, to the great and ancient churches built by Constantine (himself venerated as a saint) and a plethora of ancient ruins. Medieval pilgrims' guide books, such as the *Mirabilia Urbis Romae* (written by a canon of St Peter's in the twelfth century) laid stress on all these aspects, giving visitors not only directions but also potted histories of the significance of different sites. In the *Mirabilia*, Rome becomes a city originally founded by Noah in his wanderings.[1]

34 OPPOSITE Santiago de Compostela, west front, 18th-century replacement of the original Romanesque façade. The tomb of St James the Great, venerated at Compostela in Galicia since the 9th century, became the single most important pilgrimage venue in western Christendom.

Santiago de Compostela, located in north-west Spain, emerged as a principal site of pilgrimage in western Christendom during the Middle Ages. The fact that the area was difficult and dangerous to reach increased its attractions to those who regarded perilous journeys as meritorious. Compostela's rise in importance also had distinct political and military implications. Its reputation as a holy place rested on the somewhat dubious claim that the remains of St James (Santiago in Spanish) had been carried to Spain from the Holy Land and discovered at the site in the ninth century. Such remains were important because they apparently belonged to an apostle and blood relative of Christ. They were located at the church behind the reliquary statue of the saint, and would be kissed by pilgrims at the culmination of the pilgrimage.

More significantly, however, the journey of the apostle from the Holy Land had appeared to transform him from a gentle fisherman into Matamoros (the Moor slayer), a powerful, patriotic symbol of Christian opposition to contemporary Muslim expansion. While the traditional representation of St James in painting and sculpture is that of the Pilgrim, dressed in broad-brimmed hat and cape and carrying a staff and scallop shell, in Spain he is depicted as a galloping knight, sword in one hand and cross in the other.[2] The great days of the site were to be during the years of the Crusades, when European Christianity was at its most aggressive towards Islam.[3]

Many other, smaller, sites proliferated throughout the continent, as the geography of Catholic pilgrimage became increasingly Europeanised. Walsingham in Norfolk, for instance, emerged as a shrine around 1061. Unlike Compostela, its reputation did not rely on the presence of relics. However, its founding myth revealed a desire to evoke some of the spiritual authority of Palestine. Richeldis, a local aristocrat, was said to have had a vision during which she was transported to Nazareth and the house where the angel Gabriel had announced the coming birth of Jesus to the Virgin (and where Jesus himself lived as a child). Obeying Mary's orders, conveniently conveyed to a person with sufficient resources to carry them out, Richeldis instructed her carpenters to build an exact replica of the holy house. The place became known as England's Nazareth and emerged as an international centre of pilgrimage. Visitors to the site were called palmers, a name usually reserved for those who had been to the Holy Land. A fifteenth-century ballad published by Richard Pynson records:[4]

> O England great cause thou hast glad for to be
> Compared to the Land of Promise, Sion . . .
> In thee is builded New Nazareth.

The legend of Walsingham reveals how Nazareth could be symbolically translated to Norfolk through the intercession of a holy figure and imitation of a holy place. Unlike the warlike St James, Mary proved an appropriate mediator for pilgrims seeking forgiveness and mercy. Throughout Europe as a whole, the tombs of saints and martyrs became sacred and powerful places, often appropriating the sites and the charisma of pagan predecessors. The creation of a sacred landscape in the

35 OPPOSITE Santiago de Compostela, figure sculpture from the right-hand jambs of the central doorway, Portico de la Gloria, 12th century. The great west entrance was sculpted between 1168–88, later than the construction of the rest of the cathedral. The figures represented here are all New Testament saints – from left to right, St Peter with the key, St Paul, St James himself and St John the Evangelist.

continent was reinforced by material manifestations of the divine such as tombs, relics and images, and sometimes the bodies of saints were even broken up for distribution to various sites.[5] According to theological orthodoxy, of course, veneration was due to God through the mediation of the Virgin or a saint represented by an image or embodied in a relic, rather than to the specific object itself. However, popular beliefs were often rather more parochial in implication. For instance, a story is told in the *Miracles of Our Lady of Chartres* of a lady who was apparently cured of a skin disease by praying to the Virgin.[6] When she set off for Notre-Dame de Soissons to give thanks for her deliverance, the Virgin appeared to inform her that she had in fact been healed by Notre-Dame de Chartres.

Often, it was important not only to view sacred objects, but also to touch them in order that their power be realised and made personally applicable in the prevention of plague, protection against war, assistance in religious conflicts, and so on. A small aperture called a *confessio* might be built on the top of a tomb so that the faithful could thrust in a piece of cloth to make contact with the remains. Tombs might even be scraped and the fragments consumed, or water drunk which had been used to wash the holy places. Such beliefs could claim biblical sanction by recalling episodes of healing associated with touching the garments of Jesus (although, of course, officially saints only acquired such power after death), but also gained force because they provided tangible, ritual enactments of ideas of mediation and intercession.

Although supposedly transcending the world of humanity, exemplary figures such as saints and martyrs tended to echo some of the characteristics of worldly hierarchy: a high proportion were both male and aristocratic. (In the late thirteenth and early fourteenth centuries, more men than women appeared to go on pilgrimage, and the practice was common among aristocrats, but over time increasing numbers of women, and people of lower status, began to visit holy sites.) The relationship of saints and their festivals with ordinary mortals also had other, distinctly mundane aspects. Holy sites were associated with fairs, and matchmaking could be arranged at large gatherings, not least because pilgrimages provided opportunities for courtship. In addition, saints could almost be seen as engaging in a relationship of exchange or patronage with humans, offering favours in return for honour and worship. At Compostela, pilgrims were expected to make offerings to the saint in the form of cash or jewellery, and such offerings helped provide the funds necessary to embellish the architecture of the shrine. According to one theory, the feudal system of acknowledging fealty to a lord was easily transferred to the relationship between saints and living Christians – even if the allegiance of pilgrims to their lords was often suspended during the time of the pilgrimage.[7]

One way of giving thanks for the granting of a favour was by leaving behind *ex-votos* – wax models of parts of the body which had been cured, crutches, model ships of those who had survived shipwrecks, and so on. These both propitiated the saint and, of course, advertised the efficacy of the site. Some saints even specialised in curing particular ailments. St Clare of France, for instance, became known (appropriately, given her name) for her ability to produce clarity of vision. The association of a saint with power over a particular illness or scourge lent them a somewhat double-edged character, however, since it was often assumed that the holy figure might, if displeased, cause the very problems for which he or she normally provided the cure.

While tombs embodied permanent places of worship, relics provided more portable vehicles of the sacred. They could be worn as charms or talismans, or even carried into battle in an attempt to ensure victory. Such objects might even be kept in a reliquary shaped in the form of the relic itself, such as a finger or an arm. Holy sites competed to gain power and attention through their collections of sacred objects, and every conse-crated church was required to have a relic played on its altar. As the demand for relics increased, so the methods of obtaining them became more ruthless. The bodies of saints, once 'discovered', were likely to be dismembered and spread with considerable alacrity. Not long after the discovery of St James in Spain, for instance, one of his hands appeared in Reading, and part of his arm in Liège. In the twelfth century, the pilgrims' guide to Compostela explicitly contested such claims from elsewhere, declaring 'let the folk beyond the mountains blush when they claim to have any part of it, or relics of him. For the entire body of the Apostle is there.'[8] Jesus's Cross, garments and blood also appeared to be spread across the continent. Such demands could lead to a kind of holy inflation: so much wood appeared to have come from the Cross that a theory developed that the holy wood had powers of self-reproduction.

The production of relics for the gullible was a tempting occupation, as satirised in Boccaccio's *Decameron*, which features a Father Cipolla ('Onion'), who returns from Jerusalem carrying a bottle allegedly contain-ing the sound of the bells of Solomon's temple. Already authenticated relics might also be obtained by underhand means. The institution of *furta sacra* ('pious thefts') developed, whereby the remains of a saint could be stolen and transported to another site by ambitious clerics, as in the case of the movement of the body of St Mark to Venice. Such conduct was rationalised with impressive theological ease by those who argued that saints were so powerful that they would not allow themselves to be moved against their will. A successful theft was thus argued to be a morally justifiable action – indeed, the success proved the action was justified.

If pilgrimages were a source of prestige for the guardians of sacred sites, and a potential provider of cures and miracles for many of their worshippers, they could also play a part in determining the nature of salvation. Through the system of 'indulgences' a pious act such as pilgrimage received a reward from the Church in the form of remission of punishments for sin, so that time spent in purgatory after death could be shortened dramatically. The system reinforced both the importance of the Church and the idea of pilgrimage as a transaction. It could also be used as an incentive, as Pope Urban II realised in granting such favours to crusaders to the Holy Land. However, like relics, indulgences were subject to destructive forces of supply and demand as competition between providers increased. By the end of the thirteenth century, shrines were outbidding each other in the length of remission they could offer, and professional pardoners (sellers of indulgences) had appeared throughout Europe. *Libri indulgentiarum* – texts whose purpose was to list the respective benefits to be found at sites – also began to appear.

Sacred places were sites of various forms of authority and power in the medieval world, and secular and religious institutions sometimes co-operated in providing legal protection as well as hospitality for pilgrims. One author goes so far as to claim that pilgrimages and their organisation constituted a collective phenomenon that structured the whole of western Christianity. [9] Abbeys, which at the time served as important centres of Christendom, supported religious voyages: Cluny, for instance, organised pilgrimages to Compostela. Many Romanesque churches also acted as important stopping-points along pilgrimage routes. In turn, a series of other organisations emerged, partially in order to service pilgrimages, such as military orders which protected the roads, and hostelries or hospices located at important transit points.

The institutionalised administration of the Church attempted, not always successfully, to co-opt and control the charisma of saints. The ability to designate such holy figures was of considerable importance, and although from the early Middle Ages this privilege was granted to bishops and synods, it was subsequently taken over by the Pope – a possible explanation for the preponderance of Italian saints. Political and religious authorities also incorporated pilgrimages into systems of discipline; indeed, this was a method employed by St Augustine himself as a form of sanction. Although sometimes self-imposed, these often involved punishment for some offence against God or the state, so that the pilgrimage became a contemporary equivalent of the exile of Cain. Penance could be demonstrated by methods of travel. Pilgrims might approach a holy site barefoot, on their knees, enduring a fast or a vow of silence, or possibly carrying stones around their neck. More generally, journeys to major sites were punctuated by visits to the shrines of lesser saints and the buildings of religious orders, thus turning the pilgrimage as a whole into a form of extended ritual. By carrying particular objects – a staff and scrip (or satchel) – the traveller could also copy religious functionaries who displayed their special status through their dress.

However, if the management of a shrine could bolster the authority of the Church, pilgrimage could also incorporate elements of popular religion whose implications were far from orthodox. The example of medieval Regensburg illustrates such a mixture of ecclesiastical control and popular enthusiasm. On 21 February 1519 the city expelled its large community of Jews. A workman engaged in pulling down the synagogue was badly injured, but recovered – an apparent miracle which encouraged contributions for a chapel on the site dedicated to the Virgin, incorporating a picture and statue of the Madonna. Thousands of people began to visit the site:[10]

. . . clothes that touched the statue were particularly good for curing sick cattle. On 1 June, Pope Leo X issued a bull granting indulgences of a hundred days to properly conducted pilgrimages to the chapel. In 1520 it became more and more the irrational and uncontrolled kind of movement that worried contemporary churchmen a good deal. The pilgrims came in thousands, often whole villages together; some elected to come naked, others on their knees; visions and wonders increased . . . crowds danced howling around the statue.

This description appears to reinforce one theory as to the nature of medieval pilgrimage: that in a society based on feudal economic and political structures, it could provide an opportunity not only to break the bounds of one's immediate locality but also the constraints of everyday behaviour. However, its subversive nature might also take on a more explicitly political character, depending on the nature of the holy figure commemorated at the holy site. An example is provided by a shrine that came to rival Walsingham amongst the pre-eminent English sites of pilgrimage: Canterbury. Here, the figure who received veneration was a martyr who had risen to the peak of ecclesiastical and political authority, only to oppose and be destroyed by the forces of temporal power once he had begun to incur the king's displeasure. Born to Norman settlers, Thomas Becket had become the chancellor of Henry II, and then in 1162 Archbishop of Canterbury. On 29 December 1170 four knights first tried to entice him out of the cathedral, but were eventually forced to kill him near the Lady Chapel. Many faithful were said to have dipped cloth in his blood as if he were already a saint, and miracles soon began to be recorded in his name. A mere three years later he was canonised as a result of popular pressure. The site became not only a memorial to Becket, but also a scene of regal humiliation, as Henry came to Canterbury, walked barefoot to the cathedral and was scourged at Becket's tomb as a sign of his apparent penitence. Henry VIII later destroyed the shrine, partly to

36 Enamelled reliquary casket from Limoges depicting the martyrdom of St Thomas Becket, 13th century, British Museum. Becket is shown on the main body of the casket performing mass at an altar over which hovers the hand of God. He is attacked by two knights (in reality there were four). Above, the saint's soul is shown ascending into heaven with angels.

ensure that no chance remained of the Becket cult continuing to symbolise resistance to the sovereign's authority.

STAGING THE SACRED: ART AND ARCHITECTURE AS THE SETTING FOR PILGRIMAGE

The fact that pilgrimages often provided arenas for assertions of and challenges to religious and secular authority in the medieval period is revealed not only in historical texts, but also in the architecture of pilgrimage sites. Let us take as an example one of the prime pilgrimage sites of the high Middle Ages. While Chartres was not quite as important a pilgrimage venue as Santiago or Rome, it was one of the principal centres for sacred travel in France – along with the shrines of St Michael on the Mont-St-Michel and Mary Magdalene at Vézelay. Moreover, it proved an important stopping-off point (like Vézelay) on the way to Compostela or Rome. Here is the thirteenth-century poet Guillaume le Breton on the cathedral of Chartres:[11]

> City of Chartres, enriched not by numerous burghers,
> Likewise also enriched by its clergy so mighty, so splendid,
> And by its beautiful church, for none can be found in the whole world,
> None that would equal its structure, its size and decor in my judgment.
> Countless the signs and the favours of grace by which the Blessed Virgin
> Shows that the Mother of Christ has a special love for this one church,
> Granting a minor place, as it were, to all other churches,
> Deeming it right to be frequently called the Lady of Chartres.
> This is also the place where every one worships the tunic
> Worn on the day of the birth of the Lamb, by the Virgin as garment. . . .

This quotation is from a poem completed within a few decades of the rebuilding of the cathedral at Chartres after the terrible fire of 1194 which demolished all the twelfth-century church but the west façade. Above all, Guillaume remarks on Chartres' great relic (which 'every one worships') and the 'countless signs and favours of grace' bestowed there by the Virgin. In fact, by the later Middle Ages, the Virgin's tunic (a 16-foot [5 m] long piece of silk) was but one of the many treasures possessed by the cathedral. In addition there were several hundred miraculous statues, a miraculous well containing the relics of local martyrs,[12] even the head of St Anne, the Virgin's mother,[13] purchased by Louis the Count of Chartres from the sacred booty looted from Constantinople in 1204 by the crusaders.

The pilgrim at Chartres was confronted with a dazzling display of medieval splendour in architecture, sculpture and stained glass. The nave floor boasted a huge labyrinth (whose diameter was as wide as the nave itself), a symbol of the pilgrim's path in this life and of the road to salvation in the next (see illustration on p. 169). The images in glass and stone were a complex doctrinal testament to the religion which pilgrimage to Chartres reaffirmed. Such imagery not only supported spiritual awe with all the emotional effects that early Gothic could muster; it also embodied a theological commentary on the Incarnation, redemption of humankind, and the possibility for salvation offered to the individual pilgrim as he or she arrived at the church. In a sense such art replaced texts as the 'book for the illiterate', and it functioned alongside the readings, liturgies and services whose setting it formed by providing them with a visual commentary.

One key element of the imagery – something implied also in Guillaume le Breton's reference to burghers and clergy – is the representation in the arts of Chartres of all the social stations to which its pilgrims would have belonged. From the royal arms of France and Castille in the North Rose (the rose window celebrating the Virgin) to images of peasants (such as the harvesters in the labours of the month sculptures of the Royal Porch at the west entrance or the peasant and cart represented in the stained-glass window of St Lubin, donated by the wine merchants), the art of Chartres framed all its pilgrims within the world of its own imagery. Many windows were given by local gentry or nobles, for instance that of the Clément family, depicting St Denis, the patron saint of France, with the youthful marshall Jean Clément in the south-east transept. Dressed as a crusader, with a cross on his tunic, the marshall stands as a figure of knighthood idealised, as well as a representative of the local nobility. Still more windows were donated by the merchants, guilds and burghers of the town of Chartres, including clothiers, drapers, furriers, haber-dashers, tanners, sculptors, armourers, bakers, butchers, cartwrights, coopers, masons, stone-cutters, bankers, apothecaries, fishmongers, water-carriers and vintners. These tradesmen signed their dedications by having their professions portrayed in glass. Together they provide a comprehensive portrayal, a cross-section, of medieval burgher life.

37 Chartres, sculptural detail from the left door, Royal Porch, late 12th century. The carving depicts a peasant harvesting grain, one of the Labours of the Months, representing July.

38 Chartres, window from
the clerestory of the south
transept, 13th century.
Marshall Jean Clément
receives the oriflamme from
St Denis (Dionisius), the
patron saint of France.

Combined with the images of royalty, aristocracy and the priesthood, the iconography of Chartres provides an idealised image of the whole social order, made up of groups with complementary but different roles and statuses. And yet it incorporated all the contestations and competitions of medieval culture, as local aristocratic families and tradesmen's guilds vied with each other to donate windows. The signatures of the tradesmen in fact functioned as permanent advertisements, since they were carefully placed at the bottom of windows so as not to impede the sacred narratives which the main imagery recounts, but also to be as close as possible to the viewer's eye.

The lives and professions of pilgrims and donors are therefore tied to the sacred histories which these windows record and to the total narrative of holy doctrine which the cathedral itself embodies. Moreover, the church becomes a visual representation of the totality of medieval society itself, placed symbolically as the foundation on which the sacred stories of Christ and the saints are told. The whole hierarchy of medieval culture is not only enshrined and reinforced by its representation in the images of the cathedral, but comes to underlie a sacred hierarchy of saints, the Virgin and Christ. The pilgrim at Chartres saw not only a theological narrative, but also – perhaps most crucially – an ideal portrait of him or herself (whether peasant, knight or burgher, king, priest or bishop) represented within that story.

39 ABOVE LEFT and
40 ABOVE RIGHT
Canterbury Cathedral, stained glass showing pilgrims travelling to the shrine of St Thomas and pilgrims praying at the tomb of St Thomas. These panels were part of a spectacular series completed in the early 13th century and placed in the low windows of the Trinity Chapel which surrounded the shrine to which Becket's body was transfered in 1220. They were physically very close to the pilgrims as they circled the shrine and more visible in detail than most medieval glass.

The art of Chartres thus incorporated the viewer – the pilgrim – into its network of meanings. Furthermore, the windows allude not only to local saints (such as St Chéron) or to those venerated specifically at Chartres (the Virgin or Christ), but also to other pilgrimage targets, whose worship spanned the geography of Europe. For instance, the choir windows include stories of St Martin of Tours, St Thomas Becket and St James. In alluding to such figures, Chartres incorporates, on one level of its meaning, a sacred geography of medieval pilgrimage in western Christendom, as well as a sacred history and a sociology of medieval society.

Chartres is unique – perhaps above all because it has survived so little harmed. Here, more than in any other Gothic church, we can experience the 'feel' of a pilgrimage centre in much the same form as it had in the Middle Ages. Yet the art of Chartres did not emphasise and re-emphasise the theme of pilgrimage in precisely the same way as the windows of other cathedrals. At Canterbury, as at Chartres, there is a great cycle of the genealogy of Christ, as well as windows reflecting local saints like Dunstan and Alphege.[14] Similarly, there are hagiographical cycles of other saints with important shrines, such as St Martin of Tours. But by far the most extended cycle – of windows placed remarkably close to eye level in the cathedal's great corona at the east – represents the miracles of St Thomas. Martyred in 1170, just four years before his cathedral happened to be (some have thought purposely) burnt to the ground, and only ten years before the great new edifice in the early Gothic style was being glazed, St Thomas turned Canterbury into a pilgrimage centre of the first rank. The Becket windows show not only the saint's life, but the miracles performed by him after his death. Many of these miracles took place at Canterbury itself, at the tomb which the windows were designed to surround.

In the early years of the thirteenth century, when St Thomas's relics were still in a shrine in the crypt of his new church (before being moved, on the completion of the choir, to the high altar in 1220), accounts of his miracles were read to pilgrims in the chapter house.[15] Thus the monks of Canterbury provided a verbal support to the visual message being conveyed by the glass. The Becket windows emphasise not only his life but the very pilgrimage to his tomb where the miracles took place. This was the pilgrimage which a viewer had to have undertaken in order to be looking at these windows. Like the social portraits at Chartres, the Canterbury windows show knights, burghers, peasants, priests and abbots being healed at the shrine of St Thomas. They show pilgrims riding to the tomb, arriving there, venerating it. They show the outcasts of medieval society – lepers, the insane – brought to the sacred centre and cured. In a still more active and dramatic way than the glass of Chartres, these windows map contemporary concerns – the activities of the recently martyred Thomas and of the pilgrims present at his tomb (of which every viewer was one) – upon the sacred narrative of the Incarnation and salvation of humankind. They depict a society healed through the Church, whose divisions are brought together in the unifying action of pilgrimage and divine grace through the mediation of the sainted

Thomas, who bestows blessings on king and pauper alike. In the high Middle Ages, it was the art of the pilgrimage centre that explained the significance of the place to its visitors and that incorporated them as pilgrims into Christendom's complete and ideal vision of a divine order informing and governing the human realm.

Such imagery, and the very act of pilgrimage which looking at such images involved, was a formidable affirmation of the power of the Church. St Thomas represented the triumph of the Church's authority – the spiritual rather than the temporal world – over that of his enemy, the king of England. Henry II's pilgrimage and self-abasement before the shrine of his erstwhile rival proved the supremacy of the Church over the king. But Canterbury's imagery of a sick society brought to health and harmony at the tomb of the saint could also be used to reinforce the king's authority. Henry's pilgrimage was a way of acquiring spiritual endorsement from a saint whom he had himself created. In later years, other English royal figures, such as the Black Prince and Henry IV, would be buried in the choir of Canterbury by the tomb of the saint. A figure whose initial distinction lay in his and the Church's resistance to temporal power came to bestow his spiritual aid upon the interests of the English monarchy.

OPPOSITION TO PILGRIMAGE: ICONOCLASM AND REFORMATION

The art and architecture of some pilgrimage sites could thus serve to reflect and thereby reinforce the image of an ordered, hierarchical, medieval society. Yet, as a widespread and popular phenomenon, involving the mass movement of the poor as well as the rich through the landscape, medieval pilgrimage always contained a potential threat to the authorities of Church and State. The Church's habit of granting the pilgrim special privileges, such as immunity both from taxes and from the threat of being arrested, also provided incentives for the less than spiritually pure to undertake the journey. As Chaucer's *Canterbury Tales* illustrated, those who chose to undertake a journey might do so with other than pious intentions. Thus, the Pardoner boasts in his prologue of his attitude to his profession:[16]

> I wol nat do no labour with myne handes . . .
> Nay, I wol drynke licour of the vyne
> And have a joly wenche in every toun.

Other, more specifically theological, reasons for resisting pilgrimage as a ritual practice were also evident. The Lollards, followers of John Wycliffe (*c*.1329–84), came up with a comprehensive and damning summary of criticisms in their opposition to the expense of undertaking long journeys (which used money that could have been given to the poor), the hypocrisy involved in granting indulgences and the idolatry involved in the apparent worship of images. Erasmus (*c*.1466–1536), a Dutch Catholic scholar of great international reputation, attacked the practice as a form of superstition which discouraged the internal

precious charbencle/of martirs alle

41 Worshippers before the tomb of St Edmund, King and Martyr, Harley MS 2278, fol. 9, 15th century, British Library. This image comes from a lavish manuscript of *The Lives of St Edmund and Fremund*, written by John Lydgate and presented to Henry VI in commemoration of his pilgrimage to the shrine of St Edmund in 1433–4. Lydgate himself is depicted in prayer before the shrine. Royal tombs were important destinations of pilgrimage in the Middle Ages.

cultivation of faith and increased the power of corrupt religious orders. He visited Walsingham in 1511–12 and possibly again in 1514. His 'colloquy' on the subject was first printed in 1526 in Basel, and later published in England as *The Pilgrimage of Pure Devotion*. The work consists of a dialogue between two men, and Erasmus chooses to let the defender of pilgrimage, Ogygius, condemn himself out of his own mouth. Here is the latter describing his innocent questioning of a custodian of the shrine at Walsingham:[17]

Inspecting everything carefully, I inquired how many years it was since the little house had been brought there. 'Some ages,' he replied. 'In any event,' I said, 'the walls don't look old.' He didn't deny that they had been placed there recently, and the fact was self-evident. 'Then,' I said, 'the roof and thatch of the house seem rather recent.' He agreed. 'Not even these crossbeams, nor the very rafters supporting the roof, appear to have been put here many years ago.' He nodded. 'But since no part of the building has survived, how is it known for certain,' I asked, 'that this is the cottage brought here from so far away?'

Ogygius clearly has the ability to ask the right question, but lacks the insight or desire to grasp the consequences of his interrogation:

. . . [the custodian] hurriedly showed us an old, worn-out bearskin fastened to posts and almost laughed at us for our dullness in being slow to see such a clear proof. So, being persuaded, and excusing our stupidity, we turned to the heavenly milk of the Blessed Virgin.

As part of a more general opposition to the traditional practices of the Roman Catholic Church, waves of iconoclasm emerged in Europe throughout the sixteenth century. Martin Luther had been on a pilgrimage to Rome in 1510. However, he came explicitly to oppose the system of indulgences, and argued against what he saw as the over-emphasis on 'good works' and consequent denial of justification by faith implied by such acts as pilgrimage. Luther, who, like Erasmus, criticised the excesses of the Roman Church but went further and broke with Papal authority, adopted a relatively conservative view compared with other reformers. Calvin, for instance, came to regard pilgrimage as a vain attempt to gain salvation through mere action and emphasised instead an interiorisation of faith which came to be seen as characteristically Protestant. As Jesus was to be the sole mediator to the divine (by contrast with the host of saints), so the universally applicable word was to take precedence over visual and tangible representations of particular images and objects.[18]

To make material images of the uncircumscribable all-creating creator, when the real images were already around (in the form of our fellow beings and in the manifestation of Christ as flesh), was terrible idolatry.

In England, theological arguments for reform combined easily with the politically motivated desire to appropriate the influence and wealth of monasteries and shrines. The abuse of images was often felt to be most prevalent at Marian shrines; accordingly, statues of the Virgin were burned in London in 1538, such violence almost constituting a ritual reversal of the reverence previously paid to images. At Boxley Rood, in Kent, a figure of Christ on the cross had been constructed which used wires to allow the eyes to move, the mouth to open, and the hands to make a gesture of blessing. This was made to perform to the crowd by Henry VIII's men before being broken into pieces.

As a source of considerable wealth and the site of the 'Virgin by the Sea', Walsingham was extremely vulnerable to the destructive attention of the reformers. Indeed, in 1537 it was alleged by Henry's spies that rebellion against the threat of dissolution was being planned at the shrine. A layman, George Gysborough, and the sub-prior were hung, drawn and quartered, and the priory and shrine destroyed in 1538. The site's brutal and apparently conclusive fate was lamented in an elegy attributed to Philip Howard, Earl of Arundel:[19]

> Weepe, weepe, O Walsingham
> whose dayes are nightes
> Blessings turned to blasphemies,
> holy deedes to dispites.
> Sinne is wher Our Ladie sate,
> heaven turned is to hell,
> Sathan sittes wher Our Lord did swaye,
> Walsingham, oh farewell.

Bouts of iconoclasm took place throughout Protestant Europe during the Reformation. They were directed not only at the 'idolatrous' images of the Roman Catholics, but also against other practices, rituals and sacraments sanctioned by the Catholic Church. Reforming theologians such as Karlstadt and Zwingli proclaimed that the Eucharist itself was an idol and, like other 'carnal' or material objects including relics and icons, could not contain the transcendence of God. In the second half of the sixteenth century, fierce outbursts of image-smashing and church desecration occurred in waves through northern Europe – in Scotland in the 1550s and 1560s, in France in the 1560s, and above all in the Netherlands in 1565–6. Such violence was a symptom of a new Christianity which asserted a transcendent God who disdained all the fripperies of the world and detested such 'Popish' activities as pilgrimage, relic worship and elaborate ritual.[20]

PILGRIMAGE IN THE ORTHODOX WORLD

The Orthodox Church had confronted much earlier many of the issues which came to a head in western Christianity during the Reformation. Byzantine Iconoclasm, a long period of theological and political crisis in the whole Orthodox world which lasted between AD 726 and 843, had faced many problems inherent in the veneration of images and relics, as well as the question of what material objects could be accepted in worship. The Byzantine solution, as formulated by the great eighth- and

42 Miniature from the Khludov Psalter, Moscow Historical Museum, codex 129, fol. 67r., 9th century. This illumination from a psalter produced shortly after the end of Iconoclasm in AD 843 illustrates a passage from Psalm 68: 'They gave me also gall for my food, and made me drink vinegar for my thirst'. The Crucifixion, and the offering of vinegar to Christ on a sponge, is paralleled with an image of the iconoclasts whitewashing an icon of Christ, the clear implication being that the sins of the iconoclasts are on a level with the sins of those who executed Christ.

ninth-century theologians John of Damascus and Theodore the Studite, was a full-scale acceptance of everything in the created world as in principle an image of the Incarnate God. In the words of St John of Damascus:

Sun and light and brightness, the running waters of a perennial fountain, our own mind and language and spirit, the sweet fragrance of a flowering rose, are images of the Holy and Eternal Trinity.[21]

The immediate result of this theology was a full-blown cult of icons and relics of remarkable intensity and longevity.[22]

With the loss of Jerusalem to the Muslims, and the split between the eastern and western Churches which developed through the Middle

43 Interior of the Church of St Sophia, Istanbul, looking east. The greatest church of the Byzantine empire, St Sophia was constructed under the emperor Justinian in 532–37 and swiftly became one of the principal pilgrimage centres in the Orthodox world. It was converted into a mosque in 1453, following the fall of Constantinople to the Ottoman Turks, and in 1930 it became a museum.

44 The Virgin and Child, mosaic from the apse of the Church of St Sophia, 9th century. This image was the first to be erected in St Sophia after the end of Iconoclasm in 843.

Ages on grounds of theology and around disputes about Papal authority, both Palestine and the great shrines of western Europe became somewhat inaccessible to Orthodox pilgrims. Instead the Orthodox Churches developed new patterns of pilgrimage, focused especially on the great churches, relics and icons in Constantinople, but also on the tombs of many Orthodox saints in remote monastic settlements like Mount Athos or Meteora in Greece. With the fall of Constantinople to the Ottoman Turks in 1453, the Orthodox Churches lost not only their empire but also St Sophia, 'the great Church' built by the emperor Justinian in the sixth century AD, which had become the centre of Byzantine liturgy and perhaps the major goal of eastern Christian pilgrimage. The Ottomans turned it into their imperial mosque. In the years after the fall of Byzantium, Orthodox pilgrimage became increasingly focused around

45 Icon representing the Triumph of Orthodoxy, Byzantine (probably from Constantinople), 14th century, British Museum. The panel celebrates the restoration of icons after the end of Iconoclasm. In the upper register two angels carry the famous Hodegetria icon of the Mother of God. To the left stands the empress Theodora, who ordered the restoration of icons, with her infant son, Michael III. To the right is a procession of monks and bishops led by the Patriarch Methodius. In the bottom row stand a number of saints and clerics famed for their defence of the cult of icons.

numerous local holy shrines and sites in the remaining Orthodox lands – principally Greece, Serbia and Russia.

The accounts by medieval Russian pilgrims of their trips to Constantinople present a vivid picture of pilgrimage to what W. B. Yeats called 'the holy city of Byzantium'. Stephen of Novgorod, who journeyed to Constantinople from Russia in the 1340s, wrote of his urge 'to venerate the holy places and to kiss the bodies of the saints'.[23] Stephen's account has a vivid description of one of the great icon festivals of Constantinople, the procession of the famous miracle-working Hodegetria icon. This image, traditionally ascribed to the hand of St Luke himself, was placed at the Hodegetria monastery (already famous for a miraculous fountain which cured the blind) in the fifth century. Like the Blachernae Virgin (another miraculous icon in Constantinople), this image acquired a number of relics of the Madonna and was frequently carried in procession through the city. In times of crisis it had a protective role and was carried around the walls during a siege and brought to the church of St Sophia and the imperial palace for prayers.[24] Stephen writes:

Since it was Tuesday, we went . . . to the procession of the holy Mother of God. Luke the Evangelist painted this icon while looking at Our Lady the Virgin Mother of God herself while she was still alive. They bring this icon out every Tuesday. It is quite wonderful to see. All the people from the city congregate. The icon is very large and highly ornamented and they sing a very beautiful chant in front of it, while all the people cry out with tears, 'kyrie eleison' ['Lord, have mercy']. They place the icon on the shoulders of one man who is standing upright, and he stretches out his arms as if being crucified, and then they bind up his eyes. It is terrible to see how it pushes him this way and that around the monastery enclosure, and how forcefully it turns him about, for he does not understand where the icon is taking him. . . . Two deacons carry the flabella [canopy] in front of the icon, and others the canopy.[25]

The drama of this procession, with its imitation of the Passion and the icon's remarkable effects, is emphasised in other Russian accounts of the Hodegetria. Later pilgrims reported that the icon performed miracles every Tuesday, healing the sick.[26] One effect of such civic processions of miraculous images and relics was the fusion of pilgrimage with traditions of urban festival going back to ancient times.

The man singled out to be the icon's bearer held out his arms in imitation of Christ's Passion. This quality of making present a holy world through imitation is characteristic of Orthodoxy. It was on the basis of their imitation of Christ's person and that of the saints that icons were considered holy by the Iconophile theologians. Likewise, Stephen of Novgorod's pilgrimage to the church of St Sophia (the seat of the Patriarch of Constantinople, whose hand Stephen kissed) took on the pattern of a trip to the Holy Land. After seeing 'the Lord's Passion relics which we sinful men kissed', Stephen and his party confronted an icon of 'the Saviour . . . depicted in mosaic on the wall . . .; holy water runs from the wounds of the nails in his feet'. At the eastern end of St Sophia, Stephen meets 'a truly magnificent icon of the holy Saviour. It is called the "Mount of Olives" because there is a similar one in Jerusalem.' In the main sanctuary is a fountain called the Jordan which was said to have appeared miraculously from the Jordan river in Palestine and still to be linked to it. Stephen tells of some Russian pilgrims who recognised a cup found in this fountain in St Sophia, which they had originally lost in the river Jordan in Galilee. Finally, Stephen mentions the stone table of Abraham, from Mamre where the three angels appeared to the Prophet.[27]

The trip through St Sophia becomes in effect a trip through the Holy Land transposed in the imagination and through various material objects associated with the Bible into the space of a single church in Constantinople. The imitation of Palestine inside St Sophia is accomplished through relics actually from the Passion and from Old Testament events, through miraculous prodigies such as the Jordan Fountain and through images which not only suggest Jerusalem (the 'Mount of Olives' icon) but actually enact the Passion (the holy water flowing from the wounds in the mosaic icon). Other churches in Constantinople also had the power to evoke Palestine, for instance the Church of the Holy Apostles (the burial church of the Byzantine emperors), which possessed the column to which Christ had been bound and that by which St Peter had wept bitterly.[28] But through their relics (all of which the Russian pilgrims kissed fervently) they could also recall other times, such as the golden age of Christian theology, monasticism and Orthodoxy in the fourth century (the Church of the Holy Apostles contained not only the tomb of Constantine but also those of the great Cappadocian fathers John Chrysostom and Gregory of Nazianzus).[29]

While later Protestantism attempted to spiritualise religion by abolishing the material accoutrements of worship, and indeed frowning on pilgrimage itself, Orthodoxy never rejected the sensual world of icons, incense and liturgical drama. Instead, in the practice of pilgrimage as a way of life, many Russians (both lay and clergy) found a spiritual path in the imitation of Christ. People dressed in pilgrim's costume so that their social station could vanish in the face of their sacred vocation, and they would live by begging. In the words of the Russian religious writer Catherine de Hueck Doherty, 'to the Russian mind this begging was in imitation of Christ'.[30]

A memorable self-portrait by such a pilgrim in nineteenth-century Russia is the famous spiritual diary *The Way of a Pilgrim*. The writer chooses to give up his life to saying the Jesus Prayer ceaselessly. Pilgrimage becomes the ideal way of life for someone employing this kind of spiritual practice:

I made up my mind to go to Siberia to the tomb of St Innocent of Irkutsk. My idea was that in the forests and steppes of Siberia I should travel in greater silence and therefore in a way that was better for prayer and reading. And this journey I undertook, all the while saying my oral Prayer without stopping.[31]

The diary, although essentially a private record of the pilgrim's inner life and experience, refers to a number of such journeys – to the shrines of the saints at Kiev in the Ukraine (p. 144) and to the 'wonder-working footprint of the most pure Mother of God' at Pochaev (p. 152). Getting to the goal is far less important for this pilgrim than the process of the journey itself. He sets out for Jerusalem but fails to leave Russia (p. 124):

Of course I fretted at first because I had not been able to carry out my wish to go to Jerusalem, but I reflected that even this had not happened without the providence of God, and I quieted myself with the hope that God, the lover of men, would take the will for the deed, and would not let my wretched journey be without edification and spiritual value. And so it turned out, for I came across the sort of people who showed me many things that I did not know and for my salvation brought light to my dark soul. If that necessity had not sent me on this journey I should not have met those spiritual benefactors of mine. . . .

What marks the value of this kind of pilgrimage and sets protective blessing upon it is not the outer quality of the destination, but the inner strength of the pilgrim's prayers. As a woman traveller explains to the pilgrim (p. 113):

I made up my mind to live unmarried, to go on pilgrimage to the shrines, and pray at them. However, I was afraid to travel all by myself, young as I was, I feared evil people might molest me. But an old woman-pilgrim whom I knew taught me wherever my road took me always to say the Jesus prayer without stopping, and told me for certain that if I did no misfortune of any sort could happen to me on my way. I proved the truth of this, for I walked even to far-off shrines, and never came to any harm.

Such pilgrims were a common feature of Russian life before the Revolution. Their faith was not always strictly what the Church hierarchy would have approved. In Tolstoy's late novel *Resurrection*, his hero Prince Nekhlyudov encounters such a pilgrim on a ferry:

'. . . Why is it there are different religions?', asked Nekhlyudov.
'There be different religions because people believe in other people, and don't believe in themselves. When I used to believe in other men I wandered about like I was in a swamp. I got so lost, I never thought I'd find me way out. There be Old Believers, an' New Believers, an' Sabbatarians, an' Sectarians, an' them as 'as Parsons an' them as don't, an' Austrians, an' Malakans, an' them as castrates themselves. Every faith praises itself up only. An' so they all crawl about in different directions like blind puppies. Many faiths there be but the Spirit is one. In you an' in me an' in 'im. That means, if everyman of us believes in the Spirit within 'im, us'll all be united. Let everyone be 'imself, and us'll all be as one.'[32]

PILGRIMAGE AND THE EXPANSION OF EMPIRE

Despite the strictures of the Protestant Reformers in western Europe, pilgrimage was continued by members of the Catholic and Eastern Orthodox churches, and the Counter-Reformation actually stimulated journeys to the Holy Land, to Rome and to the tombs of saints and martyrs. Furthermore, even if Catholicism were under attack in Europe, it could find new areas in which to flourish as the empires of Spain and Portugal expanded far from home. For the European missionaries, territories such as those of South America held out the prospect of encountering spiritually naïve peoples, on to whom 'pure' forms of the faith could be inscribed. Amongst the Conquistadors who journeyed to Mexico, St James was again to appear as a valuable ally – not in the role of defender against foreign invaders, as at Compostela, but instead helping the Christian soldiers to subdue the natives. However, the Europeans could not predict how their traditions would combine with indigenous beliefs, encouraging dynamic processes of syncretism that persist into the present day.

Events in the Andes have been well documented, and illustrate vividly the effects of cultural contact and mixing.[33] Pilgrimage traditions in the region stretch back to between 1000 and 500 BC, although it was not until the second half of the first millennium AD that new inter-regional shrines arose, linked to the formation of the first Andean states. With the rise of the Inca empire in the fifteenth century, local shrines were incorporated into a centralised religious geography. Imperial rituals united all the shrines through the medium of human sacrificial blood, transported – either in its living victims or in sacred vessels – between Cusco and provincial centres.

46 Oaxaca Valley, Mexico. Woman worshipping at a popular shrine.

The Spanish conquest of the central Andes aimed to replace the local pilgrimage tradition with that of the western, Christian faith. Marian and saintly images were installed as the divine patrons of ethnic and territorial groups in the hope that loyalties to corresponding pagan deities would decline. Indeed, many shrines were established at or near indigenous sacred sites. As with the early Christianisation of Europe, missionaries hoped that allegiance would simply transfer from one religion to another, not least as statues and images began to be hailed as miraculous providers of cures or rain. However, if Andean deities were Christianised, the holy figures of Christianity were themselves subject to a form of 'Andeanisation'. Missionaries may have done their best to destroy pagan shrines, but they did not take into account the fact that, according to indigenous cosmology, the sacred quality of the landscape was more important than mere effigies. By planting crosses on pagan shrines and sites, Christians merely succeeded in confirming the sacred status of these places in the eyes of local peoples. Missionaries even fostered parallels between Inca and Christian deities, in the hope that this would help the cause of evangelisation. The Christian God could thus be identified with the sun, and Mary with nature spirits. For the Spaniards their successes proved that the conquest had been divinely inspired, while for native Andeans it indicated that the innate sacred powers of the landscape were now working out not only in the familiar spirits of mountains, crags and springs, but also via the imported gods.

The new-old gods of the Andean landscape became subject to competing definitions and understandings of the nature of divinity. These processes have continued throughout the history of the region, and are well illustrated by the case of a famous image situated in Cusco City, that of El Señor de los Temblores (Lord of the Earthquakes). The Señor became the focus of a cult after an earthquake in 1650, since he was seen as a protector against such disasters. With its carved wooden face, darkened by candle smoke, the image is said to have an authentic Andean complexion, unlike the Caucasian colouring of most religious images. It therefore came to be seen as a suitable Christ for the urban poor, and an object of veneration and pilgrimage. In 1834, however, the cathedral authorities demonstrated their lack of appreciation of the ethnic identity of the god when they retouched the Temblores crucifix and cleaned off the smoke. These actions resulted in a near riot, since it was believed that a white figure would no longer work miracles for the local people.

PILGRIMAGE REGAINED: EUROPE IN THE CONTEMPORARY ERA

The scholar of religion Ingrid Lukatis has described how in post-Reformation Europe pilgrimages increasingly became symbols of Catholic renewal and a means to cure the soul.[34] During the Thirty Years' War, pilgrimages also gained new political significance as they became symbols of victory over opponents. Thus princes, the nobility, bishops and religious orders actively promoted religious journeys, and over time ever more splendid buildings were put up at significant sites.

By the nineteenth century Christianity had become widespread in the colonies of the old and new European empires, and the iconoclasm of the Protestant Reformation had long since faded. With improvements in travel, including the opening of the Suez Canal in 1869, the Near East became the focus of many a Grand Tour, as pilgrimage and tourism were combined. Towards the end of the century, Thomas Cook even began to lead group expeditions to Palestine, and 1891 saw the publication of *Cook's Tourist Handbook for Palestine and Syria*. The print of the text was made especially clear so that it could be read on horseback or in the poor light of a tent, and contained copious lists of scriptural references.[35]

Yet the century was also marked by forces which appeared to threaten the roots of Christianity itself. According to some, science (and in particular evolutionism) could replace religion as a basis for providing fundamental explanations concerning the nature of the universe, while the state could increasingly take over the educative and moral functions of the Church. Nevertheless, even if numbers attending churches declined, pilgrimage sites still provided centres of popular devotion whose extraordinary powers appeared to defy secular explanation. Between 1830 and 1933 the Virgin appeared at nine places in Europe, often proclaiming a millenarian and urgent message, thus establishing a genre of appearances suited to the concerns of post-Enlightenment Europe.

The case of Lourdes (situated on one of the main medieval pilgrimage roads of southern France, leading from Arles to Compostela) provided one of the most striking and telling examples of this phenomenon.[36] At the centre of the site's emergence was the figure of Bernadette Soubirous, born in 1844 to a poor family of nine children. When she was 14 years old, Bernadette reported having eighteen visions of the Virgin, who talked to her in the local dialect, revealed three secrets, and aided in the discovery of a spring which has since been credited with miraculous powers of healing. Similar elements were present in other visionary experiences manifested in the region, but the Lourdes story provided a particularly powerful means by which the French Church could fight against contemporary political, scientific and social forces which threatened to weaken its power. The apparent presence of miracle cures could enable Christians to assert that they possessed a form of supernatural knowledge superior to that constructed by reason. Joseph Deery, who has written a book on Lourdes, attests vividly to the force of this argument:[37]

Drunk with the sense of power, men in their proud self-sufficiency had no further use for God or the supernatural.

but:

. . . the Queen of Heaven forestalled them. By the Apparitions of Lourdes she lit up the darkness of the age as with a flash of lightning in which the actuality of the spiritual and supernatural was clearly seen, and proved by the production of effects which could not be explained by any scientific or natural process.

Other, more specific aspects of the visions made them, after a period of initial scepticism, particularly acceptable to Church authorities. According to Bernadette, the Virgin stated 'I am the Immaculate Conception', a claim that could be quoted by those who wished to argue that Mary was free of original sin at the moment of her conception. In contrast to visions that had been reported by children at nearby La Salette in 1846, strong criticisms of the French clergy were also avoided.

Once the site received approval, it had to be transformed in accordance with the demands of the Church. In 1858 there was no easy approach to the grotto where Bernadette had received her visions, but gradually the area was made convenient for pilgrims with the establishment of a broad avenue, the diversion of the river and the building of a railway to allow pilgrims to come from all over France and beyond. A statue of the Virgin was placed in a niche in the grotto, although ironically Bernadette herself never approved of it, since she felt it did not accurately reproduce the essence of her visions.

Today, the site continues to be enormously popular, attracting over four million visitors each year.[38] As in the nineteenth century, it acts as an arena for contemporary tensions over the role of the Church in relation both to secular society and its lay members. The many sick pilgrims who come to Lourdes and its baths seem to echo the bodily sufferings of Christ at the Passion, or even those of St Bernadette during her short lifetime. It is they who, in contrast with everyday practice, take centre stage at the shrine, as the able-bodied clamour to take care of total strangers who gain spiritual significance precisely because they are sick. The fact that cures may take place at the baths or elsewhere gives the Church the opportunity to proclaim the continuing function of the supernatural. Yet the Church requires stringent proofs provided by medical science to indicate that miracles are still possible. In addition, it often prefers to stress the spiritual rather than physical benefits to be gained from pilgrimage, since it feels uneasy with the magical implications of the latter. Bathing is therefore depicted in official literature as involving the purging of sins.

Other Marian sites in Europe have taken on more obviously political resonances in their perceived opposition to the forces of secular humanism. The presence of the Virgin at Fatima in Portugal, Czestochowa in

47 Lourdes, France. Statue of the Virgin at the grotto. No easy approach to the grotto existed in the 19th century when the site first became renowned, but access has since been provided by building a broad avenue and diverting the course of the river.

48 Fatima, Portugal. A mother circumambulates the shrine at Fatima on her knees, praying for the child she carries in her arms. In the early 1980s about one million people visited the site every year, many of them to participate in its annual festival.

Poland and Medjugorje in Croatia has, at certain points in history, symbolised opposition to Communist rule (as well, in the last case, as Christian renewal in the face of a perceived Islamic threat). At Medjugorje, where since 1981 the Virgin has been appearing regularly to six youngsters, the state authorities of the former Yugoslavia felt sufficiently threatened by the mass presence of Christians to keep the site under observation by helicopter.[39]

Even Walsingham, seemingly destroyed by Henry's men in the sixteenth century, has experienced an upturn in its fortunes during the past hundred years. The site's 'revival' has served to transform its nature in the name, ironically, of tradition. In 1887, at a new church built in the Sussex village of Buxted, a Lady Chapel was constructed according to the exact proportions of the original wooden house visualised by Richeldis. A visitor to the chapel was a local boy, Alfred Hope Patten, who was later to serve as a priest at Buxted before becoming the Vicar of Walsingham from 1921 to the time of his death in 1958. Patten inherited the antiquarian interests of the late Victorian age and was heavily influenced by the Anglo-Catholic movement in his desire to imitate much that was believed to be part of the medieval Church. He was also concerned at the

49 Walsingham, England. Pilgrims to the Anglican shrine at Walsingham in a procession which echoes the Via Crucis. The ritual, which involves carrying the Host out of the church and through the grounds of the shrine and back, is shown during a Sunday afternoon service in summer 1991.

possibility of increased non-Anglican influence at the site, as Catholic interest in recommencing pilgrimages to Walsingham had become all too evident.

Patten supervised the rebuilding of the original shrine, using ancient stones from abbeys and priories to make the altars. He even discovered a Saxon Well at the site, which he took to be an auspicious sign, not least because it echoed the experience of Richeldis herself. Regalia and mantles were created for the 'Guardians of the Shrine of Our Lady at Walsingham', and around a new garden he erected the Stations of the Cross. A statue of Our Lady and the Child was carved, modelled on a figure on an ancient abbey seal preserved in the British Museum. This became a focus of prayer and intercessions for increasing numbers of pilgrims.

The revival of Walsingham initially represented the apparently eccentric vision of a single man. However, it proved to have sufficient attraction for others, and has led to the creation of an Anglican tradition at the site from the 1920s up to the present. Today, the guide book once again refers to the site as 'England's Nazareth' and expresses many of the concerns of a contemporary Church keen to define its identity in the specific context of the late twentieth century:[40]

In a world where there is so much insecurity and pain many find that Walsingham testifies to the unchanging reality of God's love. Although some of our visitors find parts of the Shrine decoration not to their taste, and others do not at first understand the significance of the externals with which they are presented, thousands of people witness to the very special atmosphere engendered by the Shrine. Walsingham is one of the few places in England where religious truth is not a matter of intellectual propositions but can be experienced in the heart. . . . We are told that we live in an increasingly secular age but Walsingham with its deep roots in our national heritage seems to be able to speak powerfully to men and women of our own generation.

V. Living Saints

a. *Sadhus going to their ritual bath, Kumbh Mela at Ahmedabad, India.*

In the crypt of the church of S. Maria della Grazie at San Giovanni Rotondo, a small town in southern Italy, lies the body of Padre Pio. This holy man (Fig. Vb), a Capuchin monk, is yet to be recognised by the Vatican as a saint but has become a focus of veneration for thousands of Catholic pilgrims, some of whom actually live beside his shrine. During his life, Pio experienced numerous mystical visions, culminating (like St Francis of Assisi) in his receiving the stigmata after having a vision of the crucified Christ in 1918. Pio's mission was realised in two ways: first, as a very practical programme of relieving the poverty of San Giovanni and, second, as a spiritual vocation of redemption through suffering.

This twin mission has continued since his death in 1968, and those pilgrims who come seeking spiritual solace from his remains make a vital contribution to the local economy. As early as 1923, official Church sources declared that the phenomena attributed to Pio had no miraculous origins. Pio thus represents a particular strand in popular religion (not only in Christianity, but also in other religious traditions such as the sufi strain of Islam or Hassidic Judaism) whereby a charismatic and miracle-working individual proves a focus for devotion which by-passes and may even conflict with the authority of the hierarchy.

In one sense, Pio was an exceptional figure on the periphery of the Catholic Church in Italy. Yet his reputation derived from the fact that he was a near-perfect exemplar of the kinds of hagiographic traditions upheld most strongly by the Church. His saintly characteristics are strongly modelled on those of St Francis and include not only the meekness of his reported demeanour but also the very miracle of the stigmata for which he became most famous. In this sense Pio fits into a lineage of holy figures who, however controversial they may have been in their lives, tend later to be assimilated to the official history of Christianity. Although Pio has not yet been canonised, his material remains are venerated and preserved like those of many saints, and his cell has been kept as it was on the day of his death. Pilgrims to the shrine of Pio regard his stigmata as a manifestation both of the stigmata of St Francis and of Christ's sufferings in the Passion, so that the individual life story acquires a deeper significance by being assimilated to more established hagiographic narratives. Moreover, the site itself has resonances with older pilgrimage traditions, as it is located on the route to the shrine of St Michael in Monte Sant' Angelo.

St Francis's reception of the stigmata at Assisi (Fig. Vd) became a central icon in the later Middle Ages, and in numerous altarpieces and frescoes the wounds are shown being placed on his body directly by Christ. Francis conceived of a vocation more exalted than Pio's: he gave up his wealth, founded a monastic order, went on Crusade, and even offered to undergo a trial by fire in front of the Sultan in Cairo in order to convert him from Islam. While Pio is still at the very beginning of his saintly career, St Francis is an example of how the charisma attached to a remarkable individual can be transformed through centuries into an iconographic and mythical narrative. In his lifetime, Francis was a radical reforming influence on the Church; after his death he became one of the upholders of orthodoxy. Assisi has become one of the most important pilgrimage sites of Italy, with spectacularly decorated medieval churches.

No religious system combines an official hierarchy with a charismatic pattern of 'saints' more successfully than Tibetan Buddhism. The recognition of young children as reincarnate lamas (a practice which has recently attracted the attentions of Hollywood in the form of Bernardo Bertolucci's film *Little Buddha*) forms an important aspect of preserving the tradition. A child

b. *Padre Pio.*

recognised in this way as the reincarnation of a deceased holy person is then enthroned in the seat of that person, often as the Abbot of a monastery. Tibetan reincarnate lamas *(tulkus)* may be said to personify their monastery and its surroundings: they form a crucial link between charisma and place. The most famous of such reincarnations is His Holiness the Dalai Lama (Fig. Vc), the current incarnation being the fourteenth. He is regarded as the manifestation of Chenrezig, or the deity of infinite compassion, and Tibetans see him as the personification of the sacred land of Tibet. In the current political circumstances, where many Tibetans, including the Dalai Lama himself, are in exile following the Chinese invasion of the 1950s, the Dalai Lama embodies not only the continuation of a tradition removed from its sacred space but also the spirit of Tibet itself. Within Tibet, his person has come to embody the struggle for resistance against the

c. *The Dalai Lama receiving a scarf, the traditional greeting for high lamas in Tibet.*

Chinese. While the Catholic Church locates orthodoxy in a series of traditions and institutions to which individual charisma may even seem a threat, the Dalai Lama (and to a lesser extent other reincarnate lamas) embodies orthodoxy. As an individual he is accorded immense respect and veneration by Tibetans, who bow also to his photograph.

While a sacred site is fixed in space, a holy person (or his relics) may move. The process of establishing a pilgrimage site often involves the fixing of the charismatic influence of a holy event or person within a given space. Pio, who spent most of his life in San Giovanni Rotondo itself, provides a good example. By contrast, a site may become important by association with events in a holy person's life – for instance the eight canonical holy places of Buddhism, which reflect important places associated with the Buddha's life, or the principal pilgrimage sites of Islam, which are associated with the life of the Prophet. Just as the sacred persona of a holy figure may evolve after his or her death, so their body in the form of relics can be used to establish new sacred sites which were not necessarily associated with them in their lives. Examples include the tomb of St Mark in Venice (whose body was stolen from Alexandria), that of St Catherine at Mount Sinai (her body was miraculously translated to Sinai by angels) and the shrine of Santiago (St James) at Compostela.

Several religious traditions maintain the notion of permanent movement to sacred places as a sanctifying activity in itself. This represents an institutionalising of pilgrimage as an endless activity. The etymology of the very word *pilgrimage* lies in the Latin *peregrinatio*, which means 'wandering about' without a goal as such, 'being a foreigner'. In Christianity, Celtic monks – 'exiles for Christ' – were particularly noted for their form of permanent travel. Likewise, Jain ascetics called *munis* travel naked or in white robes between Jain shrines in India. Hindu ascetics are not necessarily required to engage in constant movement, but are one of the main religious attractions at the great twelve-yearly festivals of India such as the Kumbh Mela (see Fig. Va). Although Celtic monks, Jain *munis* and Hindu *sadhus* emerge from divergent religious contexts and traditions, they nonetheless exemplify the notion of divorce from mundane society.

d. *Giotto*, St Francis receiving the Stigmata, c. 1300, *Louvre. Originally painted for the church of St Francis at Pisa, this large altarpiece represents the central icon of medieval Franciscan spirituality. Beneath the main scene are three smaller images portraying the dream of Pope Innocent III, the confirmation of the Franciscan Order, and the sermon to the birds.*

6

Divinity Diffused: Pilgrimage in the Indian Religions

The Indian town of Brindavan lies on the river Jumna in the region of Braj, to the south of Delhi. Here, it is believed that the deity Krishna can be found in a 500 year-old temple.[1] The god inhabits an image of fossilised stone, and is regularly woken before sunrise by the songs and bells of the temple's priests. Once he has been bathed and dressed, he is presented with offerings of butter, fruit, sweets and milk. Then, while his image remains in the temple, Krishna is also thought to join his fellow cowherds in the woods of Brindavan, where he combines work with amorous adventures, for as an eternal and omnipresent deity his activity encompasses all human life.

That Krishna spent his early life in and around the location of Brindavan was established by a man called Chaitanya, a mystic and devotee, to whom this information was divinely revealed. Indeed, many now believe that Chaitanya himself was an incarnation of both Krishna and Radha. Today, in the many temples devoted to Krishna in Brindavan, the Gavdiya Vaishnava greet the god by dancing and singing, and they and others gain spiritual sustenance either from gazing at his image or from sharing the food that has been consecrated through its contact with the sacred image. Neighbouring villages are also imbued with the mythology of Krishna, so that holy legends are associated with specific, local places.

At the time of the monsoon in July and August pilgrims from all over India come to the town. They bathe every morning in the river Jumna, the presiding deity of which is thought of as a sister to the famous Ganges. Here they may collect water to take home and use sparingly at family altars situated far away from the holy site. They come particularly to see the *Ras Lila*, sacred dramas enacted by local children who adopt the roles of Krishna, Radha (his consort) and assorted cowherds. 'Lila' means play in both senses of the word, and these performances combine drama and liturgy in order to describe incidents in Krishna's life. To see them is to experience a form of sharing which has some resemblances to the Christian drama of the Eucharist: the plays are communal celebrations of the life of a god who unites the worlds of humans and deities. The divine force is invoked to be present in the static image of the god, just as the wafer and wine become the body and blood of Christ in the Mass.

Despite its distant resemblance to Christian liturgy, pilgrimage to Brindavan, in keeping with Hindu pilgrimage in general, deviates markedly from the traditions we have encountered so far. The *hajj* to Mecca or the Christian pilgrimage to the Holy Land ideally embody an archetypal journey to a supremely sacred locality. In contrast, the *Mahabharata*, the great Hindu epic, recommends in passing a form of wandering to a wide variety of holy places.[2] Hundreds of shrines and pilgrimage sites are named in an order which follows the movements of the sun. While the holy places focus mainly on northern India, the heartland of the Indo-Aryan civilisation which emerged in India in the second millennium BC, they also encompass a tour of the entire subcontinent.

This broad spreading of sacred space parallels a diffusion of the divine that is characteristic of Hindu worship. Early sacred texts of the first and second millennia BC, in particular the *Upanishads*, contain a notion of an all-pervading, abstract God, while early Vedic religion seems to have avoided worship through temples and images.[3] Yet the concept of divinity has subsequently taken on many faces, giving form to the formless by introducing anthropomorphic gods and *avataras* or human incarnations (literally, 'descents') of the gods. Krishna's representation in Brindavan shifts with the seasons and varied locales, just as the oral tradition of the *Ras Lila* may change with each performance. He himself is also part of a vast pantheon of Hindu gods, one where lesser divinities may be seen as aspects of the greater ones, creating a loosely defined and endlessly splintering hierarchy of beings.

Such fragmentation not only aids the assimilation of a variety of cults into Hinduism, but also increases the sense of the omnipresence of divine forces. The anthropologist Chris Fuller emphasises that Hinduism postulates no absolute distinction between divine and human beings.[4] A priest in a Shiva temple must install the god's power in himself before commencing worship, and ritual texts proclaim 'only Shiva can worship Shiva'. Just as humans show respect to deities through a characteristic gesture of obeisance, *namaskara* – bowing the head, with hands held high, and palms pressed together – so this is also practised from god to god, and human to human. The act implies relations of hierarchy combined with interdependence which imbue both social and divine relationships in Hinduism.

A single deity can also contain a number of apparently contending forces: Shiva, for instance, embodies principles of both fertility and death, healing and crazed destruction. Among the many Hindu goddesses, some are maternal and domestic, the embodiment of art and culture, but others are great warriors, perhaps living wild existences on the fringes of civilisation, exercising dynamic but dangerous female forces. (By marrying a goddess, a god checks and harnesses the threat of her female power.) Vishnu 'the preserver', of whom Krishna is an incarnation, and Shiva personify powers that are believed to remain active in the world, and it is they, along with aspects of the mother goddess, who today receive the most worship in shrines and pilgrimages. In contrast Brahma, a creator deity, at one stage perhaps the chief god of the early Hindus, is often thought of as sunk in deep meditation or slumber now that his task is complete.

An Indian expression used to describe the process of pilgrimage is *tirthayatra*. *Yatra* implies the act of travelling, while *tirtha* is a complex

50 Procession of pilgrims at Tanjore, India. Each red flag depicts a Shiva linga.

Sanskrit term encompassing the notion of a ford, but also sometimes used to refer to holy men and even scriptures. The common aspect of these apparently diverse meanings lies in the idea of crossing over – the possibility of moving between human and divine realms, or at least mediating between them, which is evident in holy texts, places and people. Each *tirtha* can thus represent special nodes in what one author has called a kind of 'sacred geometry'.[5] They are seen as especially good places for the performance of rites: acts performed and prayers uttered here are believed to be many times more beneficial than they would be elsewhere.

The practice of pilgrimage institutionalises the journey of the worshipper to *tirthas*. Often, such journeys imply an immersion in sacred time as well as space, since Hinduism distinguishes between auspicious and inauspicious times for performing important actions. Pilgrimages and holy gatherings therefore tend to occur at special astrological conjunctions. In 1989, for instance, the famous Kumbha Mela pilgrimage and fair was held at Prayaga (Allahabad), where the Ganges and Jumna rivers meet. On this occasion, a favourable conjunction coincided with a lunar eclipse, and the event attracted some 15 million pilgrims.

An important element in contemporary Hinduism, manifested not least in the practice of pilgrimage, is the expression of 'devotionalism' (in Sanskrit, *bhakti*).[6] This can be traced back to the sixth or seventh centuries AD, a period when itinerant devotees travelled from shrine to shrine, abandoning their lives to the worship of a deity. Such devotion, as well as inspiring a large corpus of poetry, has helped shift the focus of some Hindu worship away from ritual sacrifice and toward hymn-singing and a surrender of the self in love of and union with god. It has thereby allowed non-Brahmin sections of society to feel that they can gain direct access to their favoured deities. Chaitanya himself, amongst many other famous teachers of devotion to Krishna, may be seen as part of this tradition, and indeed in more recent centuries it has often been evident specifically in the worship of Krishna.

Through the mediating powers of the image at Brindavan, then, we have been introduced to a concept of divinity and a pilgrimage tradition that is, above all else, multi-layered and flexible. Unlike the other world religions, Hinduism – as much a social system, perhaps, as a religion – cannot look back to a single prophetic founder or decisive event in historical time for its creation. Indeed, the very idea of a single tradition called Hinduism may derive from colonial British attempts to define and demarcate an Indian system of beliefs along Judaeo-Christian lines.[7] One pilgrimage scholar warns us against assuming that western notions of piety and sacredness need be shared cross-culturally:[8]

Quite recently, and with some mirth, I observed a pilgrim taking the holiest of all possible baths at the Dasasvamedha Ghat in Varanasi, holding his transistor radio to his ear to monitor the cricket test match against the West Indies broadcast from Calcutta.

Unlike Christianity, Islam and Judaism, Hinduism's foundations are based on a series of sacred texts (often difficult to interpret) rather than a single, revealed, repository of 'truth'. Instead of the universalising and proselytising impulses that are so evident in Islam and Christianity, its traditions encompass ways of life that actually encourage syncretism and local adaptation – the Buddha and sometimes even Christ, Marx, Freud and Einstein have been perceived as incarnations of Vishnu.[9] It may be the case that pilgrimage is almost as important within Hinduism as it is, for instance, in Islam. Yet for Hindus it represents merely one possible pathway among many in the search for salvation.

IMAGE, TEXT AND PLACE

A myth is told in sacred Hindu texts about the goddess Sati, wife of Shiva. Its details vary slightly from version to version, but the elements of the story remain reasonably consistent. Sati's father is said to have performed a sacrifice to which neither Sati nor Shiva was invited. Sati went to the ceremony nevertheless, but was insulted by her father. As a result, she is said to have died of a broken heart, or possibly by suicide. Shiva, inconsolable at her death, traversed the earth in a mad dance, carrying her body. The gods became anxious to free him of his grief and decided to deprive him of Sati. They therefore dispersed her body bit by bit, and places where the body fell became holy. These sacred sites became major pilgrimage centres for goddess worship in India.

Descriptions of Sati's fate not only provide a justification for religious practice, they also construct an image of India as a mythologically charged landscape whose holy spots are as widespread as the body of Sati herself. The very soil of India is thought by many Hindus to be the body or at least the residence of the divine, particularly in its female form.[10] Yet, despite their scattered locations, the spread of Hindu pilgrimage centres is largely limited to India (where over 80% of the population is Hindu), which is defined as *the* sacred space *par excellence*.[11] There is a clear contrast here, for instance, with the spread of important Christian centres of pilgrimage. If the importance of Rome and Jerusalem, or even Lourdes and Compostela, reflects the successful spread of a faith anxious literally to conquer the world for Christ, the Hindu tradition has usually been much more parochial in its range. Even so, this apparent limitation has also brought with it certain advantages, since the sacred geography has played some part in shaping the national identity of a country which has only rarely been unified under central rule. The fact that Hindus have been able to circumambulate the whole of India, visiting hundreds of *tirthas*, has helped to impart some sense of unity in the face of political and military conflict, and has also helped in the spreading of cults. In the present era, of course, political centralisation and even nationalism have emerged, and this fact has received significant ritual expression. In Benares (also known as Varanasi and Kashi), for instance, the temple dedicated to *Bharat Mata*, or 'Mother India', does not contain an anthropomorphic image of the goddess. Instead, a large, coloured relief map of the Indian subcontinent receives the due reverence of pilgrims.

Many Hindu sites are linked not only to texts, but also to features of the landscape itself, such as hilltops, confluences of rivers, caves, outcrops of rock and forests. There are seven particularly holy rivers, of which the Ganges, believed to acquire its sanctity by issuing forth from the very locks of Shiva's hair, is nowadays considered the foremost. The goddess Ganga is said to be one of the escorts of Shiva, just as the sacred river laps 'seductively', according to one author, against the walls of Benares, a city associated particularly with the god.[12] There are also seven holy cities which, if visited, have the power to bestow salvation or *moksha* – a state similar to the Buddhist notion of *nirvana*, which implies total, final, release from all binding attachments and the cycle of reincarnation that is the lot of humanity.[13] Four *dhamas* or dwelling-places of the gods provide abodes of sanctity in the cardinal directions of the entire subcontinent: Badrinath in the Himalayas, Rameshvaram in the extreme south; Puri on the east coast; Dvaraka on the west coast.

Tirthas are often associated with running water, and ritual bathing is of considerable importance. The seven sacred rivers are said to have originated in heaven before being released to flow down to earth, and the Ganges itself is sometimes referred to as 'the flowing ladder to heaven'. Pilgrimage thus provides the occasion for self-purification by bathing, which often takes place at dawn, the most auspicious time. Such important sites as Benares (rarely a political centre, but said to have been founded at the beginning of creation) have developed a sacred architecture that reflects the importance of the act of ablution. The city reaps rich benefits from its location on the banks of the river Ganges, whose source is high up in the Himalayas (near the home of the gods) and which flows into the Bay of Bengal after some 1,560 miles. It is thought by some both to be at the centre of the world and situated high above the earth, on Shiva's trident.[14] More visibly, the city has more than seventy *ghats*, many built in the eighteenth century at a time of Hindu revival, which comprise platforms and stairs by the river up to 50 feet (15.25 m) in height. Their steps are crowded with *ghatias*, priests who aid pilgrims in the performance of complex rites of worship as well as looking after their clients' belongings while they bathe.

Movement itself, towards or between holy areas, is a sacred act. The older *Vedas* – the earliest literary documents of an Aryan culture that was originally semi-nomadic – reveal the virtues of travel by making clear the morality of its opposite: 'Evil is he who stayeth among men.' They also describe the benefits to be accrued by the pious traveller:[15]

> Flower-like the heels of the wanderer,
> His body groweth and is fruitful;
> All his sins disappear,
> Slain by the toil of his journeying.

Landscapes and movements listed in the *Mahabharata* are complemented by other texts from perhaps the third to the fifteenth centuries AD, such as the *Puranas* and *Tantras*. These parallel the epic in that they contain no details of the physical settings of sacred sites, but are more concerned with their potential to provide spiritual rewards. Here is a characteristic passage from the *Mahabharata* itself:[16]

When one has gone to the Meadow-of-Kapisthala, which is hard to find, his sins are burned off. . . . Thereupon one should go to world-renowned Saraka and approach the Bull-bannered God on the fourteenth of the dark fortnight; for thus one obtains all his desires and goes to the world of heaven. In Saraka there are three crores of holy places. . . . There is also there the Abode-of-Ila Ford: by bathing there and worshipping the ancestors and Gods one suffers no misfortune. . . .

One pilgrimage scholar has described these types of formulaic description as 'archaic advertisements',[17] an apt phrase when we remember that it has been in the interests of priests, the guardians of temples and writers of holy texts, to emphasise the importance of their own sites in relation to others. We can also see from these texts the importance of a written tradition in reinforcing the status of prominent religious places. Yet we cannot regard the sanctity of pilgrimage sites as created and justified merely through texts, not least because any pilgrimage tradition has to be

51 Benares, India. Pilgrims performing self-purification through bathing at a ghat. Whilst the Ganges has been at the centre of worship at Benares for thousands of years, the Hindu shrines currently used in the city date mostly from the 18th and 19th centuries, after the decline of the Muslim empire in northern India.

flexible enough to accommodate different and shifting local needs. The *Puranas* themselves contain various emphases which correspond to contending sectarian and regional affiliations, reflecting the fact that different religious movements may, at any one time, be engaged in the process of creating and building on their own sacred geographies. In some cases, 'ancient' texts may even have been conveniently manufactured by priests to suit the needs of the present.

In the absence of a centralised and centralising priesthood the Hindu 'tradition' is thus characterised by immensely complex relationships between 'orthodox' traditions based on Sanskrit texts and their popular forms in regional subcultures. For some scholars, the contrast can be expressed in relatively stark terms, between a religious practice administered by high-caste Brahmin priests, which emphasises long-term welfare and transcendental goals, and one whose horizons are geographically and spiritually more confined – associated with pragmatic goals of individual welfare and less prestigious containers of the divine, such as village goddesses acting also as local clan deities.

However, the relationships between so-called continental and local, great and little traditions, are often complementary rather than mutually exclusive. An extraordinary combination of perspectives may be produced in which a partisan view of the sacredness of a locality coexists with a broader, apparently conflicting view. This is illustrated by a response to the questions of an American scholar at a famous pilgrimage site:[18]

At Gaya a college teacher told me that the Phalgu River was certainly the most sacred river in all of India for the people of Gaya. To a question about the sanctity of the Ganga, the reply was that of course the Ganga was the most sacred river of India, yet the Phalgu was more sacred than it.

In some cases, a site of great importance may become a paradigm for other shrines and holy places, as if features of a sacred geography could bestow some of their prestige on to lesser replicas of themselves. One anthropologist has described how Rajasthani villagers told her that the *dhamas* could actually be found within their own village, so that a circumambulation around India could be achieved without leaving home.[19] A similar view is often maintained by worshippers at Benares, who argue not only that the 'city of light' is symbolically present in a thousand places in India, but also that it contains all the other *tirthas* – and their sacred powers – within it.[20]

These examples show how a Hindu 'structure of consciousness' can be maintained which is both pluralistic and yet also able to focus worship on a single location.[21] We also see once more the importance of Benares in the geography of Hinduism – as both a sacred centre in itself and a

52 Water-colour of Benares by Edward Lear. Lear spent over a year travelling around India between 1873–75, fulfilling numerous commissions to paint views of the subcontinent. He described Benares as one of the most 'startlingly radiant of places, full of bustle and movement'.

refraction of other sacred places. Lieutenant-Colonel Davidson described the city in 1843 as 'the Hindoo Jerusalem',[22] and although his observation perhaps reflects a desire to assimilate Hinduism within a Judaeo-Christian category, it nevertheless highlights the character of the city as an embodiment of the sacred space of India.[23] To the scholar Diana Eck, the ability of Benares to condense sacred spaces into a single location has parallels with Hindu attitudes to texts: just as the *Vedas* can be comprehended through one mantra, so travelling the pilgrimage route around the circumference of the city can be seen as akin to circling the world. Benares is even incorporated into pan-Indian ritual practice, such as on those occasions when a groom appears at the doorway of his bride's house and announces to his future father-in-law his 'intention' to renounce the world and go to Benares in order to study the *Vedas*. Such a statement in effect invites the bride's family to dissuade him from his proposed course of action. In some parts of India, part of an initiation ceremony for young men actually requires the initiate to take seven steps in the direction of Benares.

Benares illustrates, then, the ability of a paradigmatic centre both to encompass other sacred sites and to be replicated beyond its geographical borders. Part of an original site can also be appropriated in the setting-up of a new one. Indeed, a shrine can appear when a devotee of a distant deity takes home earth or perhaps a small stone from the original abode of the god. Myths may even imply that sites are literally linked in the physical landscape. According to a story connected with the temple of Biraja, a large and famous pilgrimage site in Orissa, a priest from Benares came to the temple over a thousand years ago. He threw his specially marked cane into the well at the site. When he returned to Benares he found his cane floating in the Ganges river – implying that the well is connected underground to the Ganges several hundred miles to the north.

The construction of such stories linked to place sometimes reflects the presence of competition between sites. The anthropologist Peter Van der Veer recounts a legend associated with the sacred pilgrimage centre of Ayodhya, in Uttar Pradesh.[24] According to the story, King Vikramaditya met a totally black man at a point near the town. Having bathed in Ayodhya's sacred river, the man emerged completely white from the waters. The transformed stranger told the wondering king that he was Prayaga, king of the *tirthas*, who had become black by absorbing the sins of so many humans. Why then go to Prayaga (we are encouraged to ask) when even the king of the *tirthas* comes to Ayodhya to be cleansed?

Despite such considerations of relative spiritual merit, economic considerations cannot be ruled out as factors in the foundation and continued importance of sites of worship. By the eighteenth century, groups of *sadhus* or holy men, had become the principal traders in parts of north India, not least because they were able to use their pilgrimage cycles as trading networks. Today, wealthy industrialists sometimes build temples and rest houses for pilgrims in order to gain merit both for themselves and for their ancestors.[25] Nor can the political authority associated with sacred sites be ignored. One author states:[26]

Kings and queens used to identify with the icons in temples which they built or patronized, claiming divine sanction to rule and provide both water by hydraulic engineering and social control from the sacred centre. . . .

A single site may have retained its importance as a sacred centre and yet served a wide range of political masters over time. Puri, the most important site of the cult of Lord Jagannatha, is one of the most sacred pilgrimage places in India. Jagannatha possibly evolved from tribal roots to become a Buddhist and then a Hindu deity, and is known among Hindus as an image of Krishna. Kings of various dynasties, belonging to different sects and traditions, have patronised the cult, not least by ostentatiously building shrines in order to accrue political capital. In the twelfth century, the kings of Orissa constructed a massive stone temple which still stands, rising to over 200 feet (61 m). When the British took over the area, they were well aware of the importance of not damaging the temple, and their job was made easier by the pragmatic acquiescence of the local priests. Shortly before British troops entered Puri in 1803, they were informed by the latter that:[27]

. . . the Brahmins at the holy temple had consulted and applied to Lord Jagannath to inform them what power was now to have his temple under its protection, and that he had given a decided answer that the English Govt. was in future to be his guardian.

After the priests had issued this statement, the British were able to enter Puri without resistance. Today, power has yet again shifted hands, and patronage in effect rests with the state government of Orissa. In the modern period, Jagannatha has become the patron deity of state nationalism, reflecting and justifying new political concerns.

Myths attached to a site frequently reveal tensions between groups anxious to appropriate the power of the sacred place for their own purposes. Ayodhya, for instance, is considered to be the birthplace of, and therefore holy to, the Hindu god Rama (hero of the *Ramayana* epic), and even the architecture of the railway station echoes that of a Hindu temple.[28] Although most of the buildings of the town are of relatively recent date, myth and history have merged so that temples are regarded as restorations from the time of the town's sacred foundation. In the sixteenth century, the Mughal emperor Babur came to India with the intention of becoming its ruler, and visited Ayodhya. Local Muslim fakirs promised him that when he destroyed the temple of Rama his desire would be fulfilled.[29] According to legend, although Babur succeeded in destroying the Hindu temple, his attempts to build a mosque failed because each night everything that had been built simply collapsed. Eventually, a mosque was built which left the Hindu sanctuary open to believers. However, trouble was to flare up again in the years following partition in 1947. On the night of 22–23 December 1949, Hindus managed to smuggle an image of Rama into the mosque, a form of religious defiance that was to prove a catalyst for violence and riots. In 1989, at the potentially explosive time of a general election, Hindu 'fundamentalists' attempted to build a temple to Rama with bricks taken to the town from all over India, but were prevented from completing their task by the

53 Painting of Jagannatha procession at Puri in Orissa, Bay of Bengal, by an anonymous artist. The 12th-century stone temple, built by the kings of Orissa, rises to over 200 feet (61 metres) and displays Vishnu's sacred wheel and flag at its summit.

government. In 1992, devotees of Lord Rama tore down the mosque which stood at his supposed birthplace, setting off waves of violence in the whole of India.

Most recently, the emigration of Hindus has begun to aid the diffusion of the sacred landscape beyond the boundaries of the subcontinent, even though over 90% of the world's Hindus still live in India. In the United States, a number of temples have been built, complementing the family altars of domestic, daily worship. Intriguingly, not only have many of these become new pilgrimage sites, but they have also been seen as duplicating the topography and patterning of their counterparts in India itself. The major temples are located in the cardinal directions of the country – east (New York and Pittsburgh), north (Michigan), west (California) and south (Texas), as if they were the North American version of the *dhamas*. Sites that are specially favoured are likely to have topographical features replicating those of an 'original' holy place. At a temple in Pittsburgh, the confluence of two rivers in Ohio has been explicitly compared with the confluence of the sacred Ganges, Yamuna and Sarasvati rivers. In this way: '. . . Pittsburgh was instantly made the holy Prayagraj of America; a remarkable transformation of the Steel City as a sacred centre.'[30]

We see the complex interplay between a number of elements in the construction of pilgrimage sites: topography, texts, political patronage and even individual self-interest can play a part, as can the spiritual authority of a holy figure such as Chaitanya at Brindavan. Over the past two centuries, pilgrimage has also been considerably boosted, both by better communications systems – railways, roads and even airways – and by higher standards of general education, increasing knowledge of sacred centres located far from people's homes.[31] A further element in the creation of sacred space is revealed, however, in the way that Hinduism employs physical images both to represent and make tangible the presence of divinity. As one writer has put it, the image relates to the absolute in the way a dance is related to the dancer, or a dream to the sleeper.[32] What is ultimately an immaterial and formless deity is brought, through the skill of the artist and the ritual expertise of a priest, into a physical object – usually a sculpture – and served as if it were a human of high status with bodily needs. The innermost part of a temple contains a womb-like chamber in which is located the presiding god of the temple (contained in the *mula murti* or immovable 'root image'). The retinue of the god is usually arranged in decreasing order of precedence away from this primary image: the consort of the god comes first, followed by, among others, those that stand guard over the eight directions, saints who have worked in the service of the god, local folk deities, and so on.[33]

For some Hindu authors, there is no contradiction between the belief in an all-embracing, all-pervading, omnipresent God and the worship of a variety of deities through images, even if the latter merely provide useful means of focusing devotion:[34]

It is the spirit of inmost devotion, the Formless that is given shape in the images of the deities. Though these are used as aids in religious life, 'every Hindu hopes to escape someday from the necessity of using images'.

Images are very frequently anthropomorphic, as if to emphasise the notion of the gods made human, or at least accessible to humans, but temples may also grow from a less obvious emblem of the divine entering the world, such as a special tree or stone. Shiva, a force representing, among other things, fertility, is often associated with a phallic *linga*. At the heart of such belief is not only the notion that such objects are aids to worship, but also that they contain power, even if it is often claimed that Hindus should worship the god whose power is in an image, not the image itself (reflecting a mistrust of 'idolatry' that may indicate recent Christian influences).

Worship, or *puja*, consists of several parts, one of which is made up of presenting objects before the deity which symbolise the human senses – food for taste, perfumes or flowers for smell, fine cloths for touch, bells or music for hearing. While the god may not need such substances as such, they do indicate respect for the divine presence. This may be followed by *arati*, a form of lamp-offering in which the priest sways an oil-lamp holding a number of wicks before the image. In all types of Hindu pilgrimage, worshippers seek to absorb the beneficial effects of contact with the deity via consumption or reception of sacralised substances

54 Halebid, India. Adults and children dressed in black clothes for the pilgrimage to Lord Ayyappa at Sabarimalai. The pose of the two seated boys consciously echoes that of the god himself.

(prasad), such as food, water, ash or flowers, which have been in close proximity to the deity. Benefit in the form of merit, good fortune and well-being is also derived from a sight of the deity (darshan), and, like prasad, this action provides a means of engaging in intimate transactions with the divine. According to some scholars, such transactions – or interactions – are of particular significance in relation to traditional Hindu thought, according to which the person is not perceived as sharply bounded, as in contemporary western models of the autonomous individual, but easily subject to influence from and moulding by the environment.[35]

Whatever the validity of this view, the importance of darshan both in pilgrimage and in worship more generally must be stressed. At the enormously wealthy temple of Venkateshvara at Tirupati, it was recently suggested that closed-circuit television be installed in the temple grounds to project an image of the god to the thousands of pilgrims who some-times wait for hours in the rain, queuing for darshan of their god.[36] At Sabarimalai in Kerala, devotees may only catch a glimpse of the image of the deity Ayyappa, as they are surrounded by the massed throngs of other pilgrims at the shrine, and yet this sight is still regarded by many as the centre-point of the whole pilgrimage.[37]

A frequent assumption behind the belief in the benefits of sacred 'sight-seeing' is the idea that the greater the attraction a scene has for the mortal eye, the greater the beneficial effect will be. Just as the devotee stares at the god, so the deity stares back at the devotee in an exchange of vision.[38] Temple architecture is constructed not so much to accommodate congregational worship but to channel the devotee towards this form of viewing. While the deity in its sanctuary is usually located in a straight line from the worshipper as the latter enters the temple compound, in order to reach the image one must move through the space of the temple clockwise in ever-decreasing circles.[39]

Despite the ability of physical forms to mediate between humans and gods, it is also the case that such embodiment carries with it an important price. Location in an image concentrates the attention of the worshipper but also constrains the power and scope of divinity. Thus, when gods are worshipped in temples they become tied to a locality even though the conception of their ultimately unlimited freedom of movement is also retained. It is as if they are constrained by the limited imaginations of mere humans, who cannot conceive of the true nature of the divine without bringing it – literally – down to earth.

THE FRUITS OF DENIAL: MOTIVATIONS FOR PILGRIMAGE

At one point in the *Mahabharata* it is related that Bhishma, son of the river goddess Ganges, asks a sage (who is also a 'saint of awesome austerities') about the rewards of pilgrimage:[40]

A person who makes a sunwise tour of the earth, boundlessly mighty brahmin seer, what reward does accrue to him, tell me that, ascetic!

The sage's reply is one that emphasises the fruits of denial. Religious merit is accrued from self-discipline and cultivation of the correct state of mind:

He who has mastered his hands, feet, mind, knowledge, mortification, and good repute attains to the reward of the fords. He who has retired from possession and is contented, restrained, pure, and without selfishness, obtains the reward of the fords. He who is without deceit, without designs, of lean diet, in control of his senses, and free from all vices, he obtains the reward of the fords. The man without anger, O Indra among princes, with the habit of truthfulness and firm in his vows, who sees in the creatures the images of himself, obtains the reward of the fords.

The *Mahabharata* and the *Puranas* refer to the '*tirthas* of the heart', implying that the pilgrim should not only bathe in the waters of earthly *tirthas*, but also in the inner virtues of truth, charity, patience and self-control. Discipline and denial in Hinduism can take a variety of forms, and may show some influence from Buddhist and Jain models. The path of renunciation (*sannyasa*) – the ultimate form of asceticism and self-mastery possible in life – is treated as a vocation by those who choose to become holy mendicants, wandering around the landscape. Ascetics also settle in ashrams at major pilgrimage centres and engage in lives of instruction. Both ways of life provide powerful means of achieving salvation in the Hindu tradition. The *Upanishads*, for instance, define the goal of humans as the realisation that attachments to the material world, including the self, are mere illusion. These should be renounced in order to allow the self to become one with the all-pervading God and ultimate reality. The asceticism of *sannyasis* may take dramatic forms, such as the decision to keep a fist closed until the nails enter the flesh and come out on the other side. Although according to some Hindus these displays reveal a taste for the spectacular rather than spiritual progress, for many pilgrims such outward austerity reveals the presence of an inner power.

For a 'householder' pilgrimage provides the opportunity to experience a form of temporary renunciation. Pilgrimage is described vividly by Rajasthani villagers as equivalent to what is intriguingly called 'the rice pudding of money', since:[41]

Rice pudding is only made and savored when there is a surplus of milk; tirthayatra and the attendant pleasure of seeing other lands requires a surplus of cash.

When viewed in this way, pilgrimage provides a means of divesting the self, for a time, of excess possessions and emotional attachments, and encouraging other merit-producing activities such as meditation and charity. Such travel may be associated with particular times of the year, such as festivals and/or slack periods in the agricultural cycle. Along with such common practices as prayer, the taking of a purifying bath and the throwing of flowers, fruits and money into holy rivers, pilgrimage rules ideally lay emphasis on austerities such as fasting, celibacy, the rejection of soft beds and avoidance of vehicles for making the journey. Some also emphasise that such an act of renunciation is ideally carried out alone. The pilgrimage to the temple of Ayyappa, at Sabarimalai in Kerala,

55 Mysore, India. Bus transporting Ayyappan pilgrims in 1993.

56 Madurai, India. Devotee supplicating an image of Ganesha by the entrance to the main enclosure. The statue is covered with ash, with which the worshipper marks her forehead.

involves not only the imposition of celibacy on its (almost entirely) male participants, but also the undertaking of an arduous journey that, in the past, exposed pilgrims to attack by wild animals. A devotee of the cult writes the following:[42]

. . . it may not be desirable to provide any more 'get-there-quick' approaches . . . conveniences etc. to the pilgrims. . . . If the present trend is continued, the day when womenfolk irrespective of their ages flocking [sic] Sabarimalai will not be far off!

The austerities often associated with pilgrimage need not be experienced merely at a *tirtha*, then, but are inherent within the journey itself. Some sites are very remote, which means not only that they are suitable abodes for the gods, but also that they require effort and devotion to be reached. Pilgrims may even choose to proceed by successive body-length prostrations for part or all of the route. Given the frequent difficulties of pilgrimage journeys, it is perhaps not surprising that Hindus typically give worship to Ganesh, the god of beginnings and obstacles, before departing, as well as explicitly declaring their intention to undertake pilgrimage to a given place. On returning from pilgrimage to a temple, pilgrims usually take home a holy souvenir and reminder of their arduous trip, such as a picture or model of the god of the temple.

Pilgrimage places are also associated with obsequies for the dead, and a pious pilgrim may preserve the ashes of a relative till the time when the journey can be made in order to consign them to holy water. Ashes can actually be mailed by post to temple authorities and the ritual performed vicariously for those who cannot afford the trip. To die at Benares (where the cremation grounds, unusually, are seen as auspicious) and have one's ashes sprinkled on the river is considered a possible path to liberation, and some believe that a few drops of Ganges water on the tongue at the moment of death provide a means of salvation no matter where the dying person meets their end. Other holy places can at least provide the possibility of a better rebirth, such as Braj, itself the final destination of many old people from Bengal. It is hardly surprising, then, that pilgrimage as a form of renunciation is often adopted by those who feel they have achieved and completed the duties of everyday existence. Here are the words of an old woman to one pilgrimage scholar:[43]

We have nothing more to do in the world, our children and grandchildren are married, old people are not really wanted or needed, so we walk toward the source of the Ganges, and if we die in the effort, that is the most desirable death we can meet.

Yet, despite the sage's enlightened description in the *Mahabharata* of the attitudes ideally associated with pilgrimage, the practice among Hindus is far more varied in motivation and practice than he would perhaps have hoped. The following is a passage taken from a pilgrim's guide produced by the government of West Bengal:[44]

Family men come here with devotion in their heart, sadhus come with a burning desire for moksha (spiritual liberations), singers, story-tellers, and artists come to entertain. Traders come with their wares. Even prostitutes and gamblers also crowd the place along with the blind, crippled and invalid beggars. . . . Politicians come here with the intention to mix freely with commoners, to earn popularity, social service workers come forward to help and anti-social come to snatch valuables. . . .

Thus the presence of a sacred site need not inspire an attitude of pious devotion amongst its pilgrims. Furthermore, the boons requested by such pilgrims, as we have seen, may seem remote from an austere search for salvation. At Tarakeshwar, the principal site of Shiva in West Bengal (known as Gupta Varanasi, or hidden Varanasi), the local deity, Baba Taraknath, is well-known for his capacity to cure diseases, as expressed in the words of a song:[45]

If refuge is sought . . . with a totally devoted mind, numerous acute ailments are cured. . . . Dysentery, cough, gonorrhea and fistula in ano, Colitis, tuberculosis, leprosy and ascites, piles, severe leprosy, liver problems, all sorts of diseases shall be cured.

If the distinctly earthy claims of the song are likely to provide a cause for concern among the devout sophisticates of Hinduism, there are also strains within the tradition which go so far as to deny the validity of pilgrimage as an institution. The belief, for instance, that the divine should be found *within* the self may make one devalue the enterprise, as revealed in the words of a Kashmiri woman mystic of the fourteenth century:[46]

I . . . went out far in search of Shiva, the omnipresent Lord; having wandered, I found him in my own body. . . .

Broadly similar sentiments are expressed by a Shiva devotee writing three centuries later, who criticises image worship and pilgrimage as examples of a false attachment to the material world:[47]

What can be done by these artificial gods whose honour and even existence are under human control? How can they bring salvation to me? What is the use, then, of arranging flowers near a block of stone, and what benefit accrues from the burning of incense, and the sounding of bells before an idol, and from circum-ambulating it and observing similar other practices? . . . So give up attachment and pacify the mind; the holy Benares will rise up in your heart. It is the ideal Divinity and not the artificial images that is to be worshipped.

The notion of Benares rising in the heart has a striking resemblance, at least superficially, to the ideas of the sufi mystic who invoked the notion of an inner Ka'ba, or indeed the Christian Fathers who argued that the true Jerusalem lay within the self. Indeed, Kabir, the great medieval poet, who came from a low-caste background and who drew on both Muslim and Hindu traditions, wrote somewhat satirically:[48]

> Going on endless pilgrimages, the world died,
> exhausted by so much bathing!

We see here powerful justifications for turning away from both place and movement, in other words a detachment from the very rootedness in landscape and image that is the key to the practice of Hindu pilgrimage. Yet, although these sentiments are common among holy figures, they often contain a paradox, and one which ultimately emphasises the enduring importance of the sacred journey:[49]

. . . saints who have minimized the importance of pilgrimage have constantly been on pilgrimage themselves, most of them having spent their lives as mendicants and minstrels who sang their songs at places for pilgrimage for the benefit of the pilgrim. Thus, it has become customary for the pious Hindu to go on pilgrimages, to believe in their merit, and yet to state that pilgrimage is not important. . . .

Kabir himself may have refused to die in Benares, thus denying the idea of gaining liberation through spatial location. Yet his followers subse-quently founded a centre in his name in the city. In a way, the power of the place proved too much for him in death, if not in life.

THE 'DIVINE HIERARCHY': UNITY AND DIVISION IN HINDU PILGRIMAGE

To some scholars of Hinduism, pilgrimage represents an institution whose rules are liberal and democratic. It is seen as constructing a sacred geography that not only links together holy sites and shrines, but also helps produce a form of social and religious unity.[50] Some centres of pilgrimage are indeed sacred to more than one sect, and some, such as Puri, Mathura and Ujjain, are patronised by almost all sections of Hindu society. All pilgrims bathe effectively in the same waters, and thus social boundaries may appear temporarily to be ignored or devalued. Yet these claims also force us to consider an issue that still retains huge importance in Indian society, and moreover one which appears to embody the very essence of division and hierarchy: caste.

Textual justifications for caste are present in Vedic texts which divide society up into four classes, or *varnas*. In a hymn from around 1000 BC, for instance, each of the four *varnas* emerges from a part of the body of a primeval man who is dismembered by the gods at the beginning of time:

> The Brahman was his mouth,
> of his arms was made the warrior,
> his thighs became the Vaishya,
> of his feet the Shudra was born.

This hierarchy became ratified in legal texts written by priests (of the highest *varna*), so that each class came to be seen as performing a different role according to its ordained duty: the Brahmin to study, the warrior to protect the people, the Vaishya to till the earth and trade, and the Shudra to serve the three other classes. Below such groups came the 'untouchables', those considered so low that they did not properly merit a *varna* status. Such a straightforward division is in practice full of ambiguities over the precise relationships between caste groups within the varna system, between religious status and daily occupation, and between caste and sub-caste affiliation. Yet its influence, although transformed and increasingly challenged, prevails in India. It is more than just a set of beliefs, since it recommends practices and attitudes in an idiom of purity and pollution that serves to separate groups of people through taboos on marriage, eating together and even touch. What then, does this system imply for the practice of pilgrimage?

At many sites, regional and caste structures do in fact retain control of the pilgrim's actions. *Pandas* or *purohits* – guides who issue yearly manuals stating auspicious times for pilgrims to worship at their sanctuary and who enter their names in ledgers – also typically provide food, lodging and ritual instruction according to the custom of the pilgrim's land. Sometimes, they even go on 'inverted pilgrimages' to the homes of pilgrims who have become regular patrons, bringing sacred water and *prasad* from holy sites. Agents of guides may meet pilgrims at bus or train stations, enquire about their place of origin and caste status, and then assign them to appropriate guides. Like the Turkish visitors to Mecca, Hindu pilgrims may remain for the most part culturally cocooned amongst their own people, and therefore also within the safety of their own assumptions.

Despite current, explicitly secular, legislation which bans such discrimination, deep-rooted concerns over the polluting touch of lower castes is still reflected in the exclusion of those classified as 'untouchables' from some Hindu shrines. Sacred space can thus become an arena for conflicting views on the meaning of caste. At Benares the golden temple of Vishwanath, rebuilt by the wife of the Rajah of Indore in 1777, is a place visited by almost all pilgrims, not least because of the presence of a central image of Shiva in the form of a *linga*. Since 1954, even untouchables have been admitted to this sanctuary, and as a result a second Vishwanath temple has been constructed in protest at their presence. At yet another Vishwanath temple, however, at Benares Hindu University, not only untouchables but also non-Hindus are admitted.

If guides and guardians of temples play their part in maintaining social

divisions between pilgrims at sites, these can also be all too evident during the journey itself. Irawati Karve, a former sociology and anthropology professor at the University of Poona, reports on a fifteen-day procession from Alandi in Poona to Pandharpur in Sholapur district. This is a colourful occasion, when people follow the annual march of images of saints, and spend much of their time walking and singing together. In the vanguard of the group walk the untouchables, followed respectively by horses, flag wavers, wagons with the chief image, and then the rest of the group of pilgrims. Karve, trained in an academic tradition whose values clash with these assumptions of division, feels impelled to ask:[51]

All of the people were clean, and ate their food only after taking a bath. Then why this separateness? Was all this walking together, singing together, and reciting the poetry of the saints together directed only towards union in the other world while retaining separateness in this world?

57 Varkaris from Maharashtra on their annual fortnight-long pilgrimage to Pandharpur. During this pilgrimage devotees march on foot singing hymns in praise of Lord Vithoba, an incarnation of Krishna.

JAIN AND SIKH PILGRIMAGE

The history of Hinduism in India has been marked by periods of both decline and revival. Perhaps the greatest challenge to its dominance came from the emergence and spread of Buddhism in the latter half of the first millennium BC. Much later, Muslim and Christian invaders were prompted by military and political ambitions as much as by the desire to spread their own version of spiritual enlightenment. Two further religious impulses, created out of the desire for reform and renewal, continue to exercise considerable influence in India: Jainism and Sikhism. Their religious customs in general, as well as their pilgrimage practices in particular, are related to those of Hinduism in complex but significant ways.

The emergence of Jainism in the sixth century BC was roughly contemporaneous with that of Buddhism. Like the Buddha, its 'founder'[52] Mahavira (the 'Great Hero') made converts among members of the royal houses. However, like Buddhism Jainism was a religion originally designed to be open to all, irrespective of hereditary status, even if in practice it has adopted features of the caste system. However, while the Buddha chose the 'middle way', Mahavira adopted a form of extreme asceticism as the proper pathway to enlightenment. He spent much of his life as a wandering teacher, revered by disciples, and was the last of the Jain *tirthankaras* ('ford-builders'). This term refers to twenty-four beings who have attained enlightenment and perfect bliss, removed from the cycle of reincarnation.[53] They are also referred to as *jinas* or 'conquerors' of the passions.

The religion enjoyed tolerance and patronage from political rulers up until the twelfth or thirteenth centuries in north India and one of the main areas where Jainism is still practised today is in Gujarat. Later its adherents suffered persecution under Hindu revivalism and Muslim expansion, although unlike Buddhism it was never totally forced out of India. One possible reason for its survival was its ability to 'Hinduise' by adopting the major life-cycle rituals of the dominant religion.[54] Nowadays, although Jains only number around 3.5 million people, concentrated in the west and south-west of India, they exercise much influence through their success in commercial life.

Jainism is not a religion of *the* book, but incorporates a large textual corpus covering doctrines, mathematics, poetry and astronomy. Its texts ideally advocate the single-minded pursuit of self-purification through austerity and fasting. In this way, negative *karma* accumulated in previous births can be dissipated. The notion of complete non-violence, or *ahimsa* is extremely important, since avoiding harm to the smallest living thing can be seen as an aspect of non-attachment in the world. Jains say that the air, water and earth are occupied by countless souls, and some adherents may even put cloths or masks over their mouths in order not to harm these invisible organisms.

Although some sects reject the use of images, many Jains engage in daily *pujas* in temples to *murtis* – carved stone representatives of the enlightened beings, *tirthankaras*, who are seated in eternal meditation. Ritual practice is often similar in form to Hindu worship, also incorporating *darshan* and circumambulation. However, Jains are wary of suggestions that a 'real' presence may dwell in the images. Typically, theologians argue that offerings apparently made to an image are in fact made to the abstract virtues of enlightenment, liberation and dispassion that it symbolises.[55] The enlightened beings themselves are perceived as being remote, at the top of the universe, and thus (unlike in popular Hinduism) not interacting with or choosing to bless their 'worshippers'.

Two basic forms of adherence are available. Exemplary individuals, or *munis*, follow the supreme model of non-attachment of the *tirthankaras*. Many such renouncers are organised into single-sex travelling groups which make their way between villages and towns, wearing simple white robes, carrying begging bowls and preaching the importance of non-attachment to the material world. They walk barefoot, and carry long brushes which they use to sweep insects away from their path, lest they tread on them. Lay people follow a code of practice that is rather less rigorous, and therefore further from the path of true asceticism. However, they support and may even worship living renouncers, who can be seen as forms of divinity.

Ironically, lay Jains are well known for creating extremely successful business communities. The accumulation of wealth is regarded as the proper result of honest living, but a lack of attachment to such wealth is said to be demonstrated by donations to temples and religious cere-monies. Indeed, providing money for religious purposes as well as charitable organisations such as colleges, schools and hospitals, is the most meritorious form of giving and is practised on a large scale by men.

Some Jains spend much time in buses and trains, or walking, on pilgrimages to such holy sites as Mount Abu in Rajasthan or Parasnath in Bihar. A leaflet provided by the Department of Tourism at Bangalore describes 'The Jain Circuit', a suggested route incorporating all the important Jain centres in Karnataka (a state closely associated with the religion) and gives potential visitors information on both air and road connections to the sites. Such journeys to holy sites dispersed around the country can complement widespread travel for commercial purposes, and many of the important temple sites provide venues for annual fairs, to which non-Jains, including tribal peoples, are invited. Temples may gain fame and prove attractive to visitors for their architectural merit, association with a particular *tirthankara* or reputation for miraculous events. Many families make at least annual visits to some particular *tirtha* having made a vow to do so in return for a piece of good fortune granted by divine favour. Journeys from home are also invariably accompanied by visits to local Jain shrines and any ascetics who may be present nearby.

A single individual may also choose to bear all the expenses of a communal pilgrimage, and it may be assumed that this helps to prevent *parigraha* – the sin of taking satisfaction in possessions – since it involves spending large sums of money. However, sponsors of such pilgrimages and other virtuous enterprises inevitably also gain economic as well as moral status. A sound financial reputation is earned by demonstrating an ability to spend large sums of money, so that donations are both expres-sions of piety and also, in effect, self-advertisements.

The importance of gift-giving for religious purposes can, of course, lead to situations of competition within or between sects of Jains. One scholar has described a struggle between the Digambara ('sky-clothed', i.e. ideally naked) and Svetambara (white-clothed, i.e. white-robed) sects over the local pilgrimage site of Bahubali Hill in Kolhapur district, southern Maharashtra.[56] This was expressed in a conflict over the sacred space which involved considerable conspicuous consumption. At one point, for instance, the Svetambara constructed a temple next door to that

58 OPPOSITE Rajasthan, India. Interior of the Jain Dilwara Temple on Mount Abu, 11th century and later.

59 ABOVE Shravanabelagola, India, December 1993, Jain pilgrims at the Mahamastakabhishekha, or head-anointing ceremony, performed every 12 years to the statue of Gomateshvara, which stands at the peak of the Indragiri hill.

60 LEFT Jain pilgrims pouring milk over the feet of the Gomateshvara statue (not during the festival).

of the Digambara: the new temple was designed to be just slightly more opulent than its rival.

A sense of the immediate significance of Jain pilgrimage festivals is provided by two recent newspaper articles. The first, from the *Deccan Herald* of 20 December 1993, describes the special honouring of the 58-foot (17.7 m) figure (billed as the world's tallest monolithic statue) of Gomateshvara at Shravanabelagola, Karnataka, which takes place every twelve to fourteen years. Thousands of pilgrims from around the country and abroad come to honour the statue, including not only *munis* but also local and national politicians. The presence of numerous journalists is also noted, including television reporters from the BBC, CNN, France and Japan, as is the decision of the state government to position over 200 closed-circuit televisions near the event to enable devotees to have as good a view of the proceedings as possible. A central part of the ritual is the bathing of the statue with offerings, including water, sugar-cane juice, milk and sandalwood. While the assembled dignitaries are given the opportunity of showering flowers and water on the head of the Gomateshvara, it is also reported that:

Mr. Sudhir Jain, a Delhi businessman, . . . bought the *pratama kalasha* [pot offering] for Rs. 15 lakh at the auction held here on Saturday. He was given the privilege of pouring holy water on the statue first.

By publicly dowsing the statue with holy water, the Delhi businessman proclaims not only his devotion but also his ability to amass the financial resources necessary to win an auction.

The tenor of the second article, describing the same event and published in the *Hindu* of 2 January 1994, is rather different. Entitled 'Of Kalashas and Karma', it focuses on Jain teachings and the figure of Gomateshvara himself. Thus:

He could have become the ruler of Ayodhya but instead chose to become an ascetic, spreading the message of peace and disarmament. . . . On December 6 it seemed so right somehow, to be sitting on the newly erected scaffolding, staring into the supremely calm face of the man-who-could-have-been-king of Ayodhya. In other parts of the country, trains were being blown up and buses destroyed. But, here . . . there was a feeling of peace.

Here, the pilgrimage festival is interpreted as a supreme example of *ahimsa* – non-violence – teaching the non-violent Jain way of life to the varied groups of people, including ascetics, VIPs and even tourists. The reference to Ayodhya has extra, ironic significance in that it calls to mind a holy city notorious for violence between Hindus and Muslims, and we are reminded in this context that the message of renunciation has significance not only for Jains but for the world as a whole in its advocacy of 'peace, hope and harmony'. Yet, both articles illustrate the amplification of the significance of pilgrimage through the vicarious participation provided by the media. A picture in the *Hindu* not only shows pilgrims happily anointing the head of Gomateshvara with water, but also a cameraman recording the event for others, far from the site itself, to witness.

Sikhism's accredited founder, Guru Nanak, was born at Talwandi in the Punjab in 1469.[57] He is seen as the first Sikh or 'disciple' of truth.

Although he was probably brought up in an orthodox Kshatriya family, Nanak is said to have rejected this background, embarking instead on a religious quest to the main centres of Hinduism and Islam. Nanak concluded that God was neither specifically Hindu nor Muslim, and rejected exclusivism in religion. He also rejected the caste system in principle (even if Sikh practice has contradicted this injunction), stating that moral character was more important than birth. Indeed, a Sikh proverb states that a person should be a Brahmin in piety, a Kshatriya in defence of truth and the oppressed, a Vaishya in business acumen and hard work, and a Shudra in serving fellow human beings. One scholar has also suggested that some of the symbols now seen as characteristic of Sikh identity were originally developed in opposition to the Hindu ideals of renunciation: the comb and the turban, for instance, signify the ordering of hair as opposed to the conscious disorder 'cultivated' by the renouncer.[58]

A story is recounted of a visit paid by Guru Nanak to the Jagannatha pilgrimage site at Puri. When the Hindu priests there performed the evening lamp worship of *aarti (arati)*, they demanded to know why he had not stood up during the *puja*. Nanak is said to have replied:[59]

I was performing aarti before the Lord of the Universe . . . and the whole of creation, the whole firmament joined me. Your hearts and minds, alone, were turned against it. I worshipped the supreme light. You worshipped a stone image. I contemplated the eternal word. . . . You chanted mantras without understanding them. My mind was enchanted by the unstruck music and the universe and God's presence in it. Yours was deluded by the noise of temple bells, feigned ecstasy of the dancers and the smell of incense.

Nanak did not necessarily wish to condemn Hinduism outright. Indeed, Sikhism retains notions of transmigration and liberation adapted from the earlier religion. However, he was opposed to hypocrisy and empty formalism in religion, and mistrustful of the use of images in worship. His mistrust of pilgrimage may also have been an indication of the life-affirming as opposed to life-renouncing tendencies evident in Sikh doctrine. As part of his attempt to challenge the monopoly of Brahmin priests in spiritual matters, he produced his own hymns and stressed the need for right conduct and devotion to a personal God as opposed to participation in rituals. Liberation could only be achieved by a form of interior spirituality, involving meditation on *Akal Purakh*, the 'Timeless Being'. The view that divinity could descend to the world in the specific form of an avatar was also denied, since divinity could be seen as pervading all forms. After Nanak's death in 1539 or 1540, a Sikh community consolidated itself in the Punjab and north-west India, benefiting from the rich agricultural land of the area. The religion now has some 13 million adherents, divided to some extent by geography, ethnicity, social hierarchy and ritual practices.[60]

Nanak remains the focus of much devotion from Sikhs, but he was in fact followed by nine living successors, making ten Gurus in all. Teaching in the vernacular rather than Sanskrit, they helped develop a religious community conscious of its distinctiveness and keen to adapt Hindu

61 Sikh pilgrim bathing in the lake at the shrine of Hemkund Sahib in the Bhyundar Valley, high in the Himalayas. Sikhs believe the site indicates the spot where Guru Gobind Singh meditated at God's feet.

festive occasions for its own purposes. Sikh identity and indeed militancy was also strengthened by the need to resist increasing Mughal persecution throughout the seventeenth century, and later on the threat posed by Afghan invaders. For part of the nineteenth century, the enemy was to be the British who, in 1849, took the Punjab following the bloody Anglo-Sikh war.

The line of living Gurus was ended by a conscious decision of the tenth guru, Gobind Singh. After his death in 1708 succession was invested in both the community of Sikhs and a collection of the teachings of the Gurus called the *Guru Granth Sahib* or the *Adi Granth* ('First Collection'). The latter has become a sacred text of great symbolic significance and, in theory, the only true object of veneration. The mere presence of it in any building transforms that space into a *gurdwara* or place of worship (literally, 'gateway to a guru' or preceptor).[61]

Nanak himself, an opponent of outward conventions including ritualism and the cultivation of austerity, did not approve of pilgrimage. In his *Japji*, or book of psalms, he stated: 'One gains but a seed's weight of merit/Through pilgrimages, austerities. . . .' On a visit to Mecca, he is reputed to have made pilgrims there recognise that 'God's house is everywhere and not only in the direction of *Kaaba*'.[62] Yet his views in this regard have certainly not been adopted by his successors, even if journeys to rivers are generally proscribed. Pilgrimages are practised today, frequently cross-

ing political boundaries such as that between India and Pakistan, and gatherings help to celebrate significant events in Sikh history. An outline of the religion published in India lists ten 'historic shrines of Sikhs in Delhi', with the implication that these are places which should attract pilgrims.[63] The third Guru, Amar Das, even appealed successfully to the Mughal emperor against the tax imposed on Hardwar, one of the most important north Indian pilgrimage centres. He also appears to have made his own village, Goindwal, a pilgrimage destination. A pilgrimage that has grown in the twentieth century is that to Hemkund Sahib, a lake at 16,000 feet (almost 5,000 m), surrounded by a number of peaks in the Garhwal Himalayas near Badrinath.[64] The tenth Guru, Gobind Singh, is said to have performed penance on the mountain, and to have become blended thereby with God. Sikhs have also been known to visit Hindu and other sacred centres, as well as their own. While worshippers seek divine blessing in a way similar to Hindu devotees, they reject (at least officially) the characteristically Hindu seeking of material blessings from lower deities.[65]

The most important sacred centre is at Amritsar ('tank of nectar'). The fourth Guru, Ram Das, excavated the pool there in the sixteenth century, and his son later built the Darbar Sahib, a place of worship and pilgrimage on the site which now contains the famous Golden Temple (so called because of the gold-plate covering of its dome) and the original copy of

62 The holiest of Sikh shrines, the Golden Temple at Amritsar, built in the 16th century by Guru Arjan, the fifth of the ten Sikh Gurus. Also called Harmandir, or Temple of God, it was constructed in the middle of the sacred waters of Amritsar.

the *Granth Sahib*. The settlement grew in prosperity, not least because it was situated near the Delhi–Kabul trade routes, and continued to be regarded as a holy city even though at some points in the eighteenth century Sikhs were forbidden entry on pain of death. Amritsar has thus retained its importance as a sacred centre and focal point of identity for an often beleaguered religious group that has had violent encounters with Hindu, Muslim and British political authorities.

The temple complex itself occupies some 30 acres (12 ha) in the centre of the town, and is conspicuously without images. The fact that the main temple has a doorway on each of its four sides indicates the notion that the faith is open to all. In addition, a walkway allows pilgrims to complete a ritual of circumambulation. On some occasions worship is combined with political activity, as at the time of Baisakhi (New Year's Day in the Punjab, 13 April). It has been the custom for devout Sikhs to come on this day to the Golden Temple and bathe in the pool. In the afternoon, political rallies are sometimes held, and even a large fair to the east of the town.

Sikh forms of fundamentalism and increased investment of authority in sacred scripture have emerged since the late nineteenth century, a time of perceived threat to the Sikhs from both Christian missions and Hindu propaganda.[66] Religio-political movements developed which attempted to reinforce a specific Sikh identity, separate in cultural terms from surrounding Hindu society. Thus a specifically Sikh form of sacred space was created; Punjabi was cultivated as a sacred language, and the Golden Temple was emphasised as a visual means of mobilising the community. At this time, also, the *Khalsa* (Sikh Order) tradition was promoted as a pan-Sikh means of preserving the community of faith, incorporating the wearing of a comb, a particular form of underwear, a sword and a wrist-band, as well as the practice of not cutting the hair.[67]

While the celebration of martyrdom has long been a part of the Sikh religious tradition, it has been reinforced in the past two centuries as the sense of a distinct Sikh religious and cultural identity has also developed. Demands – often violent – for the creation of a separate Sikh state have grown throughout this century, and the control of Amritsar has proved a powerful symbol of a wider conflict over the autonomy of members of the religion. For the scholar of Sikhism T. N. Madan, the contemporary situation of the Sikhs in India is rendered still more ambivalent by the state's apparently neutral recognition of its citizens' right to hold diverse religious beliefs alongside the desire of some Sikhs to choose to combine politics and religion in the conduct of community life.[68] Most recently, the Golden Temple complex has been at the centre of a bloody conflict between Sikh separatists and the Indian government. In June 1984, the government ordered units of its army, including Hindus, Sikhs and Muslims, to storm the precincts of the temple, causing extensive damage to the buildings and resulting in the killing of over 1,000 people, including pilgrims.[69] Later that year, the event took on national and world-wide significance, as it provided a motive for the assassination of Prime Minister Indira Gandhi.

This chapter on religious traditions in India has concentrated on pilgrimage within a single, albeit vast, subcontinent. Yet, above all, it has emphasised that the study of the dominant religious tradition – Hinduism – and its pilgrimage practices should make us aware of the dangers of treating any religious system as a static or homogeneous entity. Through time, Hinduism has experienced the effects of numerous religious, cultural and military impulses – Buddhist, Jain, Sikh, Muslim, Christian, and British. Through space, it can be experienced via sacrifices at a local, village, goddess shrine, or a sanctifying bathe in the Ganges at a 'pan-Indian' site like Benares.

If a *tirtha* represents a place of safe crossing between the divine and earthly worlds, the number and variety of such *tirthas* in India has allowed the pathways of pilgrims to create a sacred geography of manifold diversity. Pilgrims are given the opportunity not only to meet distinct forms of the divine, located in specific parts of the country, but also to meet a particular divine figure in a variety of sacred places. This sense of fragmentation is embodied even in a single site such as Benares. There are many ways in which to trace a sacred route through the city, just as the city itself is 'reproduced' in minor versions throughout India. Benares is simultaneously a sacred centre but also 'decentred', rendered accessible in other parts of the continent's sacred geography.

While Hinduism has often been characterised as containing both a this-worldly aspect, embodied in the life of the householder, and an other-worldly aspect, represented by the permanent ascetic, the practice of pilgrimage mediates between these two tendencies by permitting a temporary renunciation of the world.[70] Furthermore, apart from its ability to create and sometimes accommodate considerable internal diversity, Hinduism's flexibility has allowed it to assimilate as well as influence the practices of other faiths.

We have also seen how other religions have merged in India which have parallels with the dominant tradition but which are also formed partially out of opposition to it. If Sikhism today avoids the icon-worship of Hinduism by making a text the ultimate source of veneration, Jains either reject images outright or deny that they contain the real presence of a deity. Sikhism scorns the virtues of permanent renunciation, just as its mistrust of idols and minor deities removes the possibility of pilgrimage to an endlessly diffuse divine hierarchy (even if sites associated with the various Gurus provide a variegated religious landscape). Recent events at the Golden Temple have emphasised how the demarcation of a sacred space, ideally kept pure from other religious impulses, can be made central to the articulation of a sense of communal identity, but also a source of tragic conflict as the boundaries of both place and community appear to be put under threat.

VI. Mapping the Sacred: Diagrams and Narratives

a *Plan of the Temple of Sriringham, India, 19th century. This schematic and idealised plan presents the temple as a sacred palace or mandala of the deity represented at the centre. There are four principal gateways at each of the four cardinal directions, and a series of concentric walls mark ever more interior, and hence sacred, space.*

If pilgrimage involves physical movement through symbolically charged landscapes, it is also proclaimed in the way its landscapes are represented in both word and image. Diagrams and narratives not only reproduce the topography and experience of the sacred journey, but define and even constitute it. They provide the means for imagining pilgrimage, by shaping the anticipation of a pilgrim before his or her voyage and by guiding experience at the sacred centre itself. For some pilgrims the construction of a narrative or image after their return provides a means both of reinterpreting and of reliving something of the significance of the trip.

It may even represent a sort of personal rite of passage for returning from pilgrimage to one's familiar world.

Our primary knowledge of pre-modern pilgrimage comes from such representations, made over many centuries by devotees of different religions. In a sense, what we know is derived not so much from the site or experience itself but from the way it is imagined and remembered in the mundane world away from the pilgrimage centre. Our historical knowledge of Buddhist India, for instance, is very largely derived from the accounts of Chinese Buddhists who visited India during the Middle Ages to acquire holy

b. *Miniature portrait of Geoffrey Chaucer (c. 1340–1400), late 16th century. The poet holds a rosary in his left hand (a token of piety) and a pen for writing in his right (a token of his profession). The date given is one wrongly assumed for his death by the illuminator.*

SABARIMALA ROUTE GUIDE PAMBA TO SANNITHANAM

c. *Contemporary plan of the Ayyappa pilgrimage to Sabarimalai.*

scriptures and venerate the holy sites. However, the stereotypical genres that narrative so often takes may prevail over the experience itself: in the case of the Turkish villagers whom we met in Chapter 3, the stories told by returning *hajjis* refer less to their somewhat disquieting experience at Mecca than to the ideal account expected by their audience back at home.

In the case of the pilgrimage of the Hindu Ayyappans to Sabarimalai, narrative and image reinforce each other in presenting a normative view of the journey. The pilgrimage itself is regarded as arduous and austere; indeed, such qualities are an essential part of the spiritual experience it offers. Ayyappan accounts regularly speak of the wild animals which threaten the route, and these beasts are marked on the maps used by pilgrims (Fig. VIc). The idealised topography of the pilgrimage landscape controls

the maps, which reflect not the actual landscape (they are not drawn to scale) but rather a schematic environment perceived by the minds and imaginations of devotees. Such maps are accurate in their representation of an anticipated pilgrimage terrain rather than as cartographic reality.

Similarly, the map (Fig. VIa) represents the temple at Sriringham not as it actually is but as it ought to be according to the ideal plan for a Hindu temple. Such a map, probably produced at the sacred centre, was for use there but could also be taken away, not only as a souvenir, encapsulating in schematic form the totality of the temple, but also as a kind of guide for those who might one day wish to visit it. By contrast, the huge labyrinth inset into the pavement of the nave at Chartres Cathedral in the thirteenth century (Fig. VId) is not a plan of an actual journey or place. Rather, its eleven concentric rings leading by a circuitous route to a six-petalled rose at the centre offer a parable, within the cathedral itself, of the spiritual path of which pilgrimage to Chartres was but a physical manifestation.

Two-dimensional images and diagrams are but one way of mapping the process of pilgrimage. Another, perhaps still more common, method is the written text. While many pilgrimage narratives and maps present allegories of spiritual progress outside the mundane or social worlds (take for instance the Puritan journey of Christian in John Bunyan's *The Pilgrim's Progress*), Chaucer's *Canterbury Tales* places pilgrimage directly within society. The Prologue begins by referring not only to the 'holy blisful martir' of 'Caunterbury' (v.16) but also to the prototype of all Christian pilgrimage, the voyage to Palestine:

> Than longen folk to goon on pilgrimage,
> And palmers for seeken straunge strondes,
> To ferne halwes, couthe in sondry londes. . . .
>
> (vv.12–14)

This reference to palmers, foreign shores and distant shrines (implying Jerusalem) is picked up in the prologue to the Parson's Tale, when the storyteller refers to

> Thilke parfit glorious pilgrimage,
> That highte Ierusalem celestial. . . .
>
> (vv.50–1)

Yet in Chaucer, the destination (whether Canterbury or Celestial Jerusalem) is never reached. Instead, a spread of the social spectrum from the Knight to the Wife of Bath (no mean pilgrim herself – she had been to Rome, Jerusalem and Compostela), from the Prioress and the Monk to the Cook and the Merchant, is placed before the reader, evoking not an ideal interior journey (as in Bunyan) but a very social and human process.

In *The Pilgrim's Progress*, any actual landscape is eschewed in favour of an inner pilgrimage through allegorical places like the Slough of Despond or the Town of Vanity: the landscape in effect becomes part of the narrative. In Chaucer, by contrast, the landscape is peopled. Instead of an interior journey for any one pilgrim, the *Canterbury Tales* creates a microcosm of the whole of society which is seen in its contradictions and rich diversity journeying to the national shrine. Although obviously a fictional construct, the *Canterbury Tales* may be said to capture through its literary form some of the varied human and social complexities of pilgrimage. A literary text which treads with elegance between the extremes of interiority and society is Matsuo Basho's beautiful account of Japanese pilgrimage, *The Narrow Road to the Deep North* (see pp. 188–90 below). This combines poetry and prose in an autobiographical account with many hints of actuality which nevertheless carries a suggestive theme of an inner search.

d. *Diagram of the great maze in the paving of the nave at Chartres Cathedral, 13th century. Labyrinths of the same form appear in other medieval churches, for instance on a pillar in the porch of Lucca Cathedral in Italy.*

7

Translating the Sacred:
Patterns of Pilgrimage in the
Buddhist World

'Ananda, there are four places the sight of which should arouse a sense
of urgency in the faithful. Which are they? "Here the Tathagata was
born" is the first. "Here the Tathagata attained supreme enlightenment"
is the second. "Here the Tathagata set in motion the Wheel of the
Dharma" is the third. "Here the Tathagata attained Nirvana without
remainder" is the fourth. And, Ananda, the faithful monks and nuns,
male and female lay-followers will visit those places. And any who die
while making the pilgrimage to these shrines with a devout heart will, at
the breaking up of the body after death, be reborn in a heavenly world.'
MAHAPARINIBBANA SUTTA 5,8[1]

Thus, according to Buddhist tradition, the Buddha spoke to his chief
attendant Ananda in the very last discourse he delivered before his
death (probably around 400 BC).[2] Referring to himself as the
Tathagata, or Perfected One, the Buddha prescribed four places of
pilgrimage to his followers. In doing so, he enshrined the activity of
pilgrimage as an important act of the Buddhist's life – an act sanctioned by
scriptural recommendation. He tied the Buddhist conception of pilgrimage, at least in its original form, specifically and explicitly to those
places which witnessed the most significant events of his life.

These central sites were Lumbini (perhaps modern Rummindei in
Nepal), where the Buddha was born, Uruvela (now Bodhgaya in Bihar,
northern India), where he attained enlightenment, the deer park at
Isipatana (modern Sarnath near Benares), where he preached his first
sermon (described in Buddhist tradition as the turning of the Wheel of the
Dharma, or Holy Law), and Kusinara (modern Kushinagar), where the
Buddha passed away and entered his final Nirvana. These places map
the Buddha's spiritual biography into the north Indian landscape.

By extension, other holy sites associated with the Buddha's life were
soon added to this group. Most notably, these included the Vulture Peak
at Rajagriha (modern Rajgir) and the Jetavana at Shravasti. At Rajgir, the
Buddha converted his two chief disciples, Sariputra (Sariputta) the
master of wisdom, and Maudgalyayana (Moggallana) the master of
power, and in later tradition it was on the Vulture Peak that he turned the
Wheel of the *Dharma* for the second time, preaching the so-called Wisdom

63 OPPOSITE Lumbini,
Nepal. Pilgrims
circumambulate the pillar
commemorating that erected
by Ashoka to mark the place
of the Buddha's birth.
According to legend, the
Buddha's mother, Queen
Mayadevi, was visiting the
Lumbini garden on the day
of his birth. She bathed,
leant against a sala tree
facing east and immediately
the future Buddha was born
from her right side. He took
seven steps in each of the
four directions, and from his
footprints lotus flowers
sprang up.

Sutras which formed the basis of the Mahayana school of Buddhism. The Jetavana, the grove of Prince Jeta, where the Buddha lived for twenty-five rainy seasons, was the site of the monastery built for his order of monks, the *Sangha*, by the merchant Anathapindika. By analogy, other places associated with the lives of the Buddha's chief disciples and with the *Sangha* were also added to the sacred landscape of Buddhist pilgrimage. Indeed, the Buddha himself recommended this.

In the *Mahaparinibbana Sutta*, the Buddha gave instructions to his attendant Ananda about how he should be buried:

A stupa should be erected at the crossroads for the Tathagata. And whoever lays wreaths or puts sweet perfumes and colours there with a devout heart, will reap benefit and happiness for a long time. (5,11)[3]

The emphasis is on how pilgrims should behave before, and will be affected by, the relics of the Buddha or other enlightened persons worthy of a stupa:

Because, Ananda, at the thought: 'This is the stupa of a Tathagata, of a Pacceka Buddha, of a disciple of a Tathagata, of a wheel-turning monarch', people's hearts are made peaceful, and then, at the breaking-up of the body after death they go to a good destiny and arise in a heavenly world (5,12).[4]

In this additional commentary on the value of relics, the Buddha extended the notion of pilgrimage from an emphasis on his own life to the suggestion that any place or material object associated with a person who had attained enlightenment was worthy of veneration.

For the Buddha, pilgrimage was a spiritual practice capable of easing the heart, bringing happiness and taking the practitioner to a heaven-realm. Relics and pilgrimage monuments, such as stupas, were important as the material focus of such spiritual activity. The *Mahaparinibbana Sutta* ends with an account of the veneration of the Buddha's dead body, the division of his relics and the building of stupas to contain them (6,20–8). The *Sutta* prescribed not only the practice of stupa building and relic worship but also the circumambulation of a holy site in a clockwise direction as a mark of veneration. Both as a spiritual action and as a practice explicitly recommended by the Buddha, pilgrimage would have a prime role in later Buddhism, not only in its focused form of the journey to the four holy places which the Buddha had described, but also in the more diffused form of pilgrimage to any place associated with a person who had attained liberation through enlightenment.

THE JOURNEY TO THE SITES OF THE BUDDHA'S LIFE

By focusing pilgrimage on the central spiritual events of the Buddha's life, much as Christian pilgrimage was focused on the geography of Christ's life in Palestine, Buddhism offered a different paradigm from the diffuse patterns of *Tirthayatra* which came to prevail in Hindu India. Buddhist pilgrimage became a concentrated evocation of the Tathagata's life, not only geographically but also temporally, since the ideal journey began at his birth-place and finished in Kusinara, where he passed away. Precisely this model of Buddhist pilgrimage was established by the immensely influential myth of the emperor Ashoka in the Sanskrit poem the *Ashokavadana*, whose finished form dates from about the second century AD but whose oral origins go back to the second century BC. In the poem, Ashoka (who reigned on the throne of the Mauryan emperors from about 274 to 232 BC, united almost all India under his sway and was converted to Buddhism) visits all the important sites of the Buddha's life with his spiritual master, the monk Upagupta. This pilgrimage reconstructs the Buddha's life by retracing and remembering his career from birth to death. At each site, Ashoka builds a commemorative monument and Upagupta summons up local deities who were present at the actual events and provide vivid eye-witness accounts.[5]

In the *Ashokavadana* the emperor visits not only the four prescribed sites, but altogether thirty-two holy places connected with the Buddha's life. In parallel with the thirty-two marks of the Great Man in Indian tradition (marks which the Buddha himself was held to possess), these thirty-two holy places can be seen as inscribing the body of the Great Man into the geography of India through the unifying image of the Buddha's life. While the holy places of Hindu India could be seen as representing the dismembered body of Shiva's dead wife, those of Buddhism represented the ideal body of the Great Man who could become either a Buddha in his own right or a Wheel-Turning Monarch (perhaps like Ashoka himself). In addition to his pilgrimage to the thirty-two holy places, the Ashoka of the *Ashokavadana* collects all the relics of the Buddha together and redistributes them in 84,000 stupas over the face of India. Moreover, he gives honour also to the relics of Buddha's foremost disciples, making varying offerings at their stupas. He is especially drawn to the Bodhi tree at Bodhgaya, to which he accords further worship.[6]

The *Ashokavadana* was translated into other Buddhist languages, such as Chinese, and was influential on the great fifth-century AD chronicle of Sri Lanka, the Pali *Mahavamsa*. The poem presented a model of the ideal Buddhist pilgrim which had the merit of being not entirely unrelated to actuality. The real Ashoka did indeed convert to Buddhism and has left numerous edicts carved on pillars and rock faces attesting to his concern for the *Dharma*. Ashoka was the first Buddhist pilgrim of whom we know for certain:

Twenty years after his coronation, King Priyadarsi [another name of the emperor], Beloved of the Gods, visited this place in person and worshipped here because the Buddha, the sage of the Sakyas, was born here.

He ordered a stone wall to be constructed round the place and erected this stone pillar to commemorate his visit.

He declared the village of Lumbini free of taxes and required to pay only one eighth of its produce [about half the usual amount] as land revenue.

(Rummindei Pillar Edict)[7]

In other edicts, Ashoka attests his concern for pilgrimage by improving the roads, building rest houses and watering stations.

These are trifling comforts. For the people have received various facilities from previous kings as well as from me. But I have done what I have primarily in order that the people may follow the path of Dharma with faith and devotion.

(from Pillar Edict VII).[8]

64 The Damekha Stupa, Sarnath, India. The Deer Park at Sarnath is where the Buddha 'turned the wheel of the Dharma', inaugurating his vocation as teacher of gods and men. It subsequently became one of the great centres of Buddhist monasticism and pilgrimage, with stupas and viharas built from the time of Ashoka onwards.

The importance of Ashoka was that his deep piety was coupled with the power and force of imperial patronage. While the Buddha's own words may have established the principle of pilgrimage for his followers, Ashoka's actions and buildings established the possibility and practicality of pilgrimage. Moreover, the emperor's own life itself became the ideal model, through the text of the *Ashokavadana*.

In this sense Ashoka's actions as emperor, convert to a new religion and pilgrim-builder extraordinaire form a remarkable parallel to those of Constantine and his mother St Helena in conquering an empire, converting to a new religion and building a series of exceptional pilgrim churches (see Fig. 25). Such rulers transformed not only the sacred landscape but the very means of travel within it, as well as the whole environment of the sacred centres which were the pilgrim's goals. In effect they created something radically new out of pilgrimage in their given tradition. At the same time they stood to gain the support of a religious system and the immense prestige of being the executors of a holy order, whether the Buddha's *Dharma* or the Church of Christ.

Like Muhammad, Buddha was seen as having recommended pilgrimage. But, unlike Islam, Buddhism never enshrined the holy places as a doctrinal *sine qua non*. Like Christianity, Buddhism focused its sacred sites on the life of a single individual, his disciples and (in the case of

65 Face of the recumbent statue of the Buddha at Kushinagar, India, where the Buddha entered his final Nirvana.

Christianity) his mother. It built biography into the landscape. With imperial patronage and the support of a formidable monastic system, Buddhism prefigured Christianity by enshrining its holy places and practices into a land and people originally devoted to different gods. Its long heyday as the principal religion of India was to attract many pilgrims from far away, who came to discover, and to transplant, the sacred places, texts and spiritual exercises of Buddhist India.

THE JOURNEY TO INDIA IN ACTUALITY AND IMAGINATION

In about AD 400, only a few years after Egeria made her trip from Spain to Palestine (see Chapter 4), a Chinese monk called Fa-hsien (also trans-literated as Fa-Hian or Faxian), made the long pilgrimage to India. In company with a number of other Buddhist monks, regretting 'the imperfect condition of the *Vinaya Pitaka* (or book of rules for Buddhist monks)' in the then current Chinese translation, Fa-hsien decided to go to India to search for a more complete version. His travels in the Indian subcontinent took him as far as Sri Lanka and lasted fourteen years.[9] Something of the enormity of this venture, its dangers and personal hardships, can be grasped from the section of his account in which he describes his feelings on arriving at the Jetavana Grove at Shravasti, where the Buddha delivered many of his most famous teachings:

When Fa-hsien and To-Ching arrived at this temple of the Jetavana, they reflected that this was the spot where the Lord of men had passed twenty-five years of his life; they themselves, at the risk of their lives, were now dwelling amongst foreigners; of those who had with like purpose travelled through a succession of countries with them, some had returned home, some were now dead; and now, gazing on the place where the Buddha once dwelt but was no longer to be seen, their hearts were affected with very lively regret.   (*Travels of Fa-hsien*, 20)[10]

Fa-hsien's account reveals many of the qualities inherent in Buddhist pilgrimage. He frequently remarked on the works and legends of Ashoka, which by his time had become a paradigm for Buddhist pilgrims. In thus reproducing the works of Ashoka through his writings, Fa-hsien, like the other Chinese pilgrims who would follow him, transformed (for a Chinese readership) the sacred map of India created by Ashoka, much as Ashoka himself had transformed the sacred topography implied in the Buddha's own *suttas*. He made great efforts to visit the holy places as well as to collect the various books he came to seek. He was strongly aware of being a foreigner in India. When the monks of the Jetavana discovered where he came from, they exclaimed

Wonderful! To think that men from the frontiers of the earth should come so far as this from a desire to search for the Law.   (*Travels*, 20).

As Buddhism spread to China and South-East Asia, pilgrims would increasingly be foreigners in the Buddha's homeland, until – with the extinction of Buddhism in India in about the thirteenth century (following Muslim and some Hindu persecutions, as well as the loss of royal patronage and a certain amount of Buddhist-Hindu syncretism) – the only pilgrims at the Ashokan holy sites would come from abroad.

Fa-hsien is interested not only in sites associated with the Buddha, his disciples and the *Sangha* generally, but also in places that feature in the Jataka tales of the Buddha's previous lives. For instance, the country of Taxila (which, according to a folk etymology recorded as if it were accurate by Fa-hsien, means 'Cut-off-head') is so named because

Buddha, when he was a Bodhisattva [one who has dedicated his life to attaining enlightenment for the liberation of others], gave his head in charity to a man in this place, and hence comes the name.   (*Travels*, 11)[11]

He remarks on the stupa 'adorned with every kind of precious jewel' which commemorated the spot. His pilgrimage-India is not only Buddha's biography inscribed as a map onto the landscape, but a hagiography of past lives in which previous incarnations of the Buddha themselves sanctified the land. Important too were spots associated with previous Buddhas, which Buddhist tradition believed had arisen before Gautama, the sage of the Sakyas. Some places were holy because all Buddhas would come to them – for instance the Vulture Peak at Rajgir which possessed 'the place where the four Buddhas sat down' (*Travels* 29).[12]

Perhaps most impressive in Fa-hsien's narrative is his deep sense of emotion at places of profound religious significance. This seems precisely in keeping with the 'sense of urgency' and the 'devout heart' recommended by the Buddha himself in the *Parinibbana Sutta*. Indeed, one might say that Fa-hsien's narrative enacts the injunctions implied by the Buddhist scriptures. Take, for instance, his actions at the Vulture Peak:

Fa-hsien, having bought flowers, incense, and oil and lamps in the new town, procured the assistance of two aged monks as guides. Fa-hsien, ascending the Gridhrakuta mountain, offered his flowers and incense and lit his lamps for the night. Being deeply moved he could scarcely restrain his tears as he said, 'Here it was in bygone days Buddha dwelt and delivered the *Surangama Sutra*. Fa-hsien, not privileged to be born when the Buddha lived, can but gaze on the traces of his presence and the place which he occupied.' Then he recited the *Surangama* in front of the cave and remaining there all night, he returned to the new town.

(*Travels* 29)[13]

Fa-hsien was followed by many other Chinese pilgrims to India. Among those who left records of their trips were Sung-yun, who went in the early sixth century AD, and I-ching, who travelled there from about 672 to 693. Most famous, however, and most influential of all the Chinese pilgrims and translators was Hsuan-tsang (whose name is also transliterated as Huien-tsiang and Yuan-chwang), who spent the years from 629 to 645 AD in India. Hsuan-tsang not only wrote an extensive account of his pilgrimage in twelve books, the *Si-Yu-Ki* or 'Records of the Western World',[14] but as soon as he died became the subject of a hagiographical account by his students Hwui-li and Yen-thsong. This biography dwells in detail on his trip to India, turning it into a paradigmatic pilgrimage.[15] If the myth of Ashoka had been the model for Buddhist pilgrimage within India, that of Hsuan-tsang became the paradigm for pilgrimage to India from China. It became romanticised and mythologised into folk tale in cycles of miraculous stories, being retold for instance during the sixteenth century in the famous novel *The Journey to the West* (also known as *Monkey*), probably written by Wu Ch'eng-en.[16]

Hsuan-tsang's *Records of the Western World* is a mine of information about India in the seventh century. At the beginning of Book II, he gives a sketch of Indian life and manners. With every region within India which he describes, he tends to give practical and geographic information as a prelude to his description of religious sites and relics. Like other pilgrims, such as the Greek Pausanias, he frames his pilgrimage account with quantities of other information, such as rather precise, if brief, sketches of the terrain, soil, produce, customs and local habits of the many countries which he records. Hsuan-tsang invariably describes the kinds of coinage used by the local people and often gives a short account of the king. After this introductory material, he turns to matters of religion.

Hsuan-tsang's prime project is to detail the Buddhist remains, monasteries and relics of India. He is precise about the kind of Buddhism practised in every monastery. He himself was an adherent of the Mahayana (or Great-Vehicle) school which developed around the first century BC; but in his time many of the earlier schools (Mahasamghika, Theravada and Sarvastivada) – each with a slightly different philosophical, doctrinal and scriptural emphasis – still existed. Of these early schools only the Theravada survives today, while the Mahayana has itself split and expanded into many forms and countries from Zen to Tantra (both Indian in origin) and from Japan to Tibet. Hsuan-tsang goes to great pains to describe the various relics (from bones, teeth and nail parings to the Buddha's various sticks, bowls and robes), as well as to tell the stories associated with each relic and each place. He remarks on all the Ashokan monuments he sees. As they gather pace and length, Hsuan-tsang's *Records* become a veritable biography of the Buddha through the stories associated with the sites and objects. They reconstruct a portrait of the Tathagata out of the remains which survive in material culture through the narratives which those remains evoke. Often, there is little left but ruins – even in the most prestigious sites which Ashoka and Fa-hsien had venerated.

Take for instance the Jetavana:

This is where Anathapindada . . . built for Buddha a *vihara*. There was a *sangharama* here formerly, but now all is in ruins.

On the left and right of the eastern gate has been built a pillar about 70 feet high; on the left-hand pillar is engraved on the base a wheel; on the right-hand pillar the figure of an ox is on the top. Both columns were erected by Ashoka. The residences of the priests are wholly destroyed; the foundations only remain, with the exception of one solitary brick building, which stands alone in the midst of the ruins, and contains an image of Buddha. (*Records*, V I)[17]

This is an archaeology of Buddhist India – recording not only the Buddha's own presence here (upon which Fa-hsien had explicitly commented) but also that of Ashoka. The sorry state of the present is evoked through the ruins of this once flourishing monastery where so many of the sacred texts which Hsuan-tsang had come to India to collect and translate were first spoken. But from these traces, half-vanished from the landscape, Hsuan-tsang passes to what they mean: stories of Anathapindada, as he calls Anathapindika, of the Buddha's disciples Sariputra and Maudgalyayana, of the Buddha's own miracles. The brief factual record of the remains at the Jetavana evokes a lengthy and colourful mythic portrait of the site as witness to so many sacred events.

Within a few years of Hsuan-tsang's death in China, where he lived for twenty years after returning from India in AD 645 and supervised many translations, his pilgrimage had become the subject of a biographical narrative by his pupils Hwui-li and Yen-thsong. In this *Life of Hsuan-tsang*, the hero – now referred to as 'Master of the Law' and given an impeccable pedigree reaching back to the Han emperors – proclaims his purpose:

I desire to go and gaze on the sacred traces, and earnestly to search for the Law.[18]

The journey is presented as a ritual, in which Hsuan-tsang adopts the clockwise route which worshippers use in circumambulating a stupa for his pilgrimage through India.[19] Miracles, which in his own *Records* are associated with the pilgrimage sites in former times, are in the *Life* brought forward to the pilgrim's own experience. For instance, at Bodhgaya:

After a little while the light of the lamps in the building was suddenly eclipsed, and within and without there was a supernatural illumination produced. On looking out they saw the relic-tower bright and effulgent as the sun, whilst from its summit proceeded a lambent flame of five colours, reaching to the sky. Heaven and Earth were flooded with light, the moon and stars were no longer seen, and a subtle perfume seemed to breathe through and fill the courts and the precincts. (*Life of Hsuan-tsang*, IV)[20]

66 OPPOSITE Bodhgaya, India. View of the Mahabodhi Temple built on the site of the Buddha's Enlightenment beneath the Bodhi tree.

The process of mythologising a pilgrim and the very act of pilgrimage, which we examined in medieval Christian culture in the case of Egeria's travels and the use made of them by Valerius three centuries later (see Chapter 4), is here in evidence over a single generation. The relics Hsuan-tsang visits are presented as immanent with sanctity and potent in his own time. They exhibit the miraculous qualities of the stories of the times of the Buddha, which he recounted in his *Records*. In effect, in the *Life*, the sacred power of the Buddha's traces (as described in the *Records*) is transposed to Hsuan-tsang's own experience and witness. The pilgrim himself, as well as the place of pilgrimage, becomes a sacred paradigm.

By the time Wu Ch'eng-en wrote *Monkey* in the sixteenth century, the pilgrimage of Hsuan-tsang (now given the surname Tripitaka) had become a parable which could be read on a number of levels. It was a vivid tale of travel and adventure in which Tripitaka's various magical companions, Monkey, Pigsy, Sandy and the white horse, surmount all kinds of dangers, quell demons, rescue ladies in distress and generally fulfil all the demands of a good fairy tale. Socially speaking, this transformation of the tradition of the highly learned pilgrimage account and the saint's life directed to a monastic audience, was most important. It presented the ideal of pilgrimage in a highly popular form, accessible through oral retellings to illiterate lay people. But *Monkey* was also a parable in which the various adventures and experiences of the characters were so structured as to represent a picture of the Buddhist doctrine of *karma* (or the relations of cause and effect in one's actions). The progress of the pilgrimage itself was portrayed as an allegory of the progress to enlightenment in the Buddhist tradition: at the end of their journey both Hsuan-tsang and Monkey become Buddhas.

The Lands of the West, to which Tripitaka (whose name means the three baskets of Buddhist scriptures) and his pilgrim party come, are described not as the 'real' India of Hsuan-tsang's *Records* but as an ideal world:

Everywhere they came across gem-like flowers and magical grasses, with many ancient cypresses and hoary pines. In the villages through which they passed every family seemed to devote itself to the entertainment of priests and other pious works. On every hill hermits were practising austerities, in every wood pilgrims were chanting holy writ.[21]

Passing through this perfect landscape of piety and Chinese aesthetics, the pilgrims arrive at the Vulture Peak itself. They are met by a heavenly bureaucrat named, with wonderful Chinese precision, the Golden Crested Great Immortal of the Jade Truth Temple at the Foot of the Holy Mountain. Buddha himself greets them and orders his disciples to give them the scriptures to take back to China. Yet the scriptures Tripitaka receives have nothing on them, and the pilgrims must return for new scriptures with written texts. As the Buddha explains,

It is such blank scrolls as these that are the true scriptures. But I quite see that the people of China are too foolish and ignorant to believe this, so there's nothing left for it but to give them copies with some writing on.[22]

The real India, which by the time Wu Ch'eng-en was writing was no longer a Buddhist country at all, is here completely subsumed in a divine world. The Buddha's court at the Holy Mountain, with its attendant saints and deities ('Boddhisattvas, Vajrapanis, Protectors, Arhats, Planets and Temple Guardians') is a reflection of the bureaucratic Imperial Court in China. The empty scrolls of blank scriptures are an allegory for the philosophical idea of Emptiness underlying all the manifestations of the phenomenal world, which was taught as the supreme doctrine by the Mahayana and Tantric schools of Buddhism that flourished in China in the sixteenth century. In effect, as the pilgrimage of Hsuan-tsang became embroidered and elaborated in the folklore of Buddhist China, it became a rich parable for the process of Buddhism itself. What remained were not the facts and actualities of the India visited by the real Hsuan-tsang long ago, nor even many of the myths and stories which he himself retold. Rather, what was evoked was the sense of a purposeful journey, a pilgrim's progress, to an ideal and celestial sacred place from which the pilgrim could bring back a relic that would be useful for everyone back home. That relic was the scriptures which Tripitaka had come to the West to seek.

PILGRIMAGE DIFFUSED: SECTS AND SACRED CENTRES OUTSIDE INDIA

Even as the Chinese were visiting India to gaze at the holy places and gather the writings of the Law, other pilgrims from other countries were themselves travelling for the same purpose. In the seventh century AD, Buddhist influence reached Tibet, and in the eighth the Tantric master Padmasambhava came from India and definitively established Buddhism there. From the eighth to the eleventh centuries Tibetan scholar-mystics such as Marpa the Translator were visiting India to gather Tantric initiations and writings in order to diffuse them in Tibet. Thus it was that the Mahayana tradition of Sanskrit Buddhist sutras and commentaries was translated and adapted to the needs of both Chinese and Tibetans.

In the sixth century, the translated and adapted Buddhism of China made its way via Korea to Japan. For Japanese Buddhist pilgrims China, rather than India, would become the goal for the discovery of sacred texts and the visiting of the central temples and holy mountains associated with particular sects or schools of Buddhism. In the early ninth century, the Japanese monk Saicho visited China and in 805 brought the T'ien-t'ai (Japanese, Tendai) school to Kyoto. In 816, his countryman the monk Kukai brought the Milgyo (in Japanese, Shingon) school from China to Japan. In the twelfth century the Zen master Eisai introduced the Lin-chi form of Ch'an Buddhism to Japan, where it was renamed the Rinzai school of Zen. And in the thirteenth century, a former Tendai monk called Dogen brought the Ts'ao-tung school from China, which was renamed Soto Zen in Japan. Just as the history of the transmission of Buddhism in China is inseparable from the history of pilgrimage to India, so the process of bringing Buddhism to Japan was one of pilgrimage to China.

These Japanese pilgrims to China were remarkable scholar-monks, like Hsuan-tsang himself. Something of the flavour of their project is caught in the diary of Ennin (later known as Jikaku Daishi), a senior disciple of Saicho in the Tendai school and later Abbot of Enryakuji, the great monastic headquarters of the sect at Mount Hiei near Kyoto.[23] Ennin was in China from 838 to 847, surviving the persecution of Buddhism which prevailed there in the 840s. His diary, the first in Japanese literature, is an immensely revealing account of the practice and flavour of Buddhism in late T'ang China. His major pilgrimage was to Mount Wu-t'ai, which was sacred to the Boddhisattva of Wisdom, Manjushri (Monju).

Ennin is keenly aware of the sanctity of the place:

When one enters the region of His Holiness (Monju), if one sees a lowly man, one does not dare to feel contemptuous, and if one meets a donkey, one wonders if it might be a manifestation of Monju. Everything before one's eyes raises thoughts of Monju. The holy land makes one have a spontaneous feeling of respect for the region.[24]

The ordinary expectations of social status are transformed in a place where anything can be a divine sign and where miracles are to be expected. Ennin captures not only the sense of reverence but also of heightened emotion:

For the first time we saw the summit of the central terrace. This then is Mt Ch'ing-ling, where Monjushiri resides, the central terrace of Wu-t'ai. We bowed to the ground and worshipped it from afar, and our tears rained down involuntarily.[25]

For Ennin, this precious mountain complex of monasteries and holy sites is the equivalent of the holy places of the Buddha's life in the experience of Fa-hsien and Hsuan-tsang. Wu-t'ai is immanent with magical potency, like the relic-tower Hsuan-tsang's biographers had him encounter in Bodhgaya. Ennin records a miracle image that 'emitted light from time to time and continually emitted auspicious signs'.[26] He experiences miraculous happenings himself:

In the hall I suddenly saw five beams of light, shining straight into the hall, and then suddenly they were no more to be seen. Isho, Igyo and the others were with me in the hall, but all said they saw nothing, and they marvelled without end.[27]

He finds numerous relics from India, including bones of the Buddha and even (buried apparently beneath a pagoda) 'a pagoda of king Ashoka which they do not let people see. It is one of the 84,000 pagodas made by king Ashoka.'[28]

Ennin's Mount Wu-t'ai fulfils the emotional and devotional needs of, say, Bodhgaya in the experience of Fa-hsien and Hsuan-tsang. But, while it retains some of the potency of the Buddha's life through its displays of relics, it is not directly associated with the Buddha himself. Instead, like many of the sacred mountains of eastern Asia, it is the residence of a Buddhist deity (in this case Manjushri) whose own life, powers or teaching can bring about enlightenment. In effect, in the great diffusion of Buddhism through north-east Asia, the importance of the historical Buddha became exemplary in a general sense rather than the unique paradigm of the Buddhist path. Many other deities, enlightened masters and human beings who had achieved Buddhahood provided sacred places, relics and stories (in regions much more accessible than India) to

67 A Soto Zen novice from Eheiji temple prepared to set out on pilgrimage. In his travelling pack he carries eating utensils, a selection of passages from the works of Dogen, the founder of Soto Zen in Japan, and a letter of recommendation from his abbot.

the faithful of China and Japan. Such spiritual people, although often specifically associated with a particular sect, were revered by devotees of other Buddhist sects. Despite Ennin's own preference for the Tendai sect, he notes that such sacred centres as Mount Wu-t'ai (or indeed Mount T'ien-t'ai itself, from which the Tendai sect came) were also sacred to Buddhists from other Chinese schools, such as Ch'an (Zen) or Hua-Yen.

In Japan, the places established by or associated with the Japanese pilgrim-monks and religious reformers themselves swiftly became holy.

183

In the same imperial embassy which had dispatched Ennin's teacher Saicho to China to bring back the Tendai school in 805, was another monk, called Kukai. When he returned to Japan in 816, Kukai (later to be known by the title of Kobo Daishi) founded the Shingon sect and established its headquarters at Mount Koya, fifty miles from Kyoto. He was eventually buried there, and Mount Koya became and still is an important pilgrimage centre. But even more significant was the island of Shikoku, to the south of the main island Honshu, not far from Mount Koya. In Shikoku, Kukai had been born; there he became enlightened and there he performed many of the esoteric practices of Shingon.

The pilgrimage to the eighty-eight holy places of Shikoku is one of the most important in Japan. It has been brilliantly described in English in Oliver Statler's vivid account.[29] The pilgrim's path at Shikoku follows Kobo Daishi's footsteps, circumambulating the island clockwise, as if it were a stupa. It begins at Kukai's mausoleum on Mount Koya, from where pilgrims go to the coast and take a boat to Shikoku. Temple no. 1, where the traditional pilgrim's route starts, is closest to the Kii peninsula on the mainland, where Mount Koya is located. The pilgrimage route stops at eighty-eight specifically numbered temples, most of them belonging to the Shingon sect but some to other schools such as Zen and Tendai. There are also numerous unnumbered temples en route.

Although the pilgrimage evokes other saints who visited the island, it is essentially a ritual enactment of Kobo Daishi's life, taking in his myths, spiritual activities and the places where he dwelt. It is also a trip in the footsteps of Emon Saburo, a man who had refused the Daishi alms and who had come to seek him out in Shikoku and ask forgiveness. Nearing death and worn out from continuous encircling of Shikoku, Emon Saburo finally met Kobo Daishi at the site of Temple no. 12, where he received absolution and died. The Daishi buried him and planted his staff beside the grave. The staff grew into a cedar tree, which still marks the spot.[30]

The pilgrimage to Shikoku is thus an enactment of Saburo's penitence, but it is performed in the alms-begging manner of the Daishi which Saburo had failed to revere. In an *Exhortation for Pilgrims to the Sacred Places of Shikoku*, handed out by the priests of Temple no. 1, the pilgrim is advised to perform

ascetic training in the form of standing before the gates of strangers and asking for alms . . . every day at about twenty-one houses, following the example set by the Daishi.[31]

The pilgrimage is seen as an opportunity to cultivate one's spiritual life in ritual abstinence essentially through faith in Kobo Daishi. The pilgrim is to imagine Kukai accompanying him on his journey. As the *Exhortation* puts it:

he who merely follows the Daishi with his whole heart can have his prayer granted.[32]

Pilgrims evoke this faith by circumambulating the island, often dressed in a traditional pilgrim's outfit (which includes sedge-hats, walking staff and a bell) and reciting the Daishi's mantra, 'Namu Daishi Henjo Kongo'. As the *Exhortation* advises its readers:

Without other intention or thought, calmly and without haste, with 'Namu Daishi Henjo Kongo' on one's lips – that is how to make the true pilgrimage.[33]

Through a display of relics and other treasures brought from China (whether actually by the Daishi or not), the original pilgrimage of Kukai to China is evoked. At Temples 24, 25 and 26, at Muroto where Kukai attained enlightenment, Statler was shown among the relics scrolls of the original fundamental scriptures of Shingon, said to have been those Kukai himself brought back from China.[34] The pilgrimage to Shikoku evokes memories of a previous pilgrimage, that of Kukai to China, which was itself made by the enlightened one whom the pilgrim to Shikoku comes to worship.

The whole pattern of Buddhism in China and Japan became indebted to the pilgrim seekers of the Law not only for its physical introduction but also in its very ideology and practice. To be a Buddhist in Japan is hardly separate from occasionally (or often) undertaking a pilgrimage. This may be to a sacred mountain such as Fuji, to a string of temples sacred to a particular deity (for instance the 33 sanctuaries of Kannon), to the holy places of a particular sect (such as the 25 temples of the Pure Land School or the 100 temples of the Nichiren school), or to a series of sanctuaries

68 Pilgrim party climbing Mt Fuji, 19th century. Just as pilgrimage to Fuji was celebrated as a national ritual in representations such as Hokusai's series of prints in the early 19th century, so the new technique of photography was used later in the century to record and disseminate the image of pilgrimage to the sacred mountain.

69 Japanese pilgrim beggars wearing traditional garb and carrying drums, 19th century.

located in a sacred place, like the 88 shrines on Shikoku or the 1,000 temples in the Higashiyama section of Kyoto. In Shikoku, such pilgrimage involves not only the confrontation with relics and myths, but also the acquisition of talismans that bring healing, the writing of letters by pilgrims to the Daishi and the fulfilment of a whole nexus of personal anxieties, problems and desires.[35] The importance of Shikoku was such that miniature versions of the 88 holy places were subsequently established in other parts of Japan, such as Tokyo and Soma. Here, those who could not make the arduous trip to the real Shikoku could nonetheless fulfil a penitential vow and attempt to walk alongside Kobo Daishi.

MANDALAS AND EMPTINESS: PILGRIMAGE AS METAPHOR FOR THE PATH TO ENLIGHTENMENT

Ultimately, in Mahayana Buddhism pilgrimage became a symbol for the spiritual path itself. On the level of fairy tale we have seen this in the way the novel *Monkey* transformed the travels of Hsuan-tsang. In Japanese culture, the image of pilgrimage took a peculiarly poetic and haunting turn. It suffuses the writings not only of monks like Ennin or Dogen, but also of the great Japanese poets. Take this poem by Issa (1763–1827), one of the finest of all masters of the haiku form, the succinct medium of writing a poem in only seventeen syllables. He describes visiting Mount Kamji, the consecrated hill in the inner precincts of the Ise Shrine (in fact a centre not of Buddhism but of Shinto):

> Kamji Yama.
> My head bent
> Of itself.[36]

In a single image the poet juxtaposes the grandeur of a famous sacred site with a very private and simple act of veneration. Likewise, many Zen masters caught the flavour of spiritual experience in pilgrimage poems like this one by Tesshu (1879–1939):

> On Visiting Sokei, Where the Sixth Patriarch Lived.
>
> The holy earth is overspread with leaves,
> Wind crosses a thousand miles of autumn fields.
> The moon that brushes Mount Sokei silvers,
> This very instant, far Japan.[37]

The specificity of a place sacred to Zen practitioners as the home of the sixth Patriarch Hui-neng is both generalised in the wind sweeping the thousand miles of fields and made to bring back the instantaneous memory of something personal to the writer – the image of far Japan. Tesshu's pilgrimage poem brings him not only to Hui-neng but also to himself as a Japanese far from home. In an ideal and yet very personal sense, pilgrimage in Japanese literature became an image for the whole path of personal progress leading to enlightenment.

Perhaps the supreme blend of poetry with the theme of pilgrimage came in the classic writings of Japan's most celebrated haiku master, Matsuo Basho (1644–94). Basho was born into a Samurai family and became known as a poet fairly young. He trained in Zen meditation under the priest Butcho, whose hermitage he visited in his pilgrimage to the north. Basho spent the last ten years of his life going on a number of pilgrimages, 'dressed', as he puts it, 'like a priest, but priest I am not, for the dust of the world still clings to me'.[38] In the opening of his *Records of a Weather Exposed Skeleton* Basho describes his motivation for pilgrimage:

Following the example of the ancient priest who is said to have travelled thousands of miles caring naught for his provisions and attaining to the state of ecstasy under the pure beams of the moon, I left my broken house on the River Sumida in the August of the first year of Jyokyo (1684) among the wails of autumn wind.[39]

For Basho the particular goal was less important than the wandering itself and the deep motivation for attaining an interior state, an ecstasy. He wrote several diaries of these journeys, which included poems within a prose account in the tradition of Ennin. He died on such a pilgrimage at the age of 50.

Basho's poems evoke very concrete and simple images. But through these images – their juxtaposition, the associations of their words, almost their very shape – he touches on the many moods of pilgrimage, and the changes of mood:

When worn out
And seeking an inn:
Wisteria flowers![40]

He does not need to describe relief or joy; the image of the wisteria, placed where it is, does the work. His poems also evoke moods and experiences not often recorded by those who idealise the pilgrims' path:

Fleas, lice,
A horse pissing
By my bed.[41]

In addition to his pilgrimage poetry, Basho wrote a number of prose travel sketches. He worked on and perfected the tradition of the prose account of pilgrimage in Japanese literature, and ultimately created *The Narrow Road to the Deep North* (also translatable as *The Narrow Way Within*), which is quite simply one of the most masterly and evocative travel books ever written. In the *Narrow Road*, the pilgrim's journey becomes an external metaphor for an inner progress. For instance, after visiting an ancient willow tree celebrated in a poem by the classic poet Saigyo, where 'for the first time in my life, I had an opportunity to rest my worn-out legs under its shade',[42]

after many days of wandering I came at last to the barrier gate of Shirakawa, which marks the entrance to the northern regions. Here, for the first time my mind was able to gain a certain balance and composure, no longer a victim to pestering anxiety, so it was with a mild sense of detachment that I thought about the ancient traveller who had passed through this gate with a burning desire to write home.[43]

The stages of the journey, in this instance the gate to the north, become symbols of the traveller's inner state. The 'first time' of rest under the fabled willow tree of poetry prefigures the 'first time' of composure for the pestered mind. The pilgrim is not only the 'I' who has gained 'a certain balance and composure', but also the ancient traveller with his burning desire to write, the 'Travel-Worn Satchel' and 'Weather-Exposed Skeleton' of Basho's earlier pilgrimage accounts. The text freely plays with Basho's earlier texts, with the great tradition of pilgrimage poetry in Japan (for instance the work of Saigyo) and with the model of pilgrimage as an activity in Japanese culture. Mirroring Zen doctrine, Basho paints a portrait of the road which is also a portrait of the mind, a picture of an outer process which is untendentiously, suggestively, a picture of an inner voyage.

The places which Basho visits and chooses to record can all be read metaphorically as states of mind. Their names – for instance, the waterfall 'See-from-behind', the 'Murder Stone', the 'Shadow Pond'; above all the 'Deep North' – are as suggestive as Bunyan's 'Slough of Despond' while masquerading as actual places rather than heavy allegories. They do not demand to be read metaphorically, and the book *can* be seen as a straightforward factual record with a few poems thrown in. But it can also be read metaphorically without any forcing. As in haiku itself, where a philosophical or metaphysical reflection is embodied in a brief and concrete poetic expression (usually quite unphilosophical, apparently),

so the *Narrow Road* as a whole is an extended concrete reflection of an inner spiritual journey. As such it represents a culmination of the haiku vision by expanding it from the brevity of a seventeen-syllable poem to an extensive narrative.

Basho's journey becomes a path through many worlds – the sadness of the concubines at Ichiburi or the parting from his travel companion Sora, the aesthetic beauty of landscape, seascape or mountain, the finesse of the painter Kaemon whom he meets en route, the holy awe of the sacred sites. Like Pausanias at Eleusis, Basho does not reveal the holiest secrets to his readers:

I saw many other things of interest in this mountain [Mount Yudono], the details of which, however, I refrain from betraying, in accordance with the rules I must obey as a pilgrim.[44]

Yet his silence is not a dry silence, repressed by the rules. On the contrary, it carries powerful emotion:

> Forbidden to betray
> The holy secrets of Mount Yudono,
> I drenched my sleeves
> In a flood of reticent tears.[45]

In effect, Basho's narrative can be taken as a pilgrimage manual. It shows how any journey can become a voyage inside as well as outside. It hardly has a goal in the sense of a specific place – a Bodhgaya, Mount

70 Katsushika Hokusai, groups of pilgrims on the mountain, from the series *Thirty-six Views of Mt Fuji*, 1823–9, woodblock print. The print shows climbers at different stages of their pilgrimage to the peak of Mt Fuji. The inset at the top shows them gazing into the crater at the volcano's summit.

Wu-t'ai or Shikoku – but only the suggestive, ambivalent image of the Deep North. It takes in many places, some famous for history, some famous in poetry, some famously sacred. It also touches sites personally meaningful to Basho, such as the hermitage of his own meditation teacher Butcho, and others, unknown, just glimpsed as the traveller passes by. Basho shows pilgrimage bared to its Zen essentials as existential journey without goal, as metaphor for a spiritually lived life.

In contrast with this spiritual vision of a space without goals, a journey for the sake of the spiritual state of mind in which one travels, Tibetan Buddhism established a version of pilgrimage focused on sites of remarkably complex symbolism. For many Tibetans Mount Kailas (over 22,000 feet – 6,700 m – above sea-level in Western Tibet) represents the centre of the world. In the words of Lama Anagarika Govinda, 'to Buddhists, [Kailas] represents a gigantic Mandala of Dhyani-Buddhas and Bodhisattvas, as described in the famous *Demchog Tantra*: the "Mandala of the Highest Bliss".'[46] At least for learned and initiated Buddhist practitioners, the sacred mountain was mapped on to a Tantric text, so that the circumambulation (or *parikrama*) was a journey through a sacred space, a huge natural mandala which was held to be the abode of many gods. In the words of the Japanese monk, pilgrim and (perhaps) spy, Kawaguchi Ekai, who visited Tibet in 1897–1902,

As far as my knowledge goes, it is the most ideal of the snow-peaks of all the Himalayas. It inspired me with the profoundest feelings of pure reverence, and I looked up to it as a 'natural mandala', the mansion of a Buddha and Bodhisattvas. Filled with soul-stirring thoughts and fancies, I addressed myself to this sacred pillar of nature, confessed my sins and performed to it the obeisance of 108 bows . . .[47]

The initiate pilgrim to Kailas approaches the mountain in this spirit of 'soul-stirring' contrition. But what he or she experiences is the Tantric ritual of entering a mandala. In Lama Govinda's words, the pilgrim

approaches the mountain from the golden plains of the south, from the noon of life, in the vigour and full experience of life. He enters the red valley of Amitabha in the mild light of the sinking sun, goes through the portals of death between the dark northern and multi-coloured eastern valleys when ascending the formidable Dolma-La, the Pass of Tara, the Saviouress – and he descends, as a new born being, into the green valley of Akshobya on the east of Kailas, where the poet saint Milarepa composed his hymns, and from where the pilgrim again emerges into the open, sunny plains of the south, assigned to the Dhyani-Buddha Ratnasambhava, whose colour is that of gold.[48]

For Govinda, the *parikrama* of Mount Kailas is a meditative as well as an actual journey – a voyage through life and death. Its stages represent passages through the abodes of different deities, like the quadrants of Tibetan mandala paintings. At the peak of Kailas is located the Tantric deity Demchog (known also as Chakrasamvara, Heruka or Para-masukha), whom the ritual of this pilgrimage celebrates.

At the same time, Kailas is famous for its historical saints, such as Gotsangpa and in particular Milarepa, Tibet's most famous yogi and poet. Before their destruction after the Chinese invasion of 1959, its valley was

71 Portrait of Matsuo Basho dressed as a pilgrim. Ink and water-colour, Japanese, 17th century.

191

the site of a number of important monasteries by Lake Manasarovar. Pilgrims to Kailas venerate not only the great Mandala of Demchog, but also the cave of Milarepa and the site of the lake (Manasarovar) in which Buddha's mother, Queen Maya, was said to have bathed in a dream, to remove all human impurities before the Buddha's conception. The Buddha was described as descending into her womb from the direction of Mount Kailas, appearing like a white elephant in a cloud. So great was the faith of Tibetans in Mount Kailas and so fervent their sense of its sanctity that Kawaguchi Ekai 'noticed several young pilgrims of both sexes performing the journey according to the "one-step-one-bow" method, commonly adopted as a penance.'[49]

But, like Basho's vision of an inner journey matching the outer, the image of Kailas carried inner implications for Tibetans:

[Kailas] is called Meru or Sumeru according to the oldest Sanskrit tradition, and is regarded to be not only the physical but the metaphysical centre of the world. And as our psycho-physical organism is a microcosmic replica of the universe, Meru is represented by the spinal cord in our nervous system; and just as the various centres (Sanskrit: Cakra) of consciousness are supported by and connected with the spinal cord (Sanskrit: Meru-danda), from which they branch out like many-petalled lotus-blossoms, in the same way Mt Meru forms the axis of the various places of the supramundane world.[50]

Despite a deep difference from Japan in culture, tradition and even in its kind of Buddhism, the Tibetan pilgrimage to Kailas – at least in its ideal form – resembles that represented by Basho. The rich symbolism of deities, mandalas and mountains is mapped through microcosm and macrocosm in such a way that the *parikrama* of Kailas is both a physical journey and a metaphorical one. It is a voyage to the centre of the energies of the body as defined in Tibetan Buddhism and through the process of life and death. Like the Zen poetry of Basho's narrow road to the Deep North, the Tibetan imagery of incremental symbolism evokes a pilgrimage whose meanings are focused on the inner life as well as concerned with the outer difficulties of getting to Kailas and going round it.

TRAVEL AND SAINTHOOD: THE PILGRIM AS HOLY MAN IN BUDDHIST TRADITION

We have seen how, in subsequent literature (for instance the novel *Monkey*), pilgrims like Hsuan-tsang themselves came to be regarded as saintly, even as Buddhas. In Japanese culture, Basho as pilgrim holds a more potent position than he does as merely a classic poet. He is the archetypal Zen-poet, the Zen master as poet, the pilgrim. Just as the pilgrimages to Palestine by Christians such as Willibald or Egeria came to signify, in later accounts and hagiographies, that these were truly saintly people, so the pilgrimages of Basho came to imbue his life and works with an added charisma. This process of sanctifying the pilgrim is still very much alive in Buddhism. In the Theravada traditions of South-East Asia, the link between pilgrimage and sainthood has become a particular feature of the veneration of important Buddhist monks.

Let us take the recent case of the Thai meditation master Phra Acharn

Mun, who died in 1949 at the age of 80.[51] Not only had he trained a number of illustrious disciples, but he was himself regarded by many Thais as an *arhat*, or fully enlightened being. His life, as it has been recounted in the hagiographies written and published by his pupils since his death, was one of rigorous meditation practice and constant pilgrimage. His wanderings brought him into confrontation with wild animals and other dangers which had the effect of testing and purifying his mind. As he grew more saintly, Acharn Mun gathered many disciples around him who followed him in his wanderings; and he performed a number of what in other religious traditions would be regarded as miracles. These included curing the inhabitants of a village in Laos called Ban Tham of smallpox.[52] By the time of his death, the Acharn's ashes were regarded as relics and were much sought after.[53] In effect, pilgrimage – wandering as a monk, in the way the Buddha had himself wandered, as well as paying homage to holy places – became one of the defining features of Mun's sanctity.

According to the popular biography of another saintly monk, Luang Pu Waen (born in 1888), Waen never returned to his home village after

72 Pilgrims pressing gold leaf onto the leg and hands of the colossal stone Buddha at Wat Si Chum, Sukhothai, Thailand. Applying gold leaf in this way is a traditional practice of veneration in Thailand.

ordination. He explained this by saying that he had no home or relatives, since his affiliation was to his *wat* (or monastery) and his life was dedicated to Buddhism; for him there was no past, present or future, and because there were no parents or grandparents left in his home village, he could freely go on pilgrimage.[54] Waen's journeys as a monk led him to his spiritual master, Acharn Mun, to encounters with demons, wild beasts and a long lone pilgrimage through most of Indochina including Thailand, Laos and Burma. One of the miraculous results of his spiritual attainments, as reported in the popular stories, was the ability to fly through the air in meditative concentration.

Even today in modern Thailand, the ideal of the pilgrimage as a means of renouncing the world, one's personal history and one's home in order to confront a spiritual world is very much alive. The basic paradigm for this model is the Buddha's own life.[55] But in Thailand, instead of visiting the relics of the Buddha, ordinary pilgrims may have some access to the sanctity of exceptional monks by visiting them with amulets to be blessed.[56] Such amulets may perhaps be seen as the modern equivalent of the cult of relics. They may represent images both of the Buddha and of illustrious monks like Luang Pu Waen. Today pilgrimage in Buddhism is seen to offer not only the possibility of venerating the sacred traces, but even the much rarer and more ideal opportunity to follow the Buddha's own path to enlightenment itself.

73 OPPOSITE Mahabodhi Temple, Bodhgaya, India. Tibetan woman pilgrim performing devotions with candles and a prayer wheel in her left hand.

Epilogue:
Landscapes Reviewed

In July 1988 an interdisciplinary conference on pilgrimage was held in London. Historians, geographers, anthropologists and theologians gathered in the same room to discuss apparently the same subject. Yet, rather as sacred space can be contested by opposed interest-groups at any pilgrimage site, the theme of pilgrimage found itself transformed into an object of controversy by scholars starting from very different academic assumptions.[1] By coming together to debate the topic, researchers seemed to reinforce rather than dissolve disciplinary boundaries. Eventually, a published volume of papers emerged from the conference. However, instead of reflecting the diversity of viewpoints and religions that had been evident, the editors (both anthropologists) decided to limit the book's purview to a single academic discipline – anthropology – and a single religion – Christianity.[2]

There are excellent reasons for publishing an edited volume exclusively devoted to the anthropology of contemporary Christian pilgrimage, but the decision to do this in the context of the original conference begs a series of questions. Was the initial idea of encouraging *interdisciplinary* discussion on the theme of pilgrimage flawed from the start? Is pilgrimage in itself a single phenomenon? Can, therefore, the pilgrimage traditions of different cultures and religions be meaningfully compared?

These questions are central to this book. It has been written by collaborators from different academic disciplines, an anthropologist and an art historian. In self-contained chapters, we have presented pilgrimage traditions in divergent religious landscapes. The topographies of each religion have been studied in their own historical and cultural contexts. We have not thus far attempted systematically to compare examples of pilgrimage, nor to fit them into a single interpretative framework. Yet by placing accounts of sacred travel in different religions within the same volume we have encouraged their implicit comparison. The traditions have been forced into dialogue quite simply by being incorporated into a single work.

Our account has, moreover, indicated some initial points of comparison between pilgrimage practices in the brief sections which appear between the main chapters. In many of the religions explored in this book, people have appeared to engage in some strikingly similar activities. Hindus at Benares, Buddhists at Bodhgaya and Muslims at Mecca have all been seen to circumambulate sacred shrines and objects. Hindus, Buddhists and Christians all take objects such as ampullae or tokens back from a sacred site. Yet in what sense are they really doing the

74 Greek Orthodox pilgrim with an icon of the Virgin, Jerusalem, Easter 1984.

same thing? If one were to ask members of different religious traditions to give an account of their actions, each would produce radically different descriptions and interpretations.

Indeed, can we even compare pilgrimages in the *same* religious tradition from different periods in history? Phenomena like the wearing down of the foot of the statue of St Peter at the Vatican or of the black stone embedded in the wall of the Ka'ba, bear testimony to the continuous reverence shown by pilgrims at these sites over many centuries. This sense of continuity is based upon and seemingly reinforces the notion of a shared faith, transcending time. But the religions of medieval Christendom or the Arab empires are in reality very distant from Christianity or Islam in the twentieth century. Pilgrimage in a context of secularisation or pluralism is a radically different phenomenon from religious travel in an age when atheism was virtually inconceivable.

Perhaps, then, we should limit the focus still further, and ask instead whether fellow pilgrims who attend the same site at the same time undergo similar experiences. On a single day, the crowds gathered for a procession at Lourdes may indeed appear to enact a convincing display of collective and collaborative piety.[3] In what sense, however, are the individual experiences of pilgrims from, say, Ireland and Mexico at the Lourdes shrine easily comparable? They may be framed by the same rituals and occasion, but worshippers' perspectives are formed by their position in the crowd, their expectations, their cultural backgrounds.

In this epilogue, we address some of these difficult issues in two ways. First, we shall present a number of the main analytic approaches to pilgrimage, each of which would have been represented at the London conference. We therefore aim to give the reader a theoretical background through which to reconsider the material presented in the body of the book. Second, we wish to suggest which of these theories we find most fruitful, and add some observations of our own. It is crucial, as we have implied, to avoid the trap of setting up spurious generalisations which elide the clear differences between cultures. For instance, pilgrimage is commonly described as a universal quest for the self. But what does the 'self' mean in the context of immeasurably different attitudes to identity and personhood? Nevertheless, it is too glib merely to assert that no possible parallels exist between the traditions of sacred movement which we have explored. We therefore invite the reader to reflect on and argue with our discussion as to how one might seek to understand pilgrimage as a cross-cultural phenomenon.

Approaching pilgrimage: academic accounts

Writing of the London conference, Glenn Bowman characterises one of the academic fault lines in the study of pilgrimage as having emerged between those scholars who attempted largely 'descriptive' accounts of pilgrimage and those who tried to be more 'analytical'.[4] Historians tended to belong to the former category, accepting the possibility of analysing pilgrimage as a recognisable, bounded phenomenon but focusing on the particularities of and differences between individual sites as a means to reconstruct the past. In effect, such a historical approach, while accepting that general features of the phenomenon of pilgrimage exist, would want to explore the precise nuances and differences of each individual instance of pilgrimage at different moments in its development. The intellectual justifications of this approach are set out in the following uncompromising statement, published elsewhere, concerning the study of pilgrimage and shrines:

[There are] two weaknesses common to many studies. . . . One is a conflation of the evidence, the tendency to use information about different saints' cults indiscriminately to create a virtually generic 'cult of the saints'; the other is chronological compression, the failure to recognise that particular cults went through phases of prominence and obscurity.[5]

By way of contrast, but again in line with the fundamental assumptions of their particular discipline, anthropologists at the conference attempted to analyse pilgrimages as reflections of broader social processes, such as the formation of particular kinds of group identity, or the operations of the state. In effect, pilgrimage was presented not so much as a distinct phenomenon in itself but instead a variegated activity that could be explained in terms of – almost dissolved into – its social, cultural and political contexts. As Bowman remarks, this emphasis caused a certain degree of friction:

One of the historians succinctly set forth the frustration felt by non-anthropologists with the apparent refusal of the anthropologists to discuss pilgrimage as a bounded entity when he said, after the late Saturday afternoon departure of the most vocal contingent . . ., 'now that the anthropologists are gone we can get down to talking about pilgrimage'.[6]

If the anthropological attempt to dismantle the category of pilgrimage proved intellectually unacceptable to academics from other disciplines, it nevertheless formed the basis of the volume which emerged from the conference. In their introduction the editors, John Eade and Michael Sallnow, saw themselves as setting up a new agenda in pilgrimage studies by asserting that 'pilgrimage is above all an arena for competing religious and secular discourses, . . . for conflict between orthodoxies, sects, and confessional groups . . .'.[7] These authors invoked the notion of the sacred in their title (Contesting the Sacred) only to reveal it – at least in its manifestation in pilgrimages – as a fragmented, ambiguous, ideological battleground. Thus Lourdes was presented in the book as a locus of conflict between lay and élite in the organisation and definition of the site, while the solid walls of Jerusalem melted into the many different holy cities experienced by pilgrims of different confessions – Catholic, Baptist, Orthodox, let alone Jewish or Muslim.[8]

In this anthropological view the idea of the sacred as a transcendent, universal and unified reality, utterly divorced from mundane concerns, is a collective fiction constructed in order to bolster particular social positions. Such a perspective has its distant roots in the work of the highly influential turn-of-the-century sociologist Emile Durkheim.[9] The latter saw religious belief and practice as emerging from, idealising and reinforcing human concerns and communities, so that the sacred existed not as a spiritual reality but rather as a product of social forces.

Some anthropologists of pilgrimage have explored the Durkheimian legacy by linking the worship of sacred symbols to the formation of group identities, for instance arguing that the Virgin of Guadalupe can be seen not merely as a pilgrimage shrine but also as a unifying symbol for the whole of Mexico.[10] Others have agreed with Durkheim that sacred symbols and ideas are regarded by humans as 'set apart' from the mundane world and unquestionable, but have gone on to note that they can therefore be used to legitimise unequal power relations in society.[11]

This, after all, is a basis of Marxist critiques of religion which see it as a false friend to the devout – a solace for the needy but also a link in the chain of their oppression.

Eade and Sallnow's analysis of pilgrimage, while opposing the Durkheimian idea of a sacred shrine functioning as a symbol of un-challenged unity and identity, nevertheless reveals its anthropological agenda by arguing that the varied cultural assumptions of pilgrims and the power struggles of society are evident at pilgrimage sites. For them, the sacred embodied in pilgrimage sites becomes 'a religious void' open to conflicting interpretations, 'a vessel into which pilgrims devoutly pour their hopes, prayers and aspirations'.[12] Following the logic of their approach, Eade and Sallnow even speculate whether one should frag-ment

the very category of 'pilgrimage' into historically and culturally specific be-haviours and meanings. For, if one can no longer take for granted the meaning of a pilgrimage for its participants, one can no longer take for granted a uniform definition of the phenomenon of 'pilgrimage' either.[13]

Ironically perhaps, this view echoes that of many historians in its plea for detailed analyses of the unique aspects of sites and the particular cultures of pilgrims rather than the forming of broad and therefore potentially vacuous generalisations. Yet, while most historians of the Middle Ages (say) would not contest the existence of pilgrimage in medieval Christendom, the implications of Eade and Sallnow's position go much further, since they are prepared to contemplate actually aban-doning the idea that pilgrimage as a socially discrete phenomenon even exists.

If anthropologists at the conference were opposed to historians (and, one suspects, almost everybody else) in their mistrust of pilgrimage as a meaningful category of behaviour, the proponents of these two disci-plines did appear to unite in their relative lack of interest in a third approach evident in London: that of religious functionaries. Professional academics at least agreed to adhere to a principle of neutrality on spiritual matters, but members of the Church were actively concerned to discuss how research could help make pilgrimages more attractive in their drawing-power and more effective as religious guides to the faithful. Pilgrimage here was regarded not so much as an object of study *per se* but as a means to a broader, religiously motivated, end.

The view that pilgrimages are, above all, opportunities to encounter a holy realm that actually does exist – and cannot be explained away by social-scientific theory – expresses a radically different perspective from that of Durkheim. For instance, the historian of comparative religion Mircea Eliade conceived of the sacred as inhabiting a realm transcending time and mundane concerns but accessible through religious experi-ence.[14] While anthropologists, then, seek to define the sacred *through* the filter of society, scholars such as Eliade – and, of course, priests and practitioners actively involved in practising or teaching their faith – have sought to affirm the existence of the sacred *beyond* society.

It is difficult to see how strong adherents of either of these positions would find it easy to engage in a common debate about any religious phenomenon. Nevertheless, possibly the most influential theory of pilgrimage (and one which was acknowledged if not followed in many of the conference papers) has been produced by two anthropologists, Victor and Edith Turner, whose writings reveal both religious and social scientific sensibilities.[15] The Turners argue that, in embarking on a sacred journey, pilgrims typically leave the demands of conventional social structure far behind and enter a world of 'antistructure'. Everyday norms of social status, hierarchy and interaction are ideally abandoned in favour of the development of spontaneous association and shared experiences. A temporary state of what is termed 'communitas' can be reached, as the pilgrim enters a special time, set apart from the everyday. Pilgrimage sites not only commemorate the lives of deceased holy figures, therefore, they also encourage the temporary 'social deaths' of their visitors.[16]

Such a view seems to be supported by the location of many sites on the political or economic periphery of societies: Mecca may be 'the navel of the earth' to Muslims but it is not a centre of secular administration as such, and nor is Benares. We have also seen how pilgrims frequently avoid the overt display of status differences by the wearing of standard clothes – one can think of the black garments of devotees of Lord Ayyappa in India, the staff and scrip of the medieval Christian pilgrim in Europe, or the white robes of Muslims at Mecca – and converge on a sacred site for the common purpose of worship. Victor Turner has even speculated that pilgrimages resurface at periods of rapid social change and consequent removal from conventional ties, such as the waning of the Roman Empire, the end of the Middle Ages, and the contemporary era.[17]

The Turners' theory provides, on one level, a neat means of sidestepping conventional anthropological views of religion as a phenomenon embedded in everyday social concerns and structures because it argues that pilgrimages are precisely those occasions when people can, temporarily, escape such constraints (although of course some pilgrimages contain a high level of obligation, such as that to Mecca, those of the early Israelites, or some medieval Christian penitential examples).[18] An element of Eliade's concept of the sacred is present: the notion of transcending the everyday world. Yet, perhaps not surprisingly, the idea of pilgrimage as providing unproblematic access to 'communitas' has been criticised sharply by social scientists who argue that the Turners ignore the secularly inspired divisions between pilgrims. Glenn Bowman, for instance, accuses the theory of separating interpretation 'from the constraints of history and society and [presenting communitas] as a transhistorical and omnipresent archetypal form'.[19] Eade and Sallnow's work also opposes the notion of communitas by replacing it with the idea of sites being arenas not of consensus and sharing but differing interpretations and contestation.

Where, then, does this discussion of varied perspectives leave us in our attempts to understand pilgrimage? Perhaps the first point that we should make is that our book has not been an attempt either to prove the correctness of any one religion, or indeed of any one academic line in the interpretation of pilgrimage, or to suggest how pilgrimage can be used as an effective means of disseminating any particular religious faith. We have, admittedly, indicated that the Turnerian notion of communitas is present as an ideal in many of the traditions we have studied (even if it is not expressed in the jargon of anthropology). Some of the key sites in the sacred geography of religious traditions have indeed been perceived by pilgrims as arenas of potential religious solidarity: Mecca for Muslims, the road to Pandharpur in Irawati Karve's account, the sites of the Buddha's life in northern India, and Jerusalem bring together believers from all backgrounds and social levels.

Yet we have also shown that communitas is only an ideal. Such sites cannot be regarded as separate from their socio-economic surroundings in their foundation or continued popularity.[20] Many pilgrimages not only involve situations of conflict and social division, but are also liable to be controlled by powers more temporal than spiritual. Mecca, Jerusalem and Amritsar have clearly been placed under considerable, often disputed, political authority during their long histories. In our picture section on contested sites (pp. 48–51), we have also suggested how symbolically charged spaces become arenas for architectural as well as ideological conflicts, as the buildings at Benares and Jerusalem indicate.

The arguments put forward by Eade and Sallnow are, therefore, clearly powerful in their assessments of the realities of pilgrimage. One cannot avoid the fact that pilgrims, even those visiting the same place, engage in a multiplicity of frequently incompatible interpretations, even if it is the case that Eade and Sallnow are describing ritual contexts particularly characteristic of contemporary, pluralist, highly mobile societies.[21] Although a pilgrimage centre is fixed in space it is not fixed in significance. Part of the fascination of studying pilgrimage lies precisely in examining the juxtaposition of varying views, as we have tried to show in our descriptions of varied perspectives on Mecca, or competing definitions of divinity in Andean pilgrimages.

However, while agreeing that *Contesting the Sacred* has set up a fruitful new agenda for study in a post-Turnerian world of analysis, one may also suggest that certain aspects of its arguments need to be modified. Eade and Sallnow have in a sense invoked the idea of pilgrimage only to dismiss it as a meaningful category for study. One can argue, however, that while virtually all social practices are open to contestation, not all have the look of pilgrimage. In other words, the emphasis on the idea of pilgrimage sites being void of intrinsic meaning does tend to ignore the considerable *structural* similarities in pilgrimage practices within and between traditions. There are indeed parallels in behaviour to be found across time and culture, even if the implications and meanings of such behaviour vary enormously. Eade and Sallnow admit this point by noting in their introduction that Christian pilgrimage, and perhaps the pilgrimage practices of all scriptural traditions, can be examined as combining co-ordinates of 'persons', 'texts' and 'places',[22] but they do not attempt to follow up this idea in any detail, nor do they discuss the fact that these elements are evident also in many other forms of ritual.

Such lack of comparison is unfortunate, given that the material we have presented indicates that pilgrimages do indeed provide rich possibilities

75 OPPOSITE Durham Cathedral from the west. The tomb of Bede in the Galilee Chapel at the western end of the cathedral serves as a counterpart to that of Cuthbert behind the high altar at the east. The sacred topography of Durham, as the vessel in which these two sets of relics are contained, is delimited by the two tombs at opposite ends of the church.

for analysis of the way in which places interact with, for instance, texts. A sacred text can provide an authoritative charter for spaces or objects, defining them as sacred or as the sites of significant events. According to the Koran, Muhammad fled from Mecca to Medina before returning in triumph, while the Suttas state that the Buddha was enlightened under the bodhi tree at Bodhgaya and delivered his first sermon at the deer park in Sarnath. These and other places both physically exist and gain mythological significance from their location in words as well as in a landscape. There are even examples of the guardians of holy sites actually 'generating' sacred texts to justify their sanctity, as we have seen in the Hindu tradition. Likewise, a revelation, such as that of the Virgin at Guadalupe or that of Krishna to Chaitanya at Brindavan in India, may establish the sacredness of a place. (Though sites which are not specifically mentioned in scripture, but are the products of human revelation, may be particularly prone to vagaries of fortune: Walsingham, for example, lay dormant for centuries as a pilgrimage centre after its destruction at the time of the Reformation.) In turn, holy locales can serve as witnesses of the truth of a text or revelatory event: as the pilgrim encounters a holy place, he or she experiences physically what had previously been known only through sacred narrative or its visual illustrations.

An examination of the relationship between persons and places raises further important questions in the comparative analysis of pilgrimage. Sacred sites, such as that of San Giovanni Rotondo associated with Padre Pio, or the tombs of Muslim sufis, often act as permanent reminders of the charisma of a person who has died years, possibly centuries, earlier. At Durham Cathedral in England are the burial-places not only of St Cuthbert but also of the Venerable Bede, the great Saxon historian of the English Church and biographer of Cuthbert. Such tombs and the relics they house represent tangible incarnations of the holy in material form.

Most pilgrims make relatively little impact on a site, except to reinforce its sanctity by their presence: their experience lasts the length of a fallible lifetime's memory. However, actions and responses of powerful pilgrims can leave a permanent mark on the pilgrimage landscape, thus illustrating a further kind of relationship between persons and places. The individual experiences and motivations of such people are transformed into permanent representations and material embodiments which alter irrevocably the journeys of future religious travellers. This is particularly evident in those instances where one person's pilgrimage acquires a special political or religious significance. St Helena transformed forever the nature of travel to the Holy Land by building churches and, according to legend, discovering the True Cross. The Indian emperor Ashoka built roads and stupas in all the holy places associated with the Buddha, and went to them on pilgrimage himself. Muhammad did not create an entirely new pilgrimage tradition at the Ka'ba, but he did transform an already existing practice by appropriating it to Islam. David and Solomon relocated and further centralised the pilgrimages of the Israelites by establishing the Ark and Temple at Jerusalem.

In actual experience (as opposed to analytical abstraction), the elements of 'person', 'place' and 'text' coincide. The pilgrim to Durham, for instance, would not know that a particular tomb in the cathedral housed the remains of a saint such as Bede or Cuthbert unless he or she were led there by guides, or unless the tomb were marked out as special by an inscription and (before the iconoclasm of the sixteenth century) by images. The cathedral itself can be seen in all its grandeur as an architectural celebration and container for the saint's relics, marking his final resting place in the landscape of northern England. The myth of St Cuthbert, moreover, tells not only how the saint exemplified Christian ideals in his lifetime (as proved by the incorruptibility of his corpse after death), but also how his body was carried on its own posthumous pilgrimage through Northumbria to keep it safe from the Vikings. The body performed a number of miracles en route, before it arrived at its final goal and resting place in Durham.[23] The medieval narratives about the person of St Cuthbert thus provided a charter for the holinesss of Durham as a pilgrimage centre through telling the story of the pilgrimage of the relics themselves in their passage to the town.

These general observations indicate how pilgrimage sites act as embodiments of myth-history, allowing adherents to reinvoke elements of their faith in words, images and physical actions. We also see how the idea of pilgrimage consisting of a series of co-ordinates is useful in that we are encouraged to think of it not so much as a static and constant entity but rather as a shifting constellation of features, often familiar from other contexts. We may even regard pilgrimage as made up of a composite of different elements – such as ritual, organised travel, objects of veneration, the construction of temporary 'communities' at special sites, sacrifices of time and effort, requests and offerings directed towards sacred figures – all of which occur in other spheres of life. Precisely because these elements are present elsewhere, pilgrimage is difficult to isolate as a discrete phenomenon. Any given pilgrimage may emphasise one or more of these elements over the others. A pious traveller to Mecca or Jerusalem, for whom the trip is likely to be a spiritual high-point, undergoes a different experience from, say, a Roman merchant who pays a visit to the Vatican as part of religious routine. Yet both these types of activity involve varying degrees of ritual, travel and worship at places of paramount spiritual import.

Mention of travel invokes one of the vital elements of pilgrimage that Eade and Sallnow's co-ordinates do not include: that of movement. Apart from involving travel across the landscape (even in those cases where the journey has no specific goal), pilgrimage practices tend to ritualise motion at a sacred site itself. Circumambulation, for instance, both echoes the broader idea of journeying and also demarcates – one can almost say 'encapsulates' – the sacred image or object which has been the goal of the pilgrimage. Even in contemporary pilgrimages, where the traveller may have arrived by bus, car or even plane, prescribed movement on foot often occurs within the site itself. In addition, and very significantly, pilgrimage in the world religions serves to link geographically dispersed peoples by giving travellers the possibility to perceive a common religious identity which transcends parochial assumptions and concerns. As a religious practice, pilgrimage has therefore complemented and incorporated other trans-local activities such as trade, exploration and even scholarly exchange.

The experience of pilgrimage, rather than being a static object or representation, involves not only movement through space but also an active process of response as the pilgrim encounters both the journey and the goal. It is the experience of travel and the constant possibility of encountering the new which makes pilgrimage distinct from other forms of ritual in the religions we have examined. An element of implicit comparison is likely to be evident between the pilgrim's home culture and those of the environments through which he or she moves. This tendency to compare indicates one of the primary differences between pilgrimage in the world religions and that in community religions such as those specific to a particular ethnic group or territorially restricted culture. (We have touched on some instances of 'community pilgrimage' in looking at classical antiquity and pre-Diaspora Judaism.) It is undoubtedly the case that small-scale cultures, groups and even nations have pilgrimages (a classic case being Shintoism in Japan, which focuses for instance on the Ise shrine as a sort of national holy of holies). But sacred travel *outside* one's home culture is perhaps a defining characteristic of the way pilgrimage has developed in the world religions.

The pilgrim in a world religion is often faced with an inevitable disjunction between the ideally universal tenets of the faith and the fact that such faith is interpreted and practised variously by members of very different societies. Thus the study of pilgrimages in such contexts consistently raises fascinating questions concerning the relationship between widely applicable tenets of faith and local cultures. To put this another way, universalising cultures of 'belief' are placed in tension with parochial cultures rooted in 'place'.

In returning home, the pilgrim can act as the agent of change, by spreading new ideas gleaned on the journey. Pilgrims may also be prompted to view their domestic environment in novel ways – as Victor Turner puts it, 'going to a far place to understand a familiar place better'.[24] Take the case of Felix Fabri, a Dominican friar from Ulm, who twice visited the Holy Land in the 1480s.[25] He recorded his travels in his long Latin *Evagatorium* written for his brother monks, as well as in a German version perhaps designed for a different audience. Fabri's first pilgrimage in 1480 did not prove a success: after a long journey from Ulm via Venice,

We did not spend more than nine days in the Holy Land, and in that time we rushed around the usual Holy Places both by day and by night, and were hardly given any time to rest. . . . When we had hurriedly visited the Holy Places . . . we were led out of the Holy City by the same road by which we had come, down to the sea where our galley waited.[26]

The speed of the journey, the mainly mercenary interests of the Venetians who brought his group of pilgrims to Palestine, and the voyage's general failure to live up to Fabri's ideals of what a pilgrimage should be, were followed by not only a storm and sea-sickness on the way back, but also by a sense of dissatisfaction. Yet far from discouraging him, this negative experience increased his desire really to see and know the Holy Land. He made a second, successful, journey in 1483 and returned after nearly a year feeling that he had been transformed. When he wrote a treatise on his home city of Ulm, some six years after his trip to Palestine, Fabri wrote of the city as 'the place from which my wandering began and where it came to an end'. Indeed, Ulm did not appear to be the same city on his return:

I would hardly have recognised the look of the city . . . if the surroundings which could not be changed, had not proved that it was the old Ulm.[27]

However, the extent to which pilgrimage involves so strong a sense of transformation or indeed an explicit confrontation with the new, either for the traveller or for those to whom he or she returns, is obviously subject to particular circumstances. Pilgrims who travel in a group of like-minded companions may not need to deal directly with the challenge of the exotic. The Turkish Muslims whom we followed on their journey to Mecca certainly faced the trial of meeting a distant holy place as well as pilgrims from other cultures; yet this experience was cushioned by the fact that they travelled in a group of fellow villagers. On returning home, their accounts conformed rather than conflicted with local assumptions.

Because some pilgrimage sites – such as Mecca – attract worshippers from widely dispersed cultural locations, their symbolic resonances must appeal on multiple, even contradictory, levels. Eade and Sallnow state that:

76 The monastery of St Catherine at Mt Sinai, 6th century AD. The monastery, a small walled fortress in the wilderness of Horeb, is here shown from the path taken by pilgrims to the mountain where Moses received the tablets of the Law.

... in the final analysis ... what confers upon a major shrine its essential, universalistic character [is] its capacity to absorb and reflect a multiplicity of religious discourses, to be able to offer a variety of clients what each of them desires.[28]

The more important a sacred centre, paradoxically, the more flexible and numerous are likely to be the meanings it encompasses. However, the title of Eade and Sallnow's book, which invokes the notion of *contesting* the sacred, rather bypasses the ways in which sites also help to *constitute* the sacred in the eyes of some believers, precisely by absorbing (even casting a discreet veil over) discrepant religious discourses. At Mecca the fact that explicit rules govern the behaviour of all pilgrims prevents, at least to some extent, the expression of idiosyncratic forms of worship. Even pilgrims at Hindu shrines are commonly encouraged to follow traditions and set routes in their passages to and round sacred places.

By being able to accommodate pilgrims from many cultures and social stations, sacred sites make divine powers accessible to far larger and more varied numbers of adherents than is often possible in everyday worship. This 'popular' aspect of much pilgrimage practice is reinforced further by the fact that sites offer religious experiences that do not rely exclusively on textual knowledge: rather, the charisma of place or person is brought 'down to earth' and embodied in tangible, often miracle-working objects, which by appearing to respond to the requests of worshippers heal or renew individual lives while also reinforcing the reputation of the shrine and even religion as a whole. Shrines frequently advertise their own efficacy by retaining records of miracles that have occurred under their auspices: the doorway of the contemporary Anglican shrine at Walsingham or the walls of the ancient Temple of Asclepius at Epidaurus, for instance, boast inscriptions and offerings of thanks from grateful pilgrims. The powers of the place are in turn diffused far and wide in the form of relics, ampullae, images and narratives. Even in a monotheistic, aniconic religion such as Islam – apparently so different from an internally variegated religion such as Hinduism – the sacred landscape consists not merely of Mecca, a textually justified place of pilgrimage, but also of many other sites of local, perhaps culturally specific, significance. Sometimes (rather as relics spread the influence of a person or site) the charisma of a place is even diffused by the 'replication' of that place far from its original location. Benares, for instance, has many smaller counterparts in the Indian subcontinent; Walsingham provides an Anglo-Saxon equivalent of Nazareth; a 'second Mecca' is said by some Muslims to exist in Ajmer.

The important function of pilgrimage in giving religious traditions concrete, tangible referents is indicated, ironically, by the fact that each world religion also contains those who forcibly deny the powers of place in the exercise of proper worship. Such attacks on pilgrimage have been waged on at least two fronts. Some, like the sufis who locate the sanctity of the Ka'ba within the self, Christians who speak of the Cross in the soul, or Hindus who find Benares rising in the heart, deny the importance of travel to an external, material location. They collapse the imagery of place into that of personal experience (in many ways, Bunyan's Puritan vision of the pilgrim's progress is an archetypal example of this tendency).[29]

Others, like the fourth-century Orthodox theologian Gregory of Nyssa, or Nanak, the first Sikh Guru, emphasise that the sacred cannot be confined or concentrated in any one place, but that it is everywhere.

Thus in our comparative survey of pilgrimages in many cultures we return – even in negative examples – to the significance of space and movement in articulating images of the sacred. Yet Eade and Sallnow's point is that pilgrimage sites have no meaning in themselves:

In the conventional view, the power of a miraculous shrine is seen to derive solely from its inherent capacity to exert a devotional magnetism over pilgrims from far and wide, and to exude of itself potent meanings and significances for its worshippers. The shrine is seen, so to speak, as *sui generis*: its power is internally generated and its meanings are largely predetermined. All the contributors to this symposium implicitly or explicitly contest this view.[30]

We do not deny that pilgrimage sites accommodate and perhaps even encourage multiple interpretations, and agree that the volume makes this point very persuasively, in well-chosen ethnographic detail. However, Eade and Sallnow's perspective runs the risk of discouraging analysis of how sacred space is orchestrated in pilgrimage sites, and how such organisation can have a considerable impact on the perspectives of pilgrims. Our chapters have shown, for instance, that sites often frame the actions of visitors in significant ways. After all, pilgrims cannot usually approach the Ka'ba at Mecca, Lord Ayyappa at Sabarimalai, or even some Christian shrines in any way they choose: their movements, and therefore their physical orientations in space, are frequently pre-scribed in ways which encourage outward conformity to religious norms. Sacred architecture and art can, after all, constrain the experience of the pilgrim, not least through giving meaning to the notion of movement itself.

At pilgrimage sites from Mecca to Benares, from ancient Olympia to modern Lourdes, official guides have existed to instruct the pilgrim in the proper sequences, forms and places for the carrying out of rites. At Lourdes, lay helpers direct people not only at the site itself but also at the local station and airport, so that their influence extends far beyond the confines of the shrine. At what for pilgrims is the most significant point of their journey, *brancardiers* (male lay assistants) facilitate and yet control the large numbers who come to bathe in the holy waters. They resist the carnival atmosphere of the bathers by regulating their exuberance through an appeal to ordered and prayerful calm, and by limiting numbers.[31] Thus the act of proceeding through a pilgrimage centre like Lourdes, which involves a number of rituals within the place, can itself take on a formalised – even a ritualised – quality. Even writing about a pilgrimage site may enshrine some of the patterns of such ritual, as when Pausanias recounts the altars of Zeus at Olympia in the order in which sacrifice was performed at them.

To illustrate and explore this argument concerning the 'constraining' functions of sites further, we shall discuss a pilgrimage centre we have analysed elsewhere in some detail: the sixth-century monastery of St Catherine at Mount Sinai.[32] The site marked the spot where Moses

77 The Transfiguration. Apse mosaic from the church of the Monastery of St Catherine at Mt Sinai. The mosaic, donated by the abbot Longinus and the deacon John in the 6th century, shows Christ transfigured between Moses (to his left) and Elijah (to his right). Beneath them are the apostles Peter (centre), James (right) and John (left). The medallion busts around the main image depict prophets and apostles.

received the tablets of the Law, and was also identified with the biblical Horeb, where he had seen the vision of the burning bush. It therefore attracted pilgrims from throughout the early Christian world – from the Latin-speaking west, the Greek north and east, the Coptic south and even from Armenia – and no doubt such a range of visitors would have brought with them very different cultural assumptions. Yet we cannot say that the site merely acted as 'an empty vessel', passively reflecting individual experience. Even before the pilgrim reached the monastery, his or her expectations would have been moulded by scripture and by the oral or written accounts of previous pious travellers (such as Egeria in the 380s, whose moving description of Sinai still survives). The monks at the site functioned in part as interpreters of and guides to the holy, using their linguistic abilities to make the site comprehensible to believers of any nationality or provenance. In addition, the layout and architecture of the place itself was significant in defining the pilgrimage experience.

Like the stational liturgies of the great capitals Constantinople and Rome, and also of the centre of Christian pilgrimage at Jerusalem, worship at Sinai involved the movement of groups of believers from sacred site to sacred site. The pilgrim not only visited the monastery, but also undertook a number of other controlled journeys, of less distance but ever increasing theological significance, such as to the rock where Moses struck water, a day's journey away from the monastery; to the burning bush, located at the eastern end of the church; to the spring where Moses watered sheep – associated in later tradition with Jethro's well where Moses met his wife Zipporah (see Exodus 2:16–22); to the cave where Elijah fled from king Ahab (I Kings 19:8), and finally to the peak of Mount Sinai, where Moses received the tablets of the Law.

The architecture of the sixth-century monastery delineated a path in its own right. The sixth-century fixtures, images and buildings of the monastery acted both to channel visitors through its sacred places and to locate the process of Sinai pilgrimage in a Christian interpretative frame. The pilgrim would arrive out of the desert into a small oasis, at the heart of which was the monastery. Inside was the church, and at its eastern (most sacred) end was the relic of the burning bush. On entering the building, the pilgrim's first sight would have been the remarkable mosaics at the eastern end which represented a hierarchy of theophanies from Moses' vision of the burning bush to his receiving of the tablets of the Law and to the vision of the Incarnate Christ at the Transfiguration. This journey into ever more interior space, the space of ever more intensive liturgical action, was emphasised by the fact that the site of the bush was the lowest part of the monastery, so that the pilgrim had to descend several steps into the church. Moreover, by completing the series of Old Testament theophanies afforded to Moses (at the burning bush and on the peak of Sinai) with the New Testament vision of Christ's Transfiguration, the arts at Sinai successfully accomplished the Christianisation of what was originally and textually a Jewish holy site.[33]

The path into and within the heart of the monastery was set against the ascent of Mount Sinai – the pilgrimage for which the monastery was the starting point. A series of prayer niches were built along the path which led up from the monastery to the summit. These marked significant spots, either places where the path joined another path, or places where pilgrims might glimpse a view of the distant mountain peak – their sacred goal. All such material marks on the local landscape not only recorded where previous believers had been, but also indicated a succession of mini-goals for pilgrims on their way to the summit of Sinai. At the top was a small church which marked the site where Moses had received the tablets of the Law. The final point of this pilgrimage was (like the descent within the monastery to the site of the bush) a descent to the cave where Moses had stood to receive the second lot of tablets and where he had been vouchsafed a vision of God.

The topography, images and architecture of sixth-century Sinai (much of it still surviving) performed a great deal of ideological work at the site. The theme of motion signifying transformation is implicit not only in the act of pilgrimage but also in the mosaic images of the church. Moses is depicted in front of the burning bush, and then again on top of the mountain, receiving the tablets of stone. This movement, expressed through representation, prefigures the actual journey of the pilgrim from the monastery to the peak of the mountain.

The Sinai example indicates further some of the close interactions between texts, places and person in the construction and maintenance of a pilgrimage site. Apart from being the physical embodiment of a place mentioned in the Bible, the site was moulded by its buildings and images into a context where the pilgrim's movement could be guided and converted into an ordered progression, culminating in the twin dramas of visiting the burning bush at the back of the church and reaching the site of the donation of the law at the mountain top. The art, architecture and narratives associated with the site celebrated, above all, sacred persons – principally Moses and Jesus – but were also presented to pilgrims at least partially through the interpretative filter of religious functionaries permanently located at Sinai.

While the Sinai case is far from, say, the pilgrimage to Lord Ayyappa in culture, geography and history, the sites are comparable in how they illustrate the funnelling of pilgrims through significant points in a sacred geography. Ayyappa does not feature prominently in canonical texts, unlike Moses (although he is present in local legends and folk songs), but images of both sacred figures are reached by a long and arduous journey punctuated by intermediate rituals and goals and culminating in a final ascent and highly charged 'vision'. In neither case is the pilgrim forced into adopting a fixed interpretation of the site or experience, but is rather prompted to move through the respective sites in ritually prescribed ways, so viewing the images and architecture from conventionalised perspectives.

In re-emphasising the importance of the physical layout of pilgrimage sites we are consciously calling to mind the image of landscape mentioned in the subtitle of this book. The word is an obvious choice in the sense that pilgrimage necessarily involves bodily movement through a physical environment. However, the image of landscape can be seen also as a powerful organising metaphor for examining pilgrimage cross-culturally and through time. If we think of pilgrimage as an institution made up of a constellation of features, the 'landscape' of any pilgrimage site consists not only of a physical terrain and architecture, but also of all the myths, traditions and narratives associated with natural and man-made features. Indeed, the word itself refers ambiguously but suggestively both to physical terrain and to the idea of representing nature in art.[34] Physical and myth-historical landscapes provide the backdrop to movement, so that in progressing through the physical geography a pilgrim travels and lives through a terrain of culturally constructed symbols.[35]

Pilgrimage in the world religions is a way of putting cultural assumptions of a given tradition to the test, precisely because it involves bringing the conceptual models belonging to one context (the pilgrim's home) into confrontation with the different conceptual frameworks evident in the cultures through which the pilgrim journeys. The particular features of a landscape partially constrain the physical movements and perceptions of pilgrims, and by retaining some continuity over years and centuries they can act to uphold the claims of transcultural and transhistorical religious traditions, yet they are also vulnerable to changes imposed by pilgrims. Choice landmarks, especially, are both attractions to communal experience and to contestation over ownership, decor and access. Moreover, a second trip through the same environment may prove surprisingly different from the first and may offer new insights and divergent interpretations.

Landscapes therefore allow for different routes to be taken and can be interpreted variously by those who move through them, but they also orient travellers in ways which the latter cannot entirely control. The job of the comparative scholar is not only to compare the pilgrimage landscapes of different religions as they exist at any given moment, but also the various features of a 'single' tradition as it changes over time, encountering processes of erosion or accretion, or perhaps theological 'earthquakes' which alter the sacred topography rather more suddenly.[36] In arguing this case, then, we hope to defend at least those aspects of the Turnerian approach to pilgrimage which emphasise the importance of analysing pilgrimages as extended case-histories, linking people, places, narratives and cultures in networks of constantly evolving relations.

PILGRIMAGE IN A 'SECULAR' AGE

While the metaphor of moving through a landscape describes any form of travel, our introduction and epilogue refer specifically to landscapes of the *sacred*.[37] We have therefore chosen to focus the body of the book on the major world faiths, and our approach fits well with conventional definitions of the religious. As a consequence, the themes we have highlighted in this epilogue, and perhaps even the book as a whole, may seem remote from the everyday lives of most people living in the modern 'secular' culture of the West. Yet there are a number of reasons why pilgrimage should not be seen as an anachronistic phenomenon. We have shown, for instance, that contemporary forms of travel have actually increased the ability of pilgrims to traverse large distances, and many sites are therefore more visited today than ever before.[38] As an institution involving the diffusion and intermingling of cultures over large distances, pilgrimage resonates with social processes that are occurring elsewhere in the increasingly globalised, plural societies of the world. Pilgrimages may even be gaining in symbolic significance in some societies, given that they constitute a potential means through which to react against an apparently dehumanised, secular world: one scholar speculates, for instance, that at least in Europe they provide people with the opportunity to explore contemporary forms of subjectivity and individualism that would have appeared distinctly puzzling to medieval travellers.[39] One can even argue that modern media of communication such as television and radio permit vicarious participation in pilgrimage for those who would otherwise lack either the will or ability to join in. The Marian pilgrimage to the site of El Rocio in Andalusia, for instance, has been filmed by both state and international television crews,[40] while the 1993 Mahamastabisheka ceremony, the climax of the twelve-yearly Jain pilgrimage to the colossal statue of Lord Gomateshvara at Shravanabelagola, was broadcast live on Indian television.

A further, more complex, reason exists for asserting the renewed vibrancy of pilgrimage in the present day. If we accept one aspect of a Durkheimian view of the sacred – the notion that the sacred is in some

78 OPPOSITE TOP
The Mausoleum of Lenin, Red Square, Moscow. This photograph was taken in the 1930s at the height of the cult of Lenin by the English photographer, travel-writer and spy, Robert Byron.

respects an embodiment and representation of societal ideals – we can argue that pilgrimage is currently taking on new forms that go far beyond standard religious practices.[41] Western society has been marked, for instance, not just by a decline in institutional support for the traditional religions but also by a notable increase in travel for its own sake. In this situation, tourism has become, itself, a kind of pilgrimage. Its devotees divide up their years between the profane cycle of work, based in their everyday environments, and brief periods of heightened leisure time. A holiday (the very word is derived from 'holy day') acquires a special quality from travel to a distant place. The objects of worship on these occasions may vary according to the tourist cult to which one subscribes. Some choose to honour the sun; others search for exotica in foreign cultures; a third category deliberately undergoes ascetic trials normally denied the inhabitant of a western city (climbing a mountain, trekking through a desert, wind-surfing or sailing). Those who undertake such journeys take as their guides not a conventional holy scripture but *Fodor's Guide to India*, the *Blue Guide to Greece*, or *Mexico on a Shoestring*. While away they prove their presence at the holiday site by sending postcards. On their return, they bring with them objects which retain the charisma of distant places – photographs, souvenirs and passport stamps.

The most famous instigator of mass leisure travel was Thomas Cook, himself a Baptist minister and social reformer, who specialised in arranging morally uplifting tours. Some of these actually involved journeys to the Holy Land itself, making explicit the association between pilgrimage and tourism. Before Cook, wealthy young men undertook the Grand Tour, whose focus was Italy. Like medieval pilgrims before them the grand tourists went to Rome and returned with relics, particularly classical remains for the private collections of stately homes.

One quality of holidays, particularly of going abroad, is the willingness to do things one would not normally do. The space of the exotic may serve as a licence for experiment and even self-discovery. In western Europe, tourism often takes the form of visiting churches or other religious monuments, which the traveller might never go to in his or her ordinary life. Locals rarely visit their churches, by comparison with the sea of foreigners in prestige sites like Notre-Dame, St Peter's, or King's College Chapel in Cambridge. (How many Londoners go to Westminster Abbey in the normal course of events, except when they have a foreign guest to show round?) The Catholic Church in Italy, in an attempt to distinguish between the entirely casual tourist and the more religiously motivated or respectful traveller (even the pilgrim), frequently bans scantily clad and 'improperly dressed' visitors from its great cathedrals. Likewise, churches have sometimes banned large groups taken round by tourist guides, or have ordained that only church-appointed guides may lead tours.

The boundaries between pilgrimage and tourism become blurred further in the case of commemoration of the dead. The mausoleum in Red Square containing the embalmed body of Lenin attracted both devotees of Communism and tourists from western countries, and a visit to the body could even be incorporated into wedding rituals.[42] The home (appropriately named Graceland) and grave of Elvis Presley have also become

79 OPPOSITE BOTTOM
Graceland, Memphis, USA. Teenage girl at Elvis' grave.

objects of veneration.[43] Presley, who flirted with Christianity and other religions in his lifetime, has become more accessible to his devotees in death than in life, and some who now visit the grave are too young to have seen him in his lifetime. Elvis T-shirts and badges can be bought, and an undercover trade in relics has also developed, including the marketing of his sweat, apparently preserved in glass phials. The grave is regularly covered with flowers, pictures and scraps of paper bearing both messages and prayers. Most who visit the site wear Elvis insignia, and some bear Christian symbols. On the anniversary of the star's death, a candlelight vigil is held by fans who progress slowly up a hill, past the house to the grave itself.

A more conventional goal for the secular pilgrim is the museum. Many museums (at least in the Anglo-Saxon world, for instance the British Museum) are traditionally designed as if they were Greek temples, imbued with a classical rather than Christian sanctity, a holiness vested in the distant past.[44] Like the relics in the treasury of a medieval cathedral, objects in a museum are enclosed within a series of frames which add to their sanctity. The glass museum case is a kind of reliquary; the museum room (labelled 'Egyptian', 'the Angerstein Collection' or 'Herbivorous Quadrupeds') is equivalent to the private chapel in the way it encases and classifies a particular selection of objects in a wider frame; finally, the museum itself proclaims architecturally its special purpose as temple of culture, just as a church's form announces its sacred function.

A medieval church encompasses a temporal as well as spiritual world. It is orientated in relation to all the points of the compass, so that the visitor locates his or her position within a much wider and more inclusive conceptual geography. Its imagery – stained-glass windows, sculpture, misericords – represents and thereby may incorporate the social levels of all the congregation. A church employs the universal Christian symbol of the cross, not only in its altarpiece and images, but also in its very form of nave and transepts. Likewise, the great museums – the Louvre, the 'Museums Island' in Berlin, the Museum complex on the Mall in Washington – are universal 'treasure chests' accumulating in one space prestige emblems of other cultures taken to represent the whole of human experience.[45] As Mary Beard has remarked of the British Museum,

. . . the Museum . . . is commonly defined by its visitors as the location of *all the world's history* – and its building signifies more than 'just a building'. It is the treasure chest itself, the (mystical) container of that totality, the frame that gives sense and order to the baffling array of the incomplete remains of all the past civilizations that lie inside.[46]

Just as pilgrimage sites include both universal and parochial centres, so museums vary in their appeal, ranging from all-inclusive reliquaries to the local exhibition of village life. While, let us say, the Museums Island in Berlin, with its spectacular architecture and state patronage, was designed as a kind of Jerusalem in its encompassment of cultural riches, so the average folk museum with its mementos of parish life in past times has counterparts in the village *tirtha* in Hindu India or the local saint's tomb in Islam.

In the larger centres of both pilgrimage and museum visiting, it is necessary to appeal to a wide range of possibly conflicting constituencies.[47] At museums and pilgrimage centres, universal and parochial, the visitor confronts a specially constructed and idealised version of the identity of a community or society. The historical overview provided by the hugely popular National Air and Space Museum in Washington DC incorporated, at least until the early 1980s, galleries on the First and Second World Wars, yet barely mentioned either the Korean or the Vietnam Wars.[48] While the world wars provided uplifting hero-tales of American triumph, the latter – far more ambiguous in their morality and outcome – constitute some of the deepest traumas in North American culture.

Like the major museums, pilgrimage centres gain from charitable benefactors, but such beneficence is also inevitably a means of control. The often idealised picture of a society presented by a sacred site or a museum corresponds to the particular vision of its powerful donors and its dominant clientele. This picture, in both museums and places of pilgrimage, is defined by its particular construction of a mythical past, a 'squeamish selection of ancestors' as one anthropologist has put it.[49] While all kinds of cultural artefacts, from newspapers to books, from films to adverts, also construct a mythologised vision of the past, what is special about pilgrimage and museum visiting is that those who come to the site play an active part in recreating the story as they proceed through its topography. The act of movement becomes itself an act of reading.

In both cases, what is read and interpreted are not only texts, but also material objects and remains. Moreover, as we have argued, movement is not usually random, but guided by particular routes, liturgies and tours. Museum guides, labelled plans and the very placement of the cases or displays tell a particular story. As Carol Duncan has put it, 'visitors to a museum follow a route through a programmed narrative'.[50] Such programmes may adopt very different forms. Many provide a crash-course through 'masterpieces'; take for example the Vatican Museum's four routes labelled A, B, C and D (each with a different colour code) which include more or less famous objects depending on the time visitors have available for their trip. At the Pitt-Rivers Museum in Oxford, objects are deliberately grouped by function rather than cultural origin or artist. At the two opposite ends of the Air and Space Museum in Washington DC, galleries in the 1980s were devoted to air travel (implying the past) and space travel (implying the future) respectively. The viewer, who moved from looking at the Wright brothers' plane to an Apollo space craft, was encouraged to retell a story of evolutionary progress, not entirely distinct from the space race and American triumphs.

Museums do not merely incorporate a 'ritual' structure: often they boast a specific material object which takes an emblematic and resonant quality as apparently defining the essence of the museum. The visitor's actions relating to this object indicate its special nature. Here is a description of the moon stone, the most significant object in the Air and Space Museum:

80 The British Museum.

The moon rock is an actual piece of the moon retrieved by the Apollo 17 mission. There is nothing particularly appealing about the rock; it is a rather standard piece of volcanic basalt some 4 million years old. Yet, unlike many other old rocks, this one comes displayed in an altar-like structure, set in glass . . . As the sign says, touch a piece of the moon. Touching the moon rock is an act of sanctification, an act that the visitor does willingly. . . . Touching it is not significantly different from genuflection.[51]

In the British Museum, meanwhile, the supreme object is the Rosetta Stone. Set on a base a couple of feet from the floor and surrounded by a rail, the Rosetta Stone stands on a main thoroughfare of the museum, at the entrance to the main gallery of Egyptian sculpture. Few visitors can comprehend the writing on the stone and yet for many its physical presence holds a certain fascination:

. . . [the] visitors' desire to make *contact* with the Stone, combined with the museum's acceptance of that desire, also confirms its talismanic properties within the context of a museum visit. Touch the Stone; touch the Museum.[52]

81 The Rosetta Stone, British Museum.

Is there any way in which such activity echoes what we have seen in conventional, overtly religious pilgrimage? Is the moon rock equivalent in any sense to the miracle-working Madonna of Czestochowa in Poland or the meteoric rock in the Ka'ba? As we have pointed out, straightforward parallels do not work. But in their particular contexts, as symbolically rich end-points of a journey to a site and controlled movement within that site, they have similar qualities. In front of such relics, a person is confronted – literally put in touch with – a tangible embodiment of all that the place might represent. As David Meltzer says of the moon rock:

Everyone touches it. Why? Because this object, perhaps more than any other piece of material culture in the Museum, hails you. The moon rock 'marks the most spectacular chapter [of the space adventure] so far' . . . On one level, it is a metaphor for the space programme . . .[53]

Or as Mary Beard puts it of the Rosetta Stone:

> The Stone itself and the decipherment that it allowed, has come to be constructed as a talisman for the museum, for museum culture and for the past time that that culture claims to embody. . . . The Stone acts as an almost mystical key to the hidden world of history.[54]

Our analogy between museum visits and pilgrimage has yet a further dimension. The final stop in a trip to a museum (and often also its starting point) is frequently the museum shop. The tokens one purchases – postcards, replicas, books – are a way of bringing home something of the charisma of a special location. They are the relics and reproductions of a cultural centre. Like pilgrim tokens, such objects represent a particular selection of that which is most significant about the museum. If Byzantine ampullae from the Holy Land frequently depicted the Holy Sepulchre, and medieval pilgrimage tokens from Rome were impressed with the motto of St Peter's keys, it is revealing that the most popular postcard on sale at the British Museum shop is the Rosetta Stone itself.[55]

It may be that conventionally secular forms of pilgrimage, from tourism to museum visiting, are no more than distant analogies for the phenomenon of sacred travel, despite their rather close structural resemblances and historical links with pilgrimage in the world religions. Certainly, the initiate into a religious system might have trouble recognising the 'sacred centre' at the heart of a trip to the sun or a Sunday afternoon in the Metropolitan Museum. Yet, it is a mark of the power of pilgrimage as a ritual structure in human experience that so many of its qualities should have taken contemporary forms. Despite revolutions in communications technology and cultural identity, pilgrimage has proved remarkably persistent in adapting to and even appropriating the innovations of secular modernity.

Notes and Bibliographies

Introduction: Landscapes Surveyed

1. For a discussion of what is meant by the 'sacred', see individual chapters and particularly the Epilogue.
2. See for instance the bibliographic volume by L. K. Davidson and M. Dunn-Wood, *Pilgrimage in the Middle Ages: A Research Guide*, New York and London, 1993.

1 Piety and Identity: Sacred Travel in the Classical World

Translations of classical sources are the author's own or taken (and often adapted) from the following versions:

Aristophanes, *The Birds*, trans. D. Barrett, Harmondsworth, 1978.
Euripides, *Ion*, trans. P. Vellacott, Harmondsworth, 1954, and trans. A. P. Burnett, Englewood Cliffs (N.J.), 1970.
Homer, *The Odyssey*, trans. E. V. Rieu, Harmondsworth, 1946.
Lucian, *The Syrian Goddess*, trans. in Attridge and Oden.
Pausanias, *Description of Greece*, trans. W. H. S. Jones, London and Cambridge (Mass.), 1918–35.
Philostratus, *The Life of Apollonius of Tyana*, trans. E. C. Conybeare, London and Cambridge (Mass.), 1912.
Pindar, *The Epinicean Odes*, trans. C. M. Bowra, Harmondsworth, 1969.
Pliny the Younger, *Letters and Panegyrics*, trans. B. Radice, London and Cambridge (Mass.), 1969.

1. Plotinus, *Ennead* 1, 6, 8, 22. On the allegorical Odysseus, see Lamberton, pp. 41–3, 106–7, 119–20, 129–33, 221–32.
2. On the Christian Odysseus, see Rahner, pp. 328–86.
3. On the Parthenon and its decoration, see for instance Boardman (1985).
4. See esp. Neils; also Boardman (1985), pp. 223–5, Simon, pp. 55–72, and Parke, pp. 33–50.
5. Barber in Neils, pp. 103–18.
6. Simon, pp. 18–24, and Parke, pp. 82–8, 158–62.
7. On the Parthenon frieze see Robertson and Frantz, Boardman (1984), Osborne, and Jenkins.
8. On Athena Parthenos and Athena Polias see Herington and Kroll; for an account of the different Athenas on the Athenian Acropolis see Ridgway in Neils, pp. 119–42; on Aphrodite Pandemos see Simon, pp. 48–51.
9. On the Dionysia, see Goldhill.
10. On athletics and music at the Panathenaea see the essays by Kyle and Shapiro in Neils.

11. See for example Drees, Finley and Pleket, and Raschke.
12. On oracles see Flacelière, with Parke and Wormell on Delphi in particular; on temple medicine see Edelstein, vol. 2, pp. 139–80.
13. On priests in general, see the essays in Beard and North.
14. On these themes in Hellenistic religion, see Martin.
15. On Asclepius and Epidaurus see Edelstein, vol. 2.
16. Ibid., vol. 1, p. 229.
17. Ibid., p. 230.
18. Ibid., p. 230.
19. On such inscriptions generally (though in a discussion focused more on the Roman world) see Beard.
20. Generally on Roman pilgrimage see MacMullen, pp. 18–48, and Lane Fox, pp. 64–261 (on Asia Minor).
21. On the imperial cult see, for example, both Price and Fishwick.
22. Beard, pp. 39–40.
23. See Nock, and Lane Fox, pp. 166–7.
24. Nock, p. 58.
25. Ibid., pp. 61f.
26. See Attridge and Oden.
27. See Frazer, introduction; Habicht; Veyne, pp. 3, 71–7, 96–102; Elsner.
28. See both Mylonas and Kerenyi.

A. H. Armstrong (ed.), *Classical Mediterranean Spirituality*, London, 1986.
H. W. Attridge and R. A. Oden, *De Dea Syria*, Missoula (Mont.), 1976.
M. Beard, 'Writing and religion: *Ancient Literacy* and the function of the written word in Roman religion', in *Literacy in the Roman World (Journal of Roman Archaeology*, Supplement 3), Ann Arbor, 1991, pp. 35–58.
M. Beard and J. North (eds), *Pagan Priests*, London, 1990.
J. Boardman, 'The Parthenon Frieze', in E. Berger (ed.), *Parthenon-Kongress Basel*, Mainz, 1984, pp. 210–15.
J. Boardman, *The Parthenon and its Sculptures*, London, 1985.
L. Drees, *Olympia*, London, 1968.
E. J. and L. Edelstein, *Asclepius* 2 vols, Baltimore and London, 1945.
J. Elsner, 'Pausanias: a Greek pilgrim in the Roman world', *Past and Present* 135 (1992), pp. 3–29.
M. I. Finley and H. W. Pleket, *The Olympic Games*, London, 1976.
D. Fishwick, *The Imperial Cult in the Latin West*, 2 vols, Leiden, 1987.
R. Flacelière, *Greek Oracles*, London, 1965.

J. G. Frazer, *Pausanias's Description of Greece*, 6 vols, London, 1898.

S. D. Goldhill, 'The Great Dionysia and civic ideology', *Journal of Hellenic Studies* 107 (1987), pp. 58–76.

C. Habicht, *Pausanias' Guide to Ancient Greece*, Berkeley, 1985.

C. J. Herington, *Athena Parthenos and Athena Polias*, Manchester, 1955.

E. D. Hunt, 'Travel, tourism and piety in the Roman empire', *Echos du Monde Classique* 28 (1984), pp. 391–418.

I. Jenkins, *The Parthenon Frieze*, London, 1994.

C. Kerenyi, *Eleusis*, London, 1967.

J. H. Kroll, 'The ancient image of Athena Polias', *Hesperia*, Supplement 20 (1982), pp. 65–76.

R. Lamberton, *Homer the Theologian*, Berkeley, 1986.

R. Lane Fox, *Pagans and Christians*, London, 1986.

R. MacMullen, *Paganism in the Roman Empire*, New Haven and London, 1981.

L. H. Martin, *Hellenistic Religions*, Oxford and New York, 1987.

G. E. Mylonas, *Eleusis and the Eleusinian Mysteries*, Princeton, 1962.

J. Neils (ed.), *Goddess and Polis: The Panathenaic Festival in Ancient Athens*, Princeton, 1992.

A. D. Nock, 'A vision of Mandulis Aion', *Harvard Theological Review* 27 (1934), pp. 53–104.

R. G. Osborne, 'The viewing and obscuring of the Parthenon Frieze', *Journal of Hellenic Studies* 107 (1987), pp. 98–105.

H. W. Parke, *Festivals of the Athenians*, London, 1977.

H. W. Parke and D. E. W. Wormell, *The Delphic Oracle*, 2 vols, Oxford, 1956.

S. R. F. Price, *Rituals and Power: The Roman Imperial Cult in Asia Minor*, Cambridge, 1984.

H. Rahner, *Greek Myths and Christian Mystery*, London, 1963.

W. J. Raschke (ed.), *The Archaeology of the Olympics*, Madison, 1988.

M. Robertson and A. Frantz, *The Parthenon Frieze*, London, 1975.

E. Simon, *Festivals of Attica*, Madison and London, 1983.

J.-P. Vernant, *Myth and Society in Ancient Greece*, London, 1980.

P. Veyne, *Did the Greeks Believe in Their Myths?*, Chicago, 1988.

2 Exile and Return: Jewish Pilgrimage

1. See Exodus 24: 14–19; 34: 22–3.
2. Quoted in Kollek and Pearlman, p. 29.
3. Benjamin of Tudela, p. 259.
4. Kollek and Pearlman, p. 30.
5. Benjamin of Tudela, p. 271.
6. Ibid., p. 271.
7. Ibid., p. 274.
8. Ibid,. p. 277.
9. Ibid., pp. 275–7.
10. Ibid., p. 275.
11. Ibid., p. 274.
12. Buber (1956a), p. 83.
13. Buber (1956b), p. 103.
14. Baron, p. 334.
15. Benjamin of Tudela, p. 322.
16. See Exodus 35–40.
17. See I Kings 8:9.
18. I Samuel 1–2.
19. De Vaux, p. 470.
20. II Samuel 7 and I Chronicles 16.
21. Kraus, p. 183.
22. II Samuel 7: 2 ; cf. I Chronicles 17: 1.
23. I Chronicles 17: 4–5.
24. Kraus, p. 183. Such opposition continued throughout the existence of the temples in Jerusalem: see Turner, p. 68.
25. II Samuel 7: 12–13.
26. On the building of the Temple see I Kings 6–7, II Chronicles 3–4.
27. Cf. de Vaux, p. 297.
28. Kraus, pp. 186–7; Rowley, pp. 78–86; Haran, pp. 42–5, 189–92; Turner, pp. 47–87.
29. Deuteronomy 17: 8–13.
30. I Kings 8: 1.
31. Ibid. 8: 10–11.
32. Ibid. 8: 12–13.
33. Ibid. 8: 33–4.
34. Turner, p. 61.
35. Smith, p. 84.
36. I Kings 8: 27–9.
37. Turner, p. 64; cf. esp. Jeremiah 3: 16–17.
38. Philo, *Special Laws*, as quoted in Bokser, p. 5.
39. See Wilkinson.
40. See R. Crossman in Villiers, p. 16.
41. See Aronoff.
42. See Weingrod.
43. Cf. Paine.

M. Aronoff, 'Civil religion in Israel', *R A I Newsletter* (January 1981), pp. 2–6.

S. W. Baron, *A Social and Religious History of the Jews*, vol. XVIII, New York, 1983.

Benjamin of Tudela, 'Travels', in M. Komroff, *Contemporaries of Marco Polo*, New York, 1989.

B. M. Bokser, *The Origins of the Seder: The Passover Rite in Early Rabbinic Judaism*, Berkeley, 1984.

M. Buber, *The Legend of the Baal Shem*, London, 1956 (=1956a).

M. Buber, *Tales of the Hassidim: The Early Masters*, London, 1956 (=1956b).

R. de Vaux, *Ancient Israel: Its Life and Institutions*, London, 1961.

M. Haran, *Temples and Temple-Service in Ancient Israel*, Oxford, 1978.

T. Kollek and M. Pearlman, *Pilgrims to the Holy Land*, London, 1970.

H. J. Kraus, *Worship in Israel: A Cultic History of the Old Testament*, Oxford, 1966.

R. Paine, 'Israel, Jewish identity and competition over "tradition"', in E. Tonkin, M. McDonald and M. Chapman (eds), *History and Ethnicity*, London, 1989, pp. 121–36.

H. H. Rowley, *Worship in Ancient Israel: Its Forms and Meaning*, London, 1967.

J. Z. Smith, *To Take Place: Toward Theory in Ritual*, Chicago, 1987.

H. W. Turner, *From Temple to Meeting House. The Phenomenology and Theology of Places of Worship*, The Hague, 1979.

D. Villiers (ed.), *Next Year in Jerusalem*, London, 1976.

A. Weingrod, 'Saints and shrines, politics, and culture: a Morocco–Israel comparison', in D. Eickelman and J. Piscatori (eds), *Muslim Travellers. Pilgrimage, Migration, and the Religious Imagination*, London, 1990, pp. 217–35.

J. Wilkinson, 'Jewish holy places and the origins of Christian pilgrimage', in R. Ousterhout (ed.), *The Blessings of Pilgrimage*, Urbana and Chicago, 1990, pp. 41–53.

3 The Centre in the Desert: Muslim Pilgrimage to Mecca

1. Gilsenan, p. 27.
2. Quoted in Goldman, p. 166.
3. Brend, p. 17, points out that the root *s-l-m* encompasses meanings of safety and peace in Arabic and gives both 'Islam' (submitting oneself to the will of God) and 'Muslim' (one who has made that submission).
4. Wellhausen, quoted in Wolf, p. 338.
5. For discussions of reactions to the Prophet, see for example Husain.
6. Husain, p. 12.
7. Shah, p. 65.
8. Peters, p. 66.
9. Calligraphy is often regarded as the supreme art in the Islamic world. Writing has a sacramental character, since it can convey the word of God and avoids the idolatry of images (see Brend, p. 33).
10. Sabini, p. 67.
11. Burckhardt, p. 111.
12. Ralli, p. 14.
13. Burckhardt, p. 273.
14. Brend, pp. 18–19, notes that Muhammad is, in orthodox terms, regarded as the messenger of God. The concept of divine incarnation, evident in Hinduism or Christianity, is not present. More generally, the antipathy to representation seems to have been evident in early Islamic thought (possibly influenced by Jewish opposition to graven images), but subsequently hardened as the doctrine evolved that the painter or sculptor was guilty of trying to usurp the creative powers of God.
15. From *Ibn Battuta's Travels*.
16. Delaney, p. 515.
17. Ibid., p. 516.
18. Ibid., p. 519.
19. Ibid., p. 520.
20. Quoted in Goldman, p. 166.
21. Ibid., p. 168.
22. The following information is taken from Birks and from Yamba (1988 and 1992).
23. Birks, p. xi.
24. Currie describes a site in India that has come to be seen almost as a second Mecca (Ajmer).
25. See *Ibn Battuta's Travels*.
26. Quoted in Eickelman, p. 61.
27. Nicholson, p. 62.
28. Clancy-Smith, pp. 200–16.
29. In Eickelman, pp. 161–2.

T. W. Arnold, *The Caliphate*, London, 1965.

R. Barber, 'Mecca', in R. Barber, *Pilgrimages*, Woodbridge, 1991.

J. S. Birks, *Across the Savannas to Mecca: The Overland Pilgrimage Route from West Africa*, London, 1978.

B. Brend, *Islamic Art*, London, 1991.

J. L. Burckhardt, *Travels in Arabia, Comprehending an Account of those Territories in Hedjaz which the Mohammedans regard as Sacred*, London, 1829.

G. S. Burne, *Richard F. Burton*, Boston, 1985.

R. F. Burton, *A Pilgrimage to Meccah and Medinah*, London, 1937.

J. A. Clancy-Smith, 'Between Cairo and the Algerian Kabylia: the Rahmaniyya *tariqa*, 1715–1800', in Eickelman and Piscatori.

M. E. Combs-Schilling, *Sacred Performances: Islam, Sexuality, and Sacrifice*, New York, 1989.

P. M. Currie, 'The pilgrimage to Ajmer', in T. N. Madan (ed.), *Religion in India*, Delhi, 1991.

C. Delaney, 'The hajj: sacred and secular', *American Ethnologist* 17, 3 (1990), pp. 513–30.

D. F. Eickelman, *Moroccan Islam: Tradition and Society in a Pilgrimage Center*, Austin, 1976.

D. F. Eickelman and J. Piscatori (eds), *Muslim Travellers. Pilgrimage, Migration, and the Religious Imagination*, London, 1990.

H. Gätje, *The Qur'an and its Exegesis. Selected Texts with Classical and Modern Muslim Interpretation*, trans. A. T. Welch, London, 1971.

M. Gilsenan, *Recognizing Islam*, London, 1982.

P. Goldman, *The Death and Life of Malcolm X*, London, 1974.

M. Hastings, *Sir Richard Burton: A Biography*, London, 1978.

A. Husain, *Prophet Mohammad and his Mission*, London, 1967.

Ibn Battuta's Travels in Asia and Africa 1325–1354, trans. and selected by H. A. R. Gibb, London, 1929.

M. Z. Khan, *The Quran*, London, 1971.

G. A. W. Makky, *Mecca the Pilgrimage City. A Study of Pilgrim Accommodation*, London, 1978.

M. B. Mcdonnell, 'Patterns of Muslim pilgrimage from Malaysia, 1885–1985', in Eickelman and Piscatori.

R. A. Nicholson, *Studies in Islamic Mysticism*, 2nd edn, Cambridge, 1967.

F. E. Peters, *Jerusalem and Mecca. The Typology of the Holy City in the Near East*, New York, 1986.

P. Rabinow, *Reflections on Fieldwork in Morocco*, Berkeley, 1977.

F. Rahman, *Islam*, London, 1966.

A. Ralli, *Christians at Mecca*, London, 1909.

J. Sabini, *Armies in the Sand. The Struggle for Mecca and Medina*, London, 1981.

E. W. Said, *Orientalism*, London, 1978.

I. Shah, *Destination Mecca*, London, 1969.

J. A. Williams, *Islam*, New York, 1962.

E. Wolf, 'The social organisation of Mecca and the social

origins of Islam', *South Western Journal of Anthropology* 7, 4 (1951), pp. 329–56.

C. B. Yamba, 'A critique of the Bunyanian perspective in the anthropological analysis of pilgrimage', paper delivered to interdisciplinary conference on pilgrimage, Roehampton Institute, 1988.

C. B. Yamba, 'Going there and getting there: the future as a legitimating charter for life in the present', in S. Wallman (ed.), *Contemporary Futures. Perspectives from Social Anthropology*, London, 1992.

4 *The Gospels Embodied: Christian Pilgrimage to the Holy Land*

1. See Hunt, pp. 28–49; Walker, pp. 186–9; K. Holum, 'Hadrian and St Helena: imperial travel and the origins of Christian Holy Land pilgrimage', in Ousterhout, pp. 66–81.
2. See Hunt, pp. 3–5.
3. On the Constantinian churches see Wilkinson (1981), pp. 36–53, 164–71; Hunt, pp. 6–27; Baldovin, pp. 45–55.
4. See J. Wilkinson, 'Jewish holy places and the origins of Christian pilgrimage', in Ousterhout, pp. 41–53; for Jewish influences on Christian pilgrimage liturgies etc., see Wilkinson (1981), pp. 298–310.
5. On fourth-century theological attitudes to Palestine see Walker.
6. Tolstoy, pp. 92–117.
7. On Eudocia see Hunt, pp. 221–48, and Holum, pp. 184–90.
8. On Paula see Wilkinson (1977), pp. 1–2, 47–52; Hunt, pp. 76, 82, 171–4.
9. See Wilkinson (1981), pp. 153–63; Hunt, pp. 55–6, 83–5.
10. On Cyril and Eusebius in particular, see Walker.
11. For discussion of Egeria see Wilkinson (1981); Hunt, pp. 83–8, 107–28; Smith, pp. 88–95; Baldovin, pp. 55–64; Campbell, pp. 15–44; and Sivan (1988a and b).
12. Wilkinson (1977), pp. 4–5, 59–62.
13. Ibid., pp. 12, 137–8.
14. Ibid., pp. 6–7, 79–89.
15. On tokens and amulets see Vikan and the essays by Hahn, Vikan, Duncan-Flowers and Bakiratzis in Ousterhout.
16. On the Sinai icons see Weitzmann, pp. 19–62, and Manafis, pp. 91–133.
17. Wilkinson (1981), pp. 54–88; Hunt, pp. 107–28; Baldovin, pp. 83–96.
18. See Baldovin.
19. On the difficulties of the journey to Palestine see Wilkinson (1977), pp. 15–28; Hunt, pp. 50–82.
20. See Wilkinson (1977), pp. 14, 147.
21. For some aspects of the growth of this process see H. Sivan, 'Pilgrimage, monasticism and the emergence of Christian Palestine in the fourth century', in Ousterhout, pp. 54–65.
22. On holy men see Chitty, and Brown, pp. 103–65.
23. The *Life of Daniel* is translated in Dawes and Baynes, pp. 1–86.
24. See Ševčenko.
25. On Nicholas see Ševčenko; on Theodore see Dawes and Baynes, pp. 87–194, and Cormack, pp. 9–49; on

Willibald see Wilkinson (1977), pp. 11, 125–35.
26. On Valerius see Wilkinson (1981), pp. 174–8, and Sivan (1988a), pp. 59–63.
27. On Adomnan see Wilkinson (1977), pp. 9–10, 93–116.
28. On Peter the Deacon see Wilkinson (1981), pp. 179–210.
29. On Daniel the Abbot see Wilkinson (1988), pp. 9–10 and, for his account, 120–71; Majeska, pp. 6–7.
30. For pilgrimage under the Muslims, see Runciman, vol. 1, pp. 38–50; Wilkinson (1977), pp. 9–14; Wilkinson (1988), pp. 24–84.
31. See Hugeberc's *Life of St Willibald*, 12, 15f., in Wilkinson (1977), p. 126.
32. Wilkinson (1977), p. 123.
33. On the Crusades, Runciman (1951–4) is a gripping account; see also Mayer. On the idea of crusade and holy war see Erdmann.
34. On Saewulf, see Wilkinson (1988), pp. 6–7 and, for his account, 94–116.
35. On Burchard, see Grabois.

J. Baldovin, *The Urban Character of Christian Worship*, Rome, 1987.

P. Brown, *Society and the Holy in Late Antiquity*, London, 1982.

M. B. Campbell, *The Witness and the Other World*, Ithaca (N.Y.), 1988.

D. J. Chitty, *The Desert a City*, London, 1966.

P. J. Coke, *The Preaching of the Crusades to the Holy Land, 1095–1270*, Cambridge (Mass.), 1991.

G. Constable, 'Opposition to pilgrimage in the Middle Ages', *Studia Gratiana* 19 (1976), pp. 123–46.

R. S. Cormack, *Writing in Gold: Byzantine Society and its Icons*, London, 1985.

E. Dawes and N. Baynes, *Three Byzantine Saints*, London, 1948.

S. Elm, 'Perceptions of Jerusalem pilgrimage as reflected in two early sources on female pilgrimage (3rd and 4th centuries AD)', in E. A. Livingstone (ed.), *Studia Patristica* 20 (1989), pp. 219–23.

C. Erdmann, *The Origins of the Idea of Crusade*, Princeton, 1977.

A. Grabois, 'Christian pilgrims in the thirteenth century and the Latin kingdom of Jerusalem', in B. Z. Kedar, H. E. Mayer and R. C. Smail (eds), *Outremer*, Jerusalem, 1982, pp. 285–96.

K. Holum, *Theodosian Empresses*, Berkeley, 1982.

E. D. Hunt, 'St Silvia of Aquitaine: the role of a Theodosian pilgrim in the society of East and West', *Journal of Theological Studies* 23 (1972), pp. 351–73.

E. D. Hunt, *Holy Land Pilgrimage in the Later Roman Empire*, Oxford, 1982.

G. P. Majeska, *Russian Travellers to Constantinople in the Fourteenth and Fifteenth Centuries*, Washington DC, 1984.

K. Manafis (ed.), *Sinai: The Treasures of the Monastery*, Athens, 1990.

H. E. Mayer, *The Crusades*, Oxford, 1988.

R. Ousterhout (ed.), *The Blessings of Pilgrimage*, Urbana and Chicago, 1990.

I. and J. Riley Smith, *The Crusades: Idea and Reality*, London, 1981.

S. Runciman, *A History of the Crusades*, 3 vols, Cambridge, 1951–4.

I. and N. P. Ševčenko, *The Life of St Nicholas of Sion*, Brookline (Mass.), 1984.

H. Sivan, 'Who was Egeria? Piety and pilgrimage in the age of Gratian', *Harvard Theological Review* 81 (1988), pp. 59–72 (= 1988a).

H. Sivan, 'Holy Land pilgrimage and western audiences: some reflections on Egeria and her circle', *Classical Quarterly* 38 (1988), pp. 528–35 (= 1988b).

J. Z. Smith, *To Take Place: Toward Theory in Ritual*, Chicago, 1987.

J. E. Taylor, *Christians and the Holy Places. The Myth of Jewish-Christian Origins*, Oxford, 1993.

R. W. Thomson, 'Jerusalem and Armenia', in E. A. Livingstone (ed.), *Studia Patristica* 18 (1985), pp. 77–93.

L. Tolstoy, 'Two old men' (1885), in *Twenty-Three Tales*, trans. L. and A. Maude, Oxford, 1905.

G. Vikan, *Byzantine Pilgrimage Art*, Washington DC, 1982.

P. W. L. Walker, *Holy City, Holy Places?*, Oxford, 1990.

K. Weitzmann, *Studies in the Arts at Sinai*, Princeton, 1982.

J. Wilkinson, *Jerusalem Pilgrims before the Crusades*, Warminster, 1977.

J. Wilkinson, *Egeria's Travels to the Holy Land*, Warminster, 1981.

J. Wilkinson, *Jerusalem Pilgrimage 1099–1185*, London, 1988.

5 *Geographies of Sainthood: Christian Pilgrimage from the Middle Ages to the Present Day*

1. See the *Mirabilia Urbis Romae* I, in Nichols.

2. Cf. Bernes.

3. Cf. Costen, p. 153. St James is still the patron saint of Spain, and Compostela remains a popular site of pilgrimage.

4. A copy survives in the Pepys Library, Magdalene College, Cambridge.

5. On this last point see Costen, p. 140.

6. Quoted in Freedberg, p. 120.

7. See Costen, p. 139.

8. Codex of Calixtus I I, 5, 9, 13.

9. See Remy, pp. 139–40.

10. Baxandall, p. 84; see also Freedberg, pp. 100–4.

11. See Katzenellenbogen, p. v. For a general introduction to Chartres see Henderson.

12. On these relics see Favier, pp. 31–3.

13. See von Simson, pp. 170–1.

14. On the glass of Canterbury see Caviness.

15. Caviness, p. 143. In general on such accounts see Ward, pp. 89–109.

16. See F. N. Robinson (ed.), *The Riverside Chaucer*, 3rd edn, Boston, 1987.

17. *The Colloquies of Erasmus*, trans. C. R. Thompson, Chicago, 1965, p. 295.

18. Freedberg, p. 427.

19. Quoted in Stephenson, p. 68.

20. On European Iconoclasm in the 16th century see Christensen and Eire.

21. *Orations on Images* III, 21, 24f.

22. On Byzantine Iconoclasm and its aftermath see for example Martin; Cormack, pp. 95–178, and Pelikan.

23. See Majeska, pp. 15–27 on Stephen and pp. 28–47 for the text of his account: the quotation is from p. 28.

24. On the Hodegetria, ibid., pp. 362–6.

25. Ibid., pp. 36, 362–3.

26. Ibid., p. 363.

27. Ibid., pp. 28–32.

28. Ibid., p. 42.

29. Ibid., p. 42.

30. De Hueck Doherty, p. 18.

31. Anon., *The Way of a Pilgrim*, trans. R. M. French, London, 1930, p. 19.

32. Tolstoy, pp. 535–6.

33. Cf. Sallnow (1987).

34. For the information in this paragraph, see Lukatis. Note also that she argues (p. 204) that the motivations for Christian pilgrimage since pre-Reformation times can be divided into salvation, penitence and expiation (voluntary or imposed), devotion (a concrete expression of piety), and political commitment.

35. Cf. Davies.

36. Cf. A. Dahlberg, 'The body as a principle of holism: three pilgrimages to Lourdes', in J. Eade and M. J. Sallnow (eds) *Contesting the Sacred. The Anthropology of Christian Pilgrimage*, London, 1991; J. Eade, 'Order and power at Lourdes: lay helpers and the organisation of a pilgrimage shrine', in Eade and Sallnow (op. cit.); and Marnham.

37. Deery, pp. 235–7.

38. The site also illustrates how many contemporary Christian pilgrimages are arranged through diocesan pastoral work.

39. Cf. Llewellyn. Pace (p. 240) points out that Medjugorje echoes earlier Marian shrines in its rural origins, apocalyptic message and involvement of adolescent visionaries.

40. *The Shrine of Our Lady of Walsingham*, 2nd edn, 1991, p. 10.

R. Barber, 'Rome and the shrines of Europe: pilgrimage and miracles', in R. Barber, *Pilgrimages*, Woodbridge, 1991.

M. Baxandall, *The Limewood Sculptors of Renaissance Germany*, New Haven, 1980.

G. Bernes, *The Pilgrim Route to Compostela. In Search of St James*, 2nd edn, London, 1986.

M. H. Caviness, *The Early Stained Glass of Canterbury*, Princeton, 1977.

C. Christensen, *Art and the Reformation in Germany*, Athens (Ohio), 1979.

R. S. Cormack, *Writing in Gold: Byzantine Society and its Icons*, London, 1985.

M. Costen, 'The pilgrimage to Santiago de Compostela in medieval Europe', in I. Reader and T. Walter (eds), *Pilgrimage in Popular Culture*, London, 1993.

J. G. Davies, *Pilgrimage Yesterday and Today: Why? Where? How?*, London, 1988.

J. Deery, *Our Lady of Lourdes*, Dublin, 1958.

C. de Hueck Doherty, *Not Without Parables*, Notre Dame (Ind.), 1977.

C. M. N. Eire, *War against the Idols: The Reformation of*

Worship from Erasmus to Calvin, Cambridge, 1986.

J. Favier, *The World of Chartres*, London, 1990.

D. Freedberg, *The Power of Images: Studies in the History and Theory of Response*, Chicago, 1989.

P. J. Geary, *Furta Sacra: Thefts of Relics in the Central Middle Ages*, Princeton, 1978.

G. Henderson, *Chartres*, London, 1968.

A. Katzenellenbogen, *The Sculptural Programs of Chartres Cathedral*, New York, 1959.

R. Llewellyn, 'A call to conversion', *Frontier*, Nov.–Dec. 1989, pp. 6–9.

I. Lukatis, 'Church meetings and pilgrimages in Germany', *Social Compass* 36, 2 (1989), pp. 201–18.

G. Majeska, *Russian Travellers to Constantinople in the Fourteenth and Fifteenth Centuries*, Washington DC, 1984.

P. Marnham, *Lourdes. A Modern Pilgrimage*, London, 1980.

E. J. Martin, *A History of the Iconoclastic Controversy*, London, 1930.

F. M. Nichols, *The Marvels of Rome*, New York, 1986.

M. L. Nolan and S. Nolan, *Christian Pilgrimage in Modern Western Europe*, Chapell Hill, 1989.

E. Pace, 'Pilgrimage as spiritual journey: an analysis of pilgrimage using the theory of V. Turner and the resource mobilization approach', *Social Compass* 36, 2 (1989), pp. 229–44.

J. Pelikan, *Imago Dei: The Byzantine Apologia for Icons*, New Haven, 1990.

J. Remy, 'Editorial: Pilgrimage and modernity', *Social Compass* 36, 2 (1989), pp. 139–43.

M. J. Sallnow, 'Communitas reconsidered: the sociology of Andean pilgrimage', *Man* (n.s.) 16 (1981), pp. 163–82.

M. J. Sallnow, *Pilgrims of the Andes. Regional Cults in Cusco*, Washington DC, 1987.

D. Sox, *Relics and Shrines*, London, 1985.

C. Stephenson, *Walsingham Way*, London, 1970.

L. Tolstoy, *Resurrection*, trans. R. Edmonds, Harmondsworth, 1966.

O. von Simson, *The Gothic Cathedral*, Princeton, 1962.

B. Ward, *Miracles and the Medieval Mind*, London, 1982.

S. Wilson (ed.), *Saints and Their Cults. Studies in Religious Sociology, Folklore and History*, Cambridge, 1983.

6 *Divinity Diffused: Pilgrimage in the Indian Religions*

1. Cf. Hawley. The temple Hawley refers to is called the Radha Raman, indicating that Krishna is to be viewed in this context as Raman, the lover of his soulmate Radha.

2. Blurton notes that today the *Mahabharata* is particularly remembered for a section known as the *Bhagavad Gita* (The Song of the Lord), in which Krishna reveals himself as the Lord who is not only worthy of love but also loves all his followers in return.

3. Cf. Klostermaier, p. 38.

4. See Fuller (1992), pp. 3 and 61.

5. See Sopher.

6. Cf. Blurton, pp. 36–9.

7. Cf. for example Babb (1987), p. 2.

8. Bharati (1990). Eck (1983, p. 34) points out that no Hindu term means quite what the Judaeo-Christian faith defines as 'sacred'. Thus words such as 'pure' (*shuchi*, *pavitra*) or 'good' (*punya*) or 'auspicious' (*shuba*, etc.) are used.

9. Cf. Klostermaier, p. 41.

10. See Blurton, p. 40.

11. Ironically, as Fuller (1992, p. 10) points out, the word 'Hindu' is Persian in origin, deriving from Sindhu, the Sanskrit name of the river Indus.

12. Blurton, p. 100.

13. For Zaehner (p. 12), Hinduism is characterised by a potential conflict between the principle of *moksha* (participation in the infinite) and that of *dharma*, roughly translatable as 'right action' – in accordance with ethical and social principles – in a more temporal sense. Note also that the seven cities are Ayodhya (capital and birthplace of Lord Rama), Mathura/Brindavan (birthplace of Krishna), Hardwar (gate of the Ganges), Benares/Kashi (a home of Shiva), Ujjain (sacred to Shiva), Dvaraka (capital of Krishna), and Kanchi (sacred to both Vishnu and Shiva).

14. See Eck (1983), p. 24.

15. Quoted in Bhardwaj (1973), p. 3.

16. *The Mahabharata*, trans. and ed. J. A. B. van Buitenen, Chicago, 1975, vol., 11, p. 381.

17. Bharati (1963), pp. 145–6.

18. Sopher, p. 7.

19. See Gold.

20. One site in the Himalayas, on the way to the headquarters of the Ganges itself, is referred to as the 'Northern Kashi'. Other Kashis exist in the south of India, as well as hundreds of temples incorporating the name, associated with local hymns which claim for the local temple the same benefits to be derived from going to the distant Kashi.

21. For this discussion of Benares, see Eck (1983).

22. Quoted in Eck (1983), p. 17.

23. Eck (1983, p. 57) notes that Benares also attracts Jain pilgrims, as it is believed to be the birthplace of two preceptors and contains a number of Jain *tirthas*.

24. Van der Veer, pp. 19–20.

25. Klostermaier, p. 171.

26. Rawson, p. 21.

27. M. Jha, 'Hindu pilgrimage and patronage. A study in the history of politicalisation of Hindu Tirtha-Jagannath Puri: a case study', in Jha (1985), p. 66.

28. See van der Veer. Jains believe that five of their preceptors were born in Ayodhya, and the town contains a temple that is regularly visited by Jains from throughout India. Buddhists associate Ayodhya with Saket, a town mentioned in Buddhist scriptures and a place where the Buddha is supposed to have meditated. Muslims associate the town with the grave of Noah.

29. This process of Muslim elimination of Hindu sacred space is also evident at Benares, temporarily renamed Muhammadabad by Aurangzeb in the 17th century.

30. Bhardwaj (1990), p. 92.

31. Sekar (p. 83) points to the importance of contemporary communications media in the development of a site's reputation: the cult of Lord Ayyappa has been encouraged by its espousal by male film stars.

32. See Rawson.

33. Blurton, p. 48.

34. Sen, p. 35.

35. E.g. Babb, p. 210.

36. See Sopher.

37. See for example Vaidyanathan, p. 164. For texts relating to the Ayyappan pilgrimage we are grateful to F. and C. Osella.

38. Fuller (1992, p. 60) notes the importance of eyes in Hindu iconography, and points out that Shiva in particular is represented with a third eye in the centre of his forehead.

39. Blurton, p. 57.

40. *Mahabharata*, trans. and ed. J. A. B. van Buitenen, Chicago, 1975, vol. II, p. 373.

41. Gold, p. 266.

42. Menon, p. 4.

43. Bharati (1963), p. 162.

44. Quoted in Morinis, p. 14.

45. Ibid., p. 84.

46. Sopher, p. 15.

47. Sen, p. 95.

48. Quoted in Eck (1983), p. 86.

49. Bharati (1963), p. 144.

50. See, for example, discussion in M. Jha, 'The origin, type, spread and nature of Hindu pilgrimage' in Jha (1985).

51. Karve, p. 19.

52. One Jain argument implies that, since the religion is eternal, it cannot have had a founder as such.

53. Cf. Banks.

54. Ibid.

55. For this and subsequent points in the paragraph, see Cort, pp. 212–23, esp. p. 220.

56. See Carrithers.

57. Guru Nanak was born in Talwandi, a village now in Pakistan and place of pilgrimage for Sikhs. He spent the first thirty years of his life as a householder before undertaking missionary travels for over twenty years and then settling in Kartarpur.

58. J. P. S. Uberoi, 'Five symbols of Sikh identity' in Madan (1991a), pp. 327–8. Uncut hair can also be interpreted as an indication of living in harmony with the will of God.

59. Cole and Sambhi, p. 146.

60. Cf. Oberoi, p. 259.

61. Lock notes that the *gurdwara* can adopt many functions apart from that of a specifically holy place, including a general meeting place, a school and a place of rest.

62. Quoted in Sahib, p. 5.

63. See Sahib, pp. 15–16. Shrines include a sacred reservoir filled with healing water which was once touched by the feet of the eighth Guru, two places associated with the martyrdom and death of the ninth Guru, a place where the first Guru produced water at a time of drought, and so on.

64. For information on this pilgrimage we are grateful to Amanda Sealy (pers. comm.).

65. For this last point we are grateful to an anonymous reviewer.

66. For much of the information in this paragraph see Madan (1991b), pp. 605–9, and Lock.

67. This tradition was originally created by the tenth Guru, Gobind Singh, in 1699. Ever since, the town where the Guru is reputed to have formalised the tradition, Anandpur in the Punjab, has been an important centre of pilgrimage.

68. Madan (1991b), p. 595.

69. Ibid.

70. In making the two final remarks in this paragraph, we are grateful for the comments of an anonymous reviewer.

J. C. Archer, *The Sikhs*, Princeton, 1946.

L. A. Babb, *The Divine Hierarchy*, New York, 1975.

L. A. Babb, *Redemptive Encounters. Three Modern Styles in the Hindu Tradition*, Delhi, 1987.

P. Banerjee, *Early Indian Religions*, New Delhi, 1973.

M. Banks, *Organizing Jainism in India and England*, Oxford, 1992.

R. Barber, *Pilgrimages*, Woodbridge, 1991.

A. Bharati, 'Pilgrimage in the Indian tradition', *History of Religions* 3 (1963), pp. 135–67.

A. Bharati, 'Grammatical and notational models of Indian pilgrimage', in Jha (1990).

S. M. Bhardwaj, *Hindu Places of Pilgrimage in India. A Study in Cultural Geography*, Berkeley, 1973.

S. M. Bhardwaj, 'Single religious shrines, multireligious pilgrimages', *National Geographical Journal of India* 33, 4 (1987), pp. 457–68.

S. M. Bhardwaj, 'Hindu pilgrimage in America', in Jha (1990).

T. R. Blurton, *Hindu Art*, London, 1992.

M. Carrithers, 'Passions of nation and community in the Bahubali affair', *Modern Asian Studies* 22, 4 (1988), pp. 815–44.

M. Carrithers and C. Humphrey (eds), *The Assembly of Listeners. Jains in Society*, Cambridge, 1991.

W. O. Cole and P. S. Sambhi, *The Sikhs, Their Religious Beliefs and Practices*, London, 1978.

J. E. Cort, 'Murtipuja in Svetambar Jain temples', in Madan (1991a).

D. P. Dubey, 'Kumbh Mela: origins and historicity of India's great pilgrimage fair', *National Geographical Journal of India* 33, 4 (1987), pp. 469–92.

D. L. Eck, 'India's tirthas: "crossings" in sacred geography', *History of Religions* 20, 4 (1981), pp. 323–44.

D. L. Eck, *Banares. City of Light*, London, 1983.

D. L. Eck, *Darsan. Seeing the Divine Image in India*, Chambersburg (Pa), 1985.

C. J. Fuller, *Servants of the Goddess: The Priests of a South Indian Temple*, Cambridge, 1984.

C. J. Fuller, *The Camphor Flame. Popular Hinduism and Society in India*, Princeton, 1992.

A. G. Gold, *Fruitful Journeys. The Ways of Rajasthani Pilgrims*, Berkeley, 1988.

G. R. Gupta (ed.), *Religion in Modern India*, New Delhi, 1983.

J. S. Hawley (with S. Goswami), *At Play with Krishna: Pilgrimage Dramas from Brindavan*, New Jersey, 1981.

M. Jha (ed.), *Dimensions of Pilgrimage: An Anthropological Appraisal*, New Delhi, 1985.

M. Jha (ed.), *Social Anthropology of Pilgrimage*, New Delhi, 1990.

I. Karve, 'On the road: a Maharashtrian pilgrimage', *Journal of Asian Studies* XXII, 1 (1962), pp. 13–30.

D. Kinsley, *Hindu Goddesses. Visions of the Divine Feminine in the Hindu Religious Tradition*, Berkeley, 1986.

K. K. Klostermaier, *A Survey of Hinduism*, Albany, 1989.

S. Konow and P. Tuxen (eds), *Religions of India*, Copenhagen, 1949.

J. Laidlaw, 'The religion of Svetambar Jain merchants in Jaipur', unpublished PhD thesis, University of Cambridge, 1990.

L. J. Lock, 'I strid för de renas land. Sikhisk "fundamentalism"', in D. Westerlund (ed.), *Sekularism ifrågasatt*, Uppsala, 1992.

W. H. McLeod, *The Sikhs. History, Religion, and Society*, New York, 1989.

T. J. Madan, 'Secularisation and the Sikh religious tradition', *Social Compass* 33, 2–3 (1986), pp. 257–73.

T. J. Madan (ed.), *Religion in India*, Delhi, 1991 (= 1991a).

T. J. Madan, 'The double-edged sword: fundamentalisms and the Sikh religious tradition', in M. E. Marty and R. S. Appleby (eds), *Fundamentalisms Observed*, Chicago, 1991 (= 1991b).

P. S. K. Menon, *The Legend of Lord Ayyappa of Sabarimala*, Bangalore, 1986.

D. A. Messerschmidt and J. Sharma, 'Hindu pilgrimage in the Nepal Himalayas', *Current Anthropology* 22, 5 (1981), pp. 571–2.

E. A. Morinis, *Pilgrimage in the Hindu Tradition. A Case Study of West Bengal*, Delhi, 1984.

H. Oberoi, 'Sikh fundamentalism. Translating history into theory', in M. E. Marty and R. S. Appleby (eds), *Fundamentalisms and the State. Remaking Polities, Economies and Militance*, Chicago, 1993.

P. S. Rawson, 'The symbolism of Indian art', in K. Werner (ed.), *Symbols in Art and Religion. The Indian and the Comparative Perspectives*, London, 1990.

G. B. Sahib, *Sikhism. An Outline*, Delhi (n.d.).

R. Sekar, *The Sabarimalai Pilgrimage and Ayyappan Cults*, Delhi, 1992.

K. M. Sen, *Hinduism*, Harmondsworth, 1961.

A. Sharma, 'What is Hinduism? A sociological approach', *Social Compass* 33, 2–3 (1986), pp. 177–83.

R. P. B. Singh, 'The pilgrimage mandala of Varanasi (Kasi): a study in sacred geography', *National Geographical Journal of India* 33, 4 (1987), pp. 493–524.

D. E. Sopher, 'The message of place in Hindu pilgrimage', *National Geographical Journal of India* 33, 4 (1987), pp. 353–69.

N. M. Srinivas, 'Religions in India in a sociological perspective', *Social Compass* 33, 2–3 (1986), pp. 159–62.

R. H. Stoddard, 'Pilgrimages along sacred paths', *National Geographical Journal of India* 33, 4 (1987), pp. 448–56.

J. P. S. Uberoi, 'Five symbols of Sikh identity', in Madan (1991a), pp. 320–33.

P. van der Veer, *Gods on Earth: The Management of Religious Experience and Identity in a North Indian Pilgrimage Centre*, London, 1988.

K. R. Vaidyanathan, *Pilgrimage to Sabari*, Bombay, 1983.

H. Wilson, *Benares*, London, 1985.

R. C. Zaehner, *Hinduism*, London 1972.

7 Translating the Sacred: Patterns of Pilgrimage in the Buddhist World

1. Walshe, pp. 263–4, quoted with some adaptations.
2. This date, which represents modern consensus, is about eighty years after that generally accepted in the older scholarly accounts: see H. Bechert, 'The date of the Buddha reconsidered', *Indologia Taurinensia* 10 (1982), pp. 29–36.
3. Walshe, p. 264.
4. Ibid., pp. 264–5.
5. See Strong, pp. 109, 119–20.
6. Ibid., pp. 109, 123–6.
7. Nikam and McKeon, p. 69.
8. Ibid., pp. 64–5.
9. See Beal (1906), pp. xi–xv and, for a translation of Fahsien's account, pp. xxiii–lxxxiii. The quotation in the previous sentence is from p. xxiii.
10. Ibid., p. xlv.
11. Ibid., p. xxxii.
12. Ibid., p. lix.
13. Ibid., p. lx.
14. Translated as the main text in Beal (1906), vols 1 and 2.
15. The first five books of this ten-book biography, which deal with the journey to India, are translated by Beal (1911). On the Chinese pilgrims to India see further K. C. Hazra, *Buddhism in India Described by the Chinese Pilgrims AD 399–689*, Delhi, 1983; I-Ching, *Chinese Monks in India*, Delhi, 1986; X. Liu, *Ancient India and Ancient China*, Oxford and Delhi, 1988.
16. See Wu, esp. pp. 215–17. Wu-Ch'eng-en's novel is partially translated in Waley.
17. Beal (1906), vol. 2, p. 4.
18. Beal (1911), p. 44. See also Falk.
19. Falk, pp. 288–90.
20. Beal (1911), pp. 156–7.
21. Waley, p. 279.
22. Ibid., p. 287.
23. See Reischauer.
24. Ibid., p. 225.
25. Ibid., p. 226.
26. Ibid., p. 233.
27. Ibid., p. 245.
28. Ibid., p. 235.
29. See Statler.
30. Ibid., p. 55.
31. Ibid., p. 182.
32. Ibid., p. 181.
33. Ibid., p. 182.
34. Ibid., pp. 85–6.
35. See for example ibid., pp. 158–9 and 189.
36. In R. H. Blythe, *Haiku*, vol. 2, Tokyo, 1950, p. 139.
37. In L. Stryk and T. Ikemoto, *The Penguin Book of Zen Poetry*, Harmondsworth, 1977, p. 83.
38. From *Records of a Weather Exposed Skeleton*, in Basho, p. 54.
39. Ibid., p. 51.
40. In R. Aitken, *A Zen Wave: Basho's Haiku and Zen*, New York, 1978, p. 43.
41. Ibid., p. 45.
42. Basho, p. 105.
43. Ibid., p. 105.
44. Ibid., p. 126.
45. Ibid., p. 126.
46. Govinda, p. 199.
47. Kawaguchi, p. 136.
48. Govinda, p. 214.

49. Kawaguchi, p. 173.

50. Govinda, p. 198.

51. See Tambiah, pp. 81–110.

52. Ibid., p. 94.

53. Ibid., pp. 109–10.

54. Ibid., pp. 268–73.

55. Ibid., pp. 111–23.

56. Ibid., pp. 258–65 and, on the cult of amulets in general, 195–289.

M. Basho, *The Narrow Road to the Deep North and Other Travel Sketches*, trans. N. Yuasa, Harmondsworth, 1966.

S. Beal, *Buddhist Records of the Western World*, 2 vols, London, 1906.

S. Beal, *The Life of Huien-Tsiang by the Shaman Hwui Li*, London, 1911.

N. Falk, 'To gaze on sacred traces', *History of Religions* 16 (1977), pp. 281–93.

R. Gombrich, *Theravada Buddhism*, London, 1988.

A. Govinda, *The Way of the White Clouds*, London, 1966.

A. G. Grapard, 'Flying mountains and walkers of emptiness: towards a definition of sacred space in Japanese religion', *History of Religions* 20 (1982), pp. 195–221.

P. Harvey, *An Introduction to Buddhism*, Cambridge, 1990.

R. Johnson and K. Moran, *Kailas: On Pilgrimage to the Sacred Mountain of Tibet*, London, 1989.

E. Kawaguchi, *Three Years in Tibet*, Madras, 1909.

J. M. Kitagawa, 'Three types of pilgrimage in Japan', in *Studies in Mysticism and Religion Presented to Gershom G. Scholem*, Jerusalem, 1967, pp. 155–64.

N. A. Nikam and R. McKeon, *The Edicts of Asoka*, Chicago, 1959.

A. Powell and G. Harrison, *Living Buddhism*, London, 1989.

E. O. Reischauer, *Ennin's Diary: The Record of a Pilgrimage to China in Search of the Law*, New York, 1955.

J. Russell, 'The eight places of Buddhist pilgrimage', in G. H. Mullin and N. Ribush (eds), *Teachings at Tushita*, New Delhi, 1981, pp. 138–61.

O. Statler, *Japanese Pilgrimage*, London, 1984.

J. S. Strong, *The Legend of King Asoka*, Princeton, 1983.

S. J. Tambiah, *The Buddhist Saints of the Forest and the Cult of Amulets*, Cambridge, 1984.

A. Waley, *Monkey*, London, 1942.

M. Walshe, *Thus Have I Heard: The Long Discourses of the Buddha*, London, 1987.

A. C. Wu, 'Two literary examples of religious pilgrimage', *History of Religions* 22 (1983), pp. 202–30.

Epilogue: Landscapes Reviewed

1. For the account from which our observations are drawn, see the comprehensive conference report by Bowman (1988), pp. 20–3. The conference itself was convened by John Eade at the Roehampton Institute of Higher Education in July 1988.

2. Eade and Sallnow.

3. Cf. the notion of 'communitas' developed by Victor and Edith Turner in, for example, *Image and Pilgrimage in Christian Culture*, Oxford, 1978.

4. Bowman (1988), p. 20. These are his terms. One might prefer to talk of analyses which accept the existence of a discrete phenomenon called 'pilgrimage' and those which contest its very existence.

5. Van Dam, p. 13. Cf. his comments on a distinguished historical treatment of the cult of the saints by Peter Brown (1981): 'he . . . failed to differentiate sharply the distinctive development and the diverse functions of different cults' (p. 5).

6. Bowman (1988), p. 20.

7. Eade and Sallnow, p. 2.

8. For Lourdes see the papers by A. Dahlberg and J. Eade and for Jerusalem see the article by G. Bowman in Eade and Sallnow.

9. See Durkheim.

10. See Wolf.

11. The anthropologist M. Bloch has explored the virtues and faults of the Marxist approach in, for example, *From Blessing to Violence. History and Ideology in the Circumcision Ritual of the Merina of Madagascar*, Cambridge, 1986.

12. Eade and Sallnow, p. 15.

13. Ibid., p. 3.

14. See Eliade (1959 and 1963). He echoes Durkheim's sharp distinction between the sacred and the profane, but does not take up the latter's sociological concerns in appearing to see the sacred as society divinised. For an explicit comparison between the Durkheimian and the Eliadian views of the sacred, see Stirrat.

15. See especially V. and E. Turner.

16. Some Cypriot Orthodox pilgrims are buried in the white shrouds they wear for baptism in the Jordan, while *hajjis* may choose to be entombed in the white clothing they wear at Mecca.

17. Turner (1974), p. 172.

18. Here we should emphasise that this passage represents a brief summary of the most distinctive features of the Turnerian theory. In fact, the Turners do at times acknowledge that pilgrimage sites are often arenas of considerable social and political conflict (e.g. 1978, chapter 4). Victor Turner also distinguishes between different kinds of 'communitas', using as one variable the extent to which social relations become routinised over time (e.g. 1974, p. 169).

19. Bowman (1985), pp. 1–9 (quotation on p. 3). There have been numerous critiques of the Turners, in particular that their view is over-Christianising and ethnocentric: see, for instance, Messerschmidt and Sharma, Morinis, and Bharati (1991).

20. Victor Turner discusses the problems raised for his theory by Karve's account, and concludes, 'while the pilgrimage situation does not eliminate structural divisions, it attenuates them, removes their sting' (1974, p. 207).

21. Pace (p. 240) goes so far as to describe contemporary pilgrimage as postmodern because of its apparent inability to invoke a common set of assumptions.

22. Eade and Sallnow, p. 9.

23. On the miracles of St Cuthbert and the various medieval records of them, see Ward, pp. 56–66.

24. Turner (1992), p. 35. He also points out the parallel between this definition of pilgrimage and the practice of anthropology.

25. On the pilgrimages of Felix Fabri see Prescott (1954 and 1957).

26. *Evagatorium* I, 41, in Prescott (1954), p. 64.

27. *Evagatorium* III, 364, in Prescott (1957), p. 275.

28. Eade and Sallnow, p. 15.

29. In this regard, it is interesting to reflect, following H. W. Turner, how much post-Reformation architecture attempted to remove architectural obstacles between pulpit and congregation: a complex arrangement of space was seen as a hindrance to unmediated reflection on the divine.

30. Eade and Sallnow, pp. 9–10. Later on p. 10 they do moderate their view: '*As well as perhaps being a symbolic power-house productive of its own religious meanings*, a pilgrimage shrine is also – perhaps predominantly – an arena for the interplay of a variety of imported perceptions and understandings . . .' (our italics).

31. J. Eade, 'Order and power at Lourdes: lay helpers and the organisation of a pilgrimage shrine', in Eade and Sallnow, pp. 51–76. This example reveals how an act of conformity – being controlled by a *brancardier* – is also an act which encourages contestation in cases where the pilgrim resents such authoritarian treatment.

32. See Coleman and Elsner.

33. On the possible Jewish origins of many early Christian pilgrimage sites in the Holy Land, see Wilkinson.

34. Cf. Kemal and Gaskell, p. 2.

35. Tambiah, pp. 106–7, refers to writings in which the contribution of the environment to perception is discussed. The general theme of these works is that of participation by people in a culturally constructed 'mythic landscape' which orientates their sense of reality in powerful ways. B. Bender has also recently edited a volume (1993) dealing with the power of the landscape in human relationships. Our attempt to examine the ways in which a physical environment acts as a potentially ideologically charged means of structuring experience has resonances with other works in archaeology and anthropology, e.g. Bourdieu, Graves, Leone, Moore. However, a particular dimension is added in the sense that while these authors variously describe how the organisation of space can act as a complex structuring symbolic system *within* a given society or culture, important pilgrimage sites juxtapose religious culture(s) with the varied assumptions of pilgrims from very *different* societies. In our conclusions, we also see some parallels with John Berger's thesis (1972) on the importance of artistic representation in suggesting particular 'ways of seeing' the world.

36. The Christian Reformation – both a theological and an aesthetic revolution – is an example of one such 'earthquake'.

37. As we have noted, the sacred is a still more problematic concept even than pilgrimage itself. Judaeo-Christian conceptions of the supramundane do not necessarily apply within Buddhism or Hinduism.

38. The simple fact of the dramatic rise in the world's population is also presumably providing a larger potential clientele for pilgrimage sites.

39. Cf. Pace, p. 240.

40. See Crain, p. 105.

41. Cf. Reader and Walter for a series of papers illustrating how apparently non-religious activities such as visits to war graves, to the tombs of dead pop stars, even to Anfield football ground (Liverpool), can take on some of the features of pilgrimage.

42. Cf. Lane, p. 81.

43. Our account of Graceland is based on both King and Windsor, pp. 56–9.

44. See, for example, Duncan and Wallach, esp. pp. 448–52; Duncan, p. 90.

45. On emblems see Greenblatt; on the universal museum see Duncan and Wallach.

46. Beard (quotation p. 513).

47. For pilgrimage centres see Eade and Sallnow, p. 15; for museums see Karp and Lavine, pp. 3–4.

48. Meltzer, p. 122.

49. On museums constructing a version of the past see, for example, Sorensen, Bann, Bal, Merriman (esp. pp. 1–41), Goswamy.

50. Duncan, p. 92.

51. Meltzer, p. 121.

52. Beard, p. 523.

53. Meltzer, p. 121.

54. Beard, p. 521.

55. Beard, p. 517, cf. tables pp. 509–10; on postcards as souvenirs see also Schor.

M. Bal, 'Telling, showing and showing off: a walking tour of the American Museum of Natural History', *Critical Inquiry* 18 (1992), pp. 556–94.

S. Bann, 'On living in a new country', in Vergo, pp. 99–118.

M. Beard, 'Souvenirs of culture: deciphering (in) the museum', *Art History* 15 (Dec. 1992), pp. 505–32.

B. Bender (ed.), *Landscape, Politics and Perspectives*, Oxford, 1993.

J. Berger, *Ways of Seeing*, London, 1972.

A. Bharati, 'Grammatical and notational models of pilgrimage', in M. Jha (ed.), *Social Anthropology of Pilgrimage*, New Delhi, 1991, pp. 19–29.

M. Bloch, *From Blessing to Violence. History and Ideology in the Circumcision Ritual of the Merina of Madagascar*, Cambridge, 1986.

P. Bourdieu, 'The Berber house', in M. Douglas (ed.), *Rules and Meanings*, Harmondsworth, 1973, pp. 98–110.

G. Bowman, 'Anthropology of pilgrimage', in M. Jha (ed.), *Dimensions of Pilgrimage: An Anthropological Appraisal*, New Delhi, 1985, pp. 1–9.

G. Bowman, 'Pilgrimage conference', *Anthropology Today* 4, 6 (1988), pp. 20–3.

S. Coleman and J. Elsner, 'The pilgrim's progress. Art, architecture and ritual movement at Sinai', *World Archaeology* 26 (1994), pp. 73–89.

M. Crain, 'Pilgrims, "yuppies", and media men. The transformation of an Andalusian pilgrimage', in J. Boissevain (ed.), *Revitalizing European Rituals*, London, 1992, pp. 95–112.

C. Duncan, 'Art museums and the ritual of citizenship', in Karp and Lavine, pp. 88–103.

C. Duncan and A. Wallach, 'The Universal Survey Museum', *Art History* 3 (1980), pp: 448–69.

E. Durkheim, *Elementary Forms of the Religious Life*, London, 1912.

J. Eade and M. J. Sallnow (eds), *Contesting the Sacred: The*

Anthropology of Christian Pilgrimage, London, 1991.

M. Eliade, *The Sacred and the Profane*, New York, 1959.

M. Eliade, 'Sacred places: temple, palace, "centre of the world"', in *Patterns in Comparative Religion*, New York, 1963.

J. Elsner and R. Cardinal, *The Cultures of Collecting*, London, 1994.

B. N. Goswamy, 'Another past, another context: exhibiting Indian art abroad', in Karp and Lavine, pp. 68–78.

C. P. Graves, 'Social space in the English medieval parish church', *Economy and Society* 18, 3 (1989), pp. 297–322.

S. Greenblatt, 'Resonance and wonder', in Karp and Lavine, pp. 42–56.

I. Karp and S. D. Lavine (eds), *Exhibiting Cultures: The Poetics and Politics of Museum Display*, Washington DC, 1991.

S. Kemal and I. Gaskell, 'Nature, fine arts, and aesthetics', in S. Kemal and I. Gaskell (eds), *Landscape, Natural Beauty and the Arts*, Cambridge, 1993.

C. King, 'His truth goes marching on: Elvis Presley and the pilgrimage to Graceland', in Reader and Walter, pp. 92–104.

C. Lane, *The Rites of Rulers. Ritual in Industrial Society – The Soviet Case*, Cambridge, 1981.

M. P. Leone, 'Interpreting ideology in historical archaeology: using the rules of perspective in the William Paca Garden in Annapolis, Maryland', in D. Miller and C. Tilley (eds), *Ideology, Power and Prehistory*, Cambridge, 1984, pp. 25–35.

D. J. Meltzer, 'Ideology and material culture', in R. A. Gould and M. B. Schiffer (eds), *Modern Material Culture: The Archaeology of Us*, New York, 1981, pp. 113–25.

N. Merriman, *Beyond the Glass Case: The Past, the Heritage and the Public in Britain*, Leicester, 1991.

D. A. Messerschmidt and J. Sharma, 'Hindu pilgrimage in the Nepal Himalayas', *Current Anthropology* 22 (1981), pp. 571–2.

H. Moore, *Space, Text and Gender. An Anthropological Study of the Marakwet of Kenya*, Cambridge, 1986.

E. A. Morinis, *Pilgrimage in the Hindu Tradition: A Case-Study of West Bengal*, New Delhi, 1984.

E. A. Morinis (ed.), *Sacred Journeys: The Anthropology of Pilgrimage*, Westport, Connecticut, 1992.

E. Pace, 'Pilgrimage as spiritual journey: an analysis of pilgrimage using the theory of V. Turner and the resource mobilization approach', *Social Compass* 36, 2 (1989), pp. 229–44.

H. F. M. Prescott, *Jerusalem Journey: Pilgrimage to the Holy Land in the Fifteenth Century*, London, 1954.

H. F. M. Prescott, *Once to Sinai: The Further Pilgrimage of Friar Felix Fabri*, London, 1957.

I. Reader and T. Walter (eds), *Pilgrimage in Popular Culture*, London, 1993.

N. Schor, 'Collecting Paris', in Elsner and Cardinal, pp. 252–74.

C. Sorensen, 'Theme parks and time machines', in Vergo, pp. 60–73.

R. L. Stirrat, 'Sacred models', *Man* (n.s.) 19 (1983), pp. 199–215.

S. J. Tambiah, *Magic, Science, Religion, and the Scope of Rationality*, Cambridge, 1991.

H. W. Turner, *From Temple to Meeting House. The Phenomenology and Theology of Places of Worship*, The Hague, 1979.

V. Turner, 'Pilgrimages as social processes', in V. Turner, *Dramas, Fields, and Metaphors. Symbolic Action in Human Society*, London, 1974.

V. Turner, 'Death and the dead in the pilgrimage process', in E. Turner (ed.), *Blazing the Trail. Way Marks in the Exploration of Symbols*, Tucson, 1992.

V. and E. Turner, *Image and Pilgrimage in Christian Culture. Anthropological Perspectives*, Oxford, 1978.

R. van Dam, *Saints and Their Miracles in Late Antique Gaul*, Princeton, 1993.

P. Vergo (ed.), *The New Museology*, London, 1989.

B. Ward, *Miracles and the Medieval Mind: Theory, Record and Event 1000–1215*, Aldershot, 1987.

J. Wilkinson, 'Jewish holy places and the origins of Christian pilgrimage', in R. Ousterhout (ed.), *The Blessings of Pilgrimage*, Urbana and Chicago, 1990, pp. 41–53.

J. Windsor, 'Identity parades', in Elsner and Cardinal, pp. 49–67.

E. Wolf, 'The Virgin of Guadalupe: a Mexican national symbol', *Journal of American Folklore* 71, 1 (1958), pp. 34–9.

Illustration Acknowledgements

FRONTISPIECE Graham Harrison
1. Graham Harrison
2. Behram Kapadia
3. The Conway Library, Courtauld Institute of Art
4. The British Museum
5. The British Museum Education Service
6. The British Museum Education Service
7. Silvia Frenk
8. Deutsches Archäologisches Institut, Rom
9. Museum of London
10. The British Museum
11. National Archaeological Museum, Athens
12. A. F. Kersting
13. The Hutchinson Library
14. Israel Government Tourist Office
15. A. F. Kersting
16. Silvia Frenk
17. Saudi Arabian Government Tourist Office
18. Staatliche Museen zu Berlin, Preussischer Kulturbesitz, Museum für Islamische Kunst
19. © Mohamed Amin, Robert Harding Picture Library
20. The British Library
21. A. F. Kersting
22. Graham Harrison
23. A. F. Kersting
24. Vatican Museums and Galleries
25. The Conway Library, Courtauld Institute of Art
26. Vatican Museums and Galleries
27. Réunion des musées nationaux, France
28. A. F. Kersting
29. Bild-Archiv der Österreichischen Nationalbibliothek, Wien
30. A. F. Kersting
31. Glenn Bowman
32. A. F. Kersting
33. Pitkin Pictorials Ltd
34. A. F. Kersting
35. A. F. Kersting
36. The British Museum

37. The Conway Library, Courtauld Institute of Art
38. Sonia Halliday Photographs
39. Woodmansterne Ltd
40. Woodmansterne Ltd
41. The British Library
42. The Conway Library, Courtauld Institute of Art
43. A. F. Kersting
44. Ernest Hawkins Archive, Courtauld Institute of Art
45. The British Museum
46. Dr K. Norget
47. The Conway Library, Courtauld Institute of Art
48. Amanda Sealy
49. Amanda Sealy
50. Silvia Frenk
51. The Hutchinson Library
52. The British Library Oriental and India Office Collections
53. The British Library Oriental and India Office Collections
54. Silvia Frenk
55. Silvia Frenk
56. Silvia Frenk
57. Rajesh Vora
58. A. F. Kersting
59. Silvia Frenk
60. The Hutchinson Library
61. Amanda Sealy
62. A. F. Kersting
63. Graham Harrison
64. Graham Harrison
65. Simon Baugh
66. Graham Harrison
67. Graham Harrison
68. The British Museum
69. The British Museum
70. The British Museum
71. Itsuo Art Museum, Osaka, Japan
72. Graham Harrison
73. Graham Harrison
74. Glenn Bowman
75. A. F. Kersting
76. John Elsner
77. Ernest Hawkins Archive, Courtauld Institute of Art
78. The Conway Library, Courtauld Institute of Art

79. Robert Harding Picture Library
80. The British Museum
81. The British Museum

PICTURE SECTIONS

Section I
a. Graham Harrison
b. Silvia Frenk
c. Deutsches Archäologisches Museum, Rom
d. The Witt Library, Courtauld Institute of Art

Section II
a. The Conway Library, Courtauld Institute of Art
b. The British Museum
c. Behram Kapadia
d. Silvia Frenk

Section III
a. Amanda Sealy
b. Mary Evans Picture Library

Section IV
a. The British Museum
b. Cambridge University Museum of Archaeology and Anthropology
c. The British Museum
d. The British Museum
e. Simon Coleman
f. Graham Harrison
g. Amanda Sealy

Section V
a. The British Library Oriental and India Office Collections
b. Archives of Capuchin Friary, San Giovanni Rotondo (FG) Italy
c. Graham Harrison
d. Réunion des musées nationaux, France

Section VI
a. Cambridge University Museum of Archaeology and Anthropology
b. The British Library
c. Dr F. and Dr C. Osella
d. The Mansell Collection

Index

Figures in bold refer to illustration numbers